# MEMOIRS OF AN

# *Unrepentant Field Geologist*

The author, about 1966. Background: varved argillite of Precambrian Gowganda formation (Cobalt Series) north of Thessalon, Ontario. Photo by Roger Walker.

# MEMOIRS OF AN

# *Unrepentant Field Geologist*

A Candid Profile of Some Geologists
and Their Science, 1921–1981

# F. J. PETTIJOHN

The University of Chicago Press • Chicago and London

The University of Chicago Press, Chicago 60637
The University of Chicago Press, Ltd., London

*Library of Congress Cataloging in Publication Data*
Pettijohn, F. J. (Francis John), 1904–
   Memoirs of an unrepentant field geologist

   Includes bibliographical references and index.
   1. Pettijohn, F. J. (Francis John), 1904–
2. Geologists—United States—Biography   I. Title.
QE22.P47A35   1984        550'.92'4  [B]        83-12347
ISBN 0-226-66403-1 (cloth); 0-226-66405-8 (paper)

# CONTENTS

# PREFACE

The second half of the nineteenth century was a time of ferment and excitement in geology. The United States Geological Survey and the Geological Society of America were established; it was the age of opening up the mines of the West and the iron ore deposits around Lake Superior, of unraveling the glacial history of the continent, of unearthing the dinosaurs. The main lines of geologic history and its major concepts took form during this period, which produced such leaders as G. K. Gilbert, C. R. Van Hise, A. C. Lawson, and T. C. Chamberlin in America and H. C. Sorby, J. J. Sederholm, H. Rosenbusch, and A. Heim in Europe. Petrography came into being with the examination of thin sections in polarized light. Glacial geology, Precambrian geology, and the study of ore deposits became disciplines in their own right.

The early twentieth century, by contrast, was mainly a period of consolidation, of backing and filling, though with expansive development in petroleum geology and exploration geophysics. Mining districts were worked out; warmed-over ideas had lost their freshness; the hypothesis of continental drift was not yet respectable. The established schools lived largely on past capital and basked in their former glory.

But at the end of World War II a new era erupted, with tremendous expansion in the fringe areas of geology and in other earth sciences—in geochemistry and geophysics, meteorology and oceanography. These developments infused new life, new techniques, and new ideas into a discipline grown stale. Radiogenic isotopes provided a new clock, stable isotopes a thermometer, the airborne magnetometer and scintillometer new exploratory tools, and other remote sensing devices a new look at the oceans and the atmosphere, while the discovery of paleomagnetism awakened interest in continental drift. Experimental petrology and X-ray crystallography came of age. The results were overwhelming. Some schools moved with the change, others resisted. The University of Chicago was one of the first to accept and promote change; it became a model for other schools. The influence of Barth, Bowen, Libby, and Urey at Chicago is felt to this day.

It was my privilege to witness these changes, to study and work when Lawson, Sederholm, and T. C. Chamberlin were still alive, and to be at Chicago during one of the most exciting periods in the history of geology. Three major developments were to take place: the revived interest in the oceans and in sedimentary deposits, and the concomitant establishment of sedimentology as a subdiscipline of geology; the explosive growth of geochemistry; and the introduction of plate tectonics, an outgrowth of paleomagnetism, marine geology, and geophysics. All three profoundly influenced the teaching of geology, its techniques of investigation, and its philosophical foundations. I was in the midst of the first two and knew the principal actors; I was an outsider in the third, but not immune to its wrenching effects on long-cherished concepts.

These historical changes are not neatly organized and analyzed here. Instead they permeate the whole text. I have chosen to tell the story for the most part in chronological order—as it actually happened—but if the reader will bear with me the picture will emerge. The participants at any moment did not see the whole picture, or even where the drama was leading or how it would end. Nor can we at this moment—but a look back gives us a perspective from which to view the present. History is but prologue. It is this look back that I attempt to provide. For me it was entangled with personal events—such is my story.

History is more interesting when told through the lives of real people, not as a dry, impersonal recitation of facts. Hence I have included anecdotes that I hope will illuminate personalities and perhaps entertain as well.

To tell the story I must begin at the beginning. One needs to know who the teller of this tale is and what kind of world he was born into. For science does not live in a vacuum, apart from its practitioners; it is a product of its time and social milieu. I will sketch very briefly, therefore, my life as a boy at the turn of the century, the years before World War I, and my career in science that began in the early twenties, first with my studies at the University of Minnesota, then at Chicago, both before and after World War II, and finally at the Johns Hopkins University.

In writing this history I have used letters from my files and have checked some facts in Fisher's *The Seventy Years of the Department of Geology, University of Chicago* and Schwartz's *A Century of Geology at the University of Minnesota*. I have also consulted the National Academy of Sciences' *Biographical Memoirs*, the memorials of the Geological Society of America, and other sources for dates and occasional facts. But for the most part what I say is based on my own recollections. Since memories are fallible I apologize in advance for any misstatements. I did not keep a diary, though I sometimes wish I had.

I am indebted to many persons, especially Paul Edwin Potter, Robert N. Ginsburg, and Raymond Siever, who read the Chicago chapter and made many helpful comments. I am likewise indebted to Dana Russell, who read the California chapter, and to Carl Dutton, who read the section on Minnesota. I wish to thank Phil Tear, editor of the *Oberlin Alumni Magazine*, for his help in preparing the Oberlin chapter and for permission to republish much of it, which appeared in the *Magazine* in 1981. A great many persons contributed pictures; their help is acknowledged in the legends.

I wish to thank Kate Francis who did most of the typing of the manuscript.

# 1

## The Turn of the Century (1904–21)

It was the end of an era; the door of history had slammed on the great western frontier. Railroads now spanned the continent, and the prairie schooners were no more. The buffalo had all but disappeared; the Indians had been herded onto reservations. Settlements dotted what had only recently been empty prairie.

Yet it was not quite over. Oklahoma was Indian Territory; Arizona and New Mexico were not yet states. The Spanish-American War was fresh in the memory of the nation. Lumbering and the cutting of pine were still in progress in Wisconsin and Minnesota, though the end was in sight. So it was when, on 20 June 1904, I was born.

Yet I was linked to the past—to the great westward migration. My grandfather Thomas Pettijohn, born in 1831 in Brown County, Ohio, had "drifted logs down the Mississippi from Minnesota." He later took work in Paris, Illinois, with Neff Brothers Packing Company of Cincinnati. Shortly thereafter he settled in Flora, in southern Illinois, where he met and married Harriet Clarke. My father was born in Flora in 1875.

He was the youngest of eight, two of whom died as children. When Thomas Pettijohn tired of the "chills and fever" of the region, he vowed he would take his family far enough northwest to leave malaria behind. So in 1879, when my father was only four years old, they embarked, with personal effects and eight horses, first by train to Columbus, Nebraska, than a few miles by buggy to Albion, where my grandfather farmed for a time. But after two years they moved on to seek "wood and water" at Willow Creek not far from Long Pine, Nebraska, this time making the journey in a covered wagon. The Pettijohns arrived in August 1881, the railroad was completed a month later, and by the spring and summer 1882 there was a large influx of settlers. The community of Long Pine attained a population of seven hundred. So it was that my father grew up in the sandhill country of Nebraska. His stories of the migration, the little sod shanty on the claim, his father's ill-fated attempt to farm the land—all these and more are still with me. Grassland, they soon discovered, was for grazing not cultivation, and so cattle, not corn, replaced the buffalo. The move to Nebraska was but the last in a series of moves that began with my forefathers in Delaware in the 1600s—an intermittent march westward.

My father reversed the trend. After an aborted career in railroading, he decided to go back to school. Since he had a married sister in Lake County in northeastern Illinois, he lived for a short period with her, worked summers as a farmhand, and in winter went to the now-defunct Rochester (Wisconsin) Academy. After further study he became a schoolteacher—principal of a school at Waterford, a small village on the Fox River of southeastern Wisconsin, where he met and married my mother, a teacher in the same school. And so it happened that I was born of schoolteacher parents in Waterford. My mother was of German extraction. Southeastern Wisconsin had received more than its share of the great German migration to America in the middle and late nineteenth century. Her father, a harness maker, was a first-generation immigrant; her mother was second generation.

It was not long before we moved to Menomonee Falls, a small country town some fifteen miles northwest of Milwaukee, where my father was principal of the high school. My first recollections are of Menomonee Falls—of rural and small-town America in the first years of this century. It was a world that had changed little in the previous hundred years. Yes, there were railroads, telegraph and telephone, and, in urban areas, factories. But life in the country or small town had changed scarcely at all. The main street, unpaved of course and lined with hitching posts, was muddy in spring and dusty in summer. The sound of church bells, the clang of the anvil in the blacksmith shop, the clop-clop of horses' hooves broke the silence; at rare intervals one could hear the moan of a distant locomotive or the shriek of a factory whistle. There were the general store, with its aproned clerk behind the counter, the butcher shop with a red-faced butcher missing a couple of fingers, a harness and shoe repair shop, and a dry goods store. There was also a printshop that put out the weekly *Menomonee Falls News*. A saloon, a water-powered gristmill, a sugar beet factory, a livery stable, and a blacksmith shop completed the business establishments. Since we had no horse and buggy, marketing required a mile walk down the road to town; a shorter walk in the other direction took us to a neighboring farm for milk and eggs. My father rode to work on his bicycle.

Our first home there was lighted by kerosene lamps and heated by a wood-fueled iron range—a cookstove—in the kitchen. Water came from a pump outside the door; the toilet was a small shanty at the end of a chilly path. The kitchen was the hub of the house—not only where cooking and baking were done, but also the place for the weekly laundry and the Saturday-night bath and where the family gathered by lamplight on winter nights.

We later moved to Madison, where my father worked in university administration—in the Extension Division. Promotion was linked to job offers elsewhere, so we shortly moved to North Dakota, then to Bloomington, Indiana, and later to Washington, D.C., back to Bloomington, then to Indianapolis, and finally to Minnesota. It seemed we moved as often as a Methodist minister. But in general it was a world of little mobility. Anyone who had been abroad was looked on with awe.

But life in a small town was not dull for a small boy; the year was punctuated by exciting events. The circus was one. The unloading of the circus train before dawn, the erection of the great tent, the parade, the elephants and the steam calliope, the clowns—vivid memories all. There was Memorial Day, with the trek to the cemetery, the few Civil War veterans, and the long-winded speeches by the leather-lunged local politicians, and of course the Fourth of July with its dawn-to-dusk explosions of firecrackers and rockets. Then there was the county fair and the balloon ascension—all part of growing up in small-town America.

Our family life was low-key. The salary of a schoolteacher with a rapidly growing family did not permit many luxuries or extended travel. Activities were largely family centered. My parents belonged to no church, though they went to hear the local Methodist preacher two or three times a year; we children went to Sunday school intermittently for a year or two. There were no organized activities for children—no Boy Scouts, no YMCA, no swimming pools or tennis courts; I learned to swim in a deep hole in Clear Creek. We had chores to do—weed the large vegetable garden in summer, fill the woodbox, or later the coal hod, and carry out the ashes, and at one time tend the chickens. We did a lot of reading, since there were many books around but, of course, no radio or television. Although we had no automobile, we did make one trip each fall, in a rented car, from Bloomington to Nashville, in neighboring Brown County, no more than twenty miles away. It was an all-day trip to see the fall colors. The unpaved road, crooked and steep, wound in and out, up and down, past small mountain farms with their stony fields and mule-operated sorghum mills, and we saw the mountain folk— straw hats, sunbonnets, bare feet, and all. In places the hills were too steep for the car, so it was get out and push for men and boys. For us boys the climax was a family-style chicken dinner and a visit to the log jail in Nashville, the county seat—a town without a railroad.

When I was fifteen my father bought a "touring car," a Dodge. He and I learned to drive—a heart-stopping experience for both. Our most notable trip was from Bloomington to Washington, D.C., during World War I. There were few paved roads and no numbered highways, so we often had to stop and ask the way—getting a set of complicated directions and a "you can't miss it," though we always did. It took us three days; we ran out of money at Frederick, Maryland.

In most small towns, university towns excepted, social contacts were limited to the church and the corner saloon—institutions frequently at odds with one another. At rare intervals there was a revival meeting—a tent meeting—that shook up the village and brought people together, or a tent chautauqua where people saw their first live theater or concert or heard such notables as William Jennings Bryan. In Bloomington in particular I became aware of the cultural schism—a great rift between the townsfolk and academia—between town and gown. There was a general distrust of books and "book larnin." Books were too theoretical and not practical. Things were "all right in theory but . . ." There was, however, one exception—the Bible. This was an infallible book, true from cover to cover. The earth and everything in it was made in six days. Fundamentalism was rampant and evolution taboo; consequently the university was looked on as a den of iniquity. Revival meetings and baptisms in the local creek were much a part of the scene.

Intellectually it was a narrow and parochial world. Catholics were suspect, as were those of German ancestry during World War I, when teaching German in the schools was banned. The language was purged: sauerkraut became liberty cabbage, kindergarten became child garden. And anyone who did not believe the stories of the German atrocities was disloyal. News spread slowly—the small towns had weekly papers, so election returns and news bulletins were posted in the window of the newspaper office. City papers never found their way into the smaller communities. It is difficult to comprehend how it was before the daily paper, radio, and television, and before the automobile, tractor, and plane—along with power mowers and chain saws—broke the great silence of the countryside. Where can one go now and not hear the internal combustion engine? It is everywhere, even the remotest part of the globe.

I must have been the despair of my parents, for I was an indifferent scholar. I had no great liking for school, and my record was rather dismal. I don't think my lack of achievement can be blamed on our frequent moves—I just didn't like school. But I did pass from grade to grade, though I flunked German and physics in high school, and finally graduated from Arsenal Technical High School in Indianapolis. I did like one subject very much—botany. I took the subject in my senior year and enjoyed every minute of it.

I liked the outdoors, tramping in the countryside, exploring the limestone caves and quarries of the Bloomington region, collecting fossils—all of which my mother encouraged. By the time I finished high school I had decided I would be a geologist. I had no contact with geology in school—not even the course in "physical geography" taught at Bloomington. We did have several books—Joseph Le Conte's *A Compend of Geology* (1898) and Tarr's *New Physical Geography* (1904). These I read from cover to cover. Le Conte furnished me with ammunition to do battle with one of my high-school classmates, Darrel Adams, who was a strict fundamentalist and of course regarded the theory of evolution as blasphemy.

But the family had no tradition in science—none of my ancestors were doctors, engineers, or scientists of any kind. My father was interested in people—in education and politics. He had no particular aptitude with tools nor any consuming interest in science. He neither encouraged nor discouraged me. A neighbor in Bloomington, Clyde Malott, then a graduate student in geology at Indiana University, gave encouragement, helped me identify my collected fossils, and even invited me to look at the collections in the Geology Department at the university. His enthusiasm was genuine and contagious, so when we moved to Minnesota and I entered the university of Minnesota as a freshman in 1921, I was fully committed to geology.

The main campus of the university, a large state school even then, is in "southeast" Minneapolis, on the east bank of the Mississippi River. One could stand on the river bluff and look across into a rather shabby part of town, at the smoky and malodorous plant where coal gas was produced for domestic use, there being no natural gas then available. Looking upriver to the northwest, one could see the milling district with its huge grain elevators clustered about the remnants of Saint Anthony Falls. I say "remnants" because diversion dams and canals and their protective aprons concealed what was once a waterfall. Most of the water had been diverted through the mills.

Saint Anthony Falls, like Niagara Falls, had retreated upstream leaving behind a gorge, one wall of which formed the bluff on which the university is situated. In the walls of the gorge, perhaps one hundred to one hundred and fifty feet high, are exposed the strata responsible for the falls—the resistant Platteville limestone over which the water spilled, undermining a weaker shale and the soft, friable Saint Peter sandstone beneath.

The university, which opened in 1870, had become an ever-expanding cluster of buildings from various architectural periods. My classes were in Folwell Hall, a general classroom building; Pillsbury

Hall, a venerable structure built of sandstone, housing Geology; and the chemistry building, one of the newer structures.

Lotus Delta Coffman was president of the university. William Watts Folwell, the first president, though over ninety was still around, and actively working on the third volume of his four-volume history of Minnesota. Such optimism! My father was assistant to the president and director of the summer session. Guy Staunton Ford, whom we came to know very well, was dean of the graduate school. Minnesota at that time was making a major effort, with considerable success, to build up its graduate school. The school had attracted some of the nation's outstanding scholars—Tate and Nier in physics, Emmons in geology, Stakman in plant pathology, and several others in the agricultural departments on the farm campus several miles distant.

I took a diversity of courses, including a freshman course in rhetoric and composition—in which I got more help from my father than from my instructor. We had read Newman and others and had to write an essay on our idea of a liberal education—a subject far from my mind at that time. I also had a course in economics, truly the dismal science, one in English history, which as it turned out was a history of the judicial system, and two courses in mathematics—college algebra and trigonometry. I also took a number of courses in chemistry, my minor subject, including general chemistry from Lillian Cohen and courses in qualitative and quantitative analysis. It was indeed a very different chemistry from that of today. The Mendeleev periodic table was not understood—it was merely a convenient way to group the elements so one could recall their properties. The Bohr atom was mentioned as one of several theories about the structure of matter—a topic touched on briefly at the *end* of the course. Protons and electrons were never mentioned.

Zoology I did not study. The department had a small but excellent natural history museum with a skilled préparateur and curator who put together some excellent dioramas depicting various Minnesota habitats—the marshland, the dry woodland, and the prairie. The museum was the pride and joy of a Dr. Roberts, a retired physician who organized a series of Sunday afternoon lectures that I greatly enjoyed. My interest in natural history was further engaged by visits to a nature sanctuary—a part of the Minneapolis park system. This was a sizable fenced-off area, including a marshland, where one could see the native flora in its natural state. The caretaker was a retired schoolteacher who, if she detected a genuine interest, would take you on a guided tour. It was she who convinced me to join the Wildflower Preservation Society—my first encounter with conservation.

The university was for the most part a commuter's school. Most of the students, like myself, lived at home and came to school by public transportation—streetcars at that time. Many a time we stood waiting on a cold street corner in subzero weather. I can recall neither dormitories nor parking lots. Out-of-town students were apparently left to shift for themselves. A considerable number belonged to fraternities and sororities and therefore lived in the chapter houses. The students were a diverse lot—the commuters being generally serious. There were, as might be expected, a fair number of "Joe College" types with their coonskin coats and fraternity life that revolved about parties and football. The latter was a gladiatorial display, more for the alumni perhaps than for the students. At one time during my residence there was a drive for funds to build a memorial—as I recall, for those who had died in World War I. Whatever the reason, we were asked to pledge a substantial sum to be paid over a period of years. The memorial was to include a stadium for athletic events—primarily football—and an auditorium for concerts and the like. Of course the stadium was built first—before the Depression years and the resulting delinquent pledges. It was not until some years later that the Northrup Auditorium was completed. This, I believe, was a fair indication of the priorities; brawn, not brains, took first place.

In my second year at the university my father became ill with cirrhosis of the liver and went to the Mayo Brothers clinic in Rochester, Minnesota, for treatment. One of the Mayos was his physician, but there was then, as even now, no cure. In less than three months he was dead, leaving my mother with six children, the youngest a baby. I was the oldest. My father's death, in 1923, was most traumatic. He left little life insurance, a house only partly paid for, and large hospital bills. But he left many friends—the Coffmans, the Fords, Nicholson, who was dean of men, A. C. Krey of the History Department, and others who assisted me in many ways.

We were poor, but somehow I recall no real hardships. My mother's frugal habits—a legacy of her German background—saw us through, though, as she put it, life was patch, patch, patch. I had four younger brothers, and as we outgrew our clothes they were patched and passed down to the next in line. As they and my sister got older, they found jobs of one sort or another—delivering newspapers or working as golf caddies. I worked one summer as an assistant in the Plant Physiology Department on the farm campus of the university, doing odd jobs in the greenhouse and in the laboratory. Later I was appointed "helper" in the Geology Department, with a stipend of $150 a school year, and still later was promoted to assistant at $225. I do not recall whether these jobs included tuition, which was then $20 a quarter. All but one of my family obtained some college education; my youngest brother, Dick, went to Dunwoody Technical Institute to become a master electrician.

# 2

# Minnesota: Stumpland and Strip Mines (1921–25, 1928–29)

My first course in geology at the University of Minnesota was taught by Dr. W. H. Emmons, the head of the department. Bill Emmons was a ruddy-faced, square-jawed man with a booming voice. He was a poor teacher by conventional standards; his lectures were largely extemporaneous. But more geology majors came out of his class than all the others put together. He considered that first course the most important and believed it was his duty to teach it; his enthusiasm knew no bounds, and it was contagious. The very first day he took the class out to show us that the venerable Pillsbury Hall was being blown away. The building, made of Kettle River sandstone, was across the street from the drill ground of the ROTC. The tramp of many feet had left little grass to hold the sandy soil, which was readily picked up by the wind and swept across the street. It scoured off the soot that had accumulated over the years, exposing the fresh pink sandstone and in many places even etching out the natural stratification of the stone itself. The building was indeed being removed grain by grain.

Before the end of the first week the class made a geologic cross section showing the rock sequence exposed in the bluff of the Mississippi River on the west edge of the campus—the Saint Peter sandstone, the Glenwood shale, and the fossiliferous Platteville limestone. Emmons also took the class to Minnehaha Falls, where by adroit questions he had us work out the retreat history of Saint Anthony Falls, the gorge that retreat produced, and the related story of Minnehaha Falls itself. The landscape took on new meaning. By the end of the course no doubt remained—if there had been any. A geologist I would be.

## THE PILLSBURY DEPARTMENT

The Geology Department at Minnesota was fairly typical of those in the midwestern universities of that time. Wisconsin and Chicago probably had the edge: Wisconsin because of the stature of Van Hise and Leith and the role they played in unraveling the Precambrian of the Lake Superior region, Chicago because of the Chamberlin and Salisbury tradition. But tradition was all that remained at Chicago in the twenties, since Salisbury was dead and Chamberlin had retired.

Geology at Minnesota was housed in Pillsbury Hall—one of the oldest buildings on the campus, named for its donor, the founder of Pillsbury Mills. It was a cavernous building with high ceilings and broad hallways, so it was only tolerable in Minnesota's below-zero weather. One cold morning Dr. Emmons taught in his shaggy coat and fur hat, much to the amusement of the students.

Why were so many geology departments of this era quartered in the oldest, and commonly, the most decrepit, buildings—all nineteenth-century structures, usually of stone? Northwestern's was in the attic of Main Hall, Wisconsin's in old Science Hall, Hopkins's in Latrobe Hall, Ohio State's in Orton Hall, Indiana's in Owen Hall, and Berkeley's in Bacon Hall, the old library now demolished. And they were usually furnished with an assortment of old wooden specimen cases with sticky drawers and diverse laboratory tables or benches that were probably hand-me-downs from the Chemistry Department. Most, too, had neglected museums with poorly lighted glass cases containing endless trays of dusty mineral and fossil specimens.

The Minnesota department at this time consisted of seven full-time faculty members. There were three senior professors—W. H. Emmons, economic geology, Clinton R. Stauffer, paleontology, and Frank F. Grout, petrology; three assistant professors—John W. Gruner, mineralogy, G. M. Schwartz, structural geology, and George A. Thiel, general geology; and one instructor, Ira S. Allison, who taught a course in sedimentation and, with Thiel, handled much of the elementary geology.

The general program at Minnesota was largely patterned after that at Chicago, which had become a model for most midwestern departments. Like Minnesota, most of these were led by Chicago men, who imprinted the Chicago stamp. Geology was then largely a field science, though laboratory study of collected materials was an important element. Both thin and polished sections were investigated under the microscope. Experimental work was uncommon, though Emmons had made his reputation through investigating the secondary enrichment of ores—a study that included some leaching experiments—and Gruner had done

W. H. Emmons, head of the Geology Department and state geologist of Minnesota,
University of Minnesota. Photo courtesy of
the University of Minnesota.

Frank F. Grout, professor of petrology,
University of Minnesota. Photo courtesy of
the University of Minnesota.

some work on iron transport, since he was interested in the origin of the
iron-bearing formations. Rock analysis—by wet chemical methods—
was an important part of the program in petrology at Minnesota. In this
respect Minnesota was unique. Grout, who had early training in chemistry, insisted that each of his doctoral candidates make their own rock
analyses, a practice not unknown in some European universities, particularly in Finland, but very unusual in America. Most of the work was
project-oriented; the era of collections and museum displays had passed.
Much of the work at Minnesota, except for that of Emmons, was
Minnesota-bound, since it was done for the Minnesota Geological
Survey.

The facilities at Minnesota would be considered primitive by today's
standards, but they probably did not differ greatly from those at comparable places. The X-ray investigation of the crystal structures of minerals was just beginning when I got to Minnesota. Gruner was quick to see
the possibilities of this new technique and put together equipment using
the powder method of X-ray diffraction. But this work was essentially a
part of his own research on mineral structure, not a tool that students
used for mineral identification. I had no work in this area, which now is

John W. Gruner, professor of mineralogy,
University of Minnesota. Photo courtesy of
the University of Minnesota.

commonplace and used by students nearly everywhere. The department did have equipment for chemical analysis of silicate rocks; it also had an assortment of petrographic microscopes.

The department strongly encouraged its students to study chemistry, both general and analytical, and so I took an undergraduate minor in the subject. They did not press us to do much in physics, since no geophysics was then taught at Minnesota, nor did they require much proficiency in mathematics. I had college algebra and trigonometry—no more.

The department offered two field courses—one two-week course on the Minnesota iron ranges and a six-week course in the Black Hills. I never took either, since I was employed as field assistant by the Minnesota Geological Survey.

Frank Grout introduced me both to petrology and to the North Woods. He was thin and wiry, with sandy brown hair and blue eyes—a man of few words, sparing in his praise, slow to reprimand but an exacting taskmaster nonetheless. He had started out in chemistry, but because of a lung condition he was advised to seek an outdoor vocation and a drier climate. He went to California, where he regained his health, but returned to Minnesota to take his bachelor's degree. Grout joined the

Minnesota faculty in 1907 but left for Yale to earn his Ph.D., then returned to Minnesota and remained until he retired in 1948.

Grout was well organized. He conducted his classes in the laboratory with microscopes and thin sections, not relying on laboratory assistants but circulating about checking, questioning, and closely following the students' work. Grout placed strong emphasis on "criteria." Just what criteria support a given concept? What does one see, in the field, in the hand specimen, or under the microscope that suggests magmatic assimilation, for example? Grout was a good disciplinarian in this respect. He was quiet and soft-spoken, not a particularly good lecturer, and he preferred to work with his students one to one—in the manner of a physician making rounds with a coterie of medical students. Grout was very critical, insisting on exactness of written expression. The first draft of my doctoral thesis was filled with his blue pencil markings. Whatever success I had in writing I owe to Grout rather than to my formal courses in rhetoric and composition.

Grout was a good scientist, but because of his self-effacing manner he never received the acclaim due him. It was rumored that he was offered the presidency of the Geological Society of America, but he declined because he thought the honor should have been offered to Emmons, the head of the department. Grout's only textbook, *Petrography and Petrology*, was largely a failure; it was too much like a notebook, and it did not convey his enthusiasm and the excitement of his courses.

Grout spent many summers in fieldwork for the Minnesota Geological Survey in the border lakes region of northern Minnesota. He learned woodcraft from the Indians employed by the Survey as packers and canoemen, but before long he became the tutor and passed his skills on to others. He had an aversion to the trappings of civilization and preferred a tent and campfire to a cabin with stove and other amenities. His campsite was usually a glaciated rock shelf on the shore of a northern lake, with the deep waters of the lake in front and the woods behind. In the field he could never pass a blueberry patch without stopping to gather a handful. He was justly proud of his skills as a woodsman, and he taught me what I know about canoeing and the North Woods.

Dr. Stauffer was totally different. He was a Chicago product; his courses were based on copious notes, no doubt rewritten, which he kept in large loose-leaf binders. These he read line by line, word for word. His students, in turn, copied down as much as was possible. His advanced general geology course was little more than a paraphrase of Chamberlin and Salisbury's three-volume *Geology*—the bible in the early twentieth century. Stauffer was a paleontologist, or more precisely a biostratigrapher, as were most American paleontologists of that time. His courses in paleontology were similar—copious notes dictated to his classes. His course in index fossils consisted of dozens of trays containing fossils typical of each geologic system. The student was expected to learn the scientific names of these fossils—a major feat of memory. This approach to paleontology was not unlike the approach to stratigraphy and historical geology then in vogue in the midwestern universities— based no doubt on the Chicago pattern. In these courses one learned— memorized—the stratigraphic sections, with all their subdivisions, of each of the geologic systems in the United States, especially the Midwest and the northeastern states, where they were first studied in detail. Such a style of teaching has gone out of fashion today, but it did have one thing in its favor. The student learned something; he knew where the Uinta, the Wasatch, or the Ouachita mountains were and had some idea of their age and their rock sequences and structures. Students today may know something about Reynolds number or the activities of ions in solution, but they are abysmally ignorant of the geology of their own country. Students also learned to read and interpret both topographic and geo- logic maps—air photographs were not yet available. Skill in map reading and interpretation became a part of their arsenal—no mean asset, but one that has deteriorated or even disappeared in many of our leading univer- sities today. I was later to witness the erosion of the teaching of the fundamentals of geology and the substitution of esoteric peripheral subjects. The product has been "geologists" with very limited under- standing of their discipline—geologists with tunnel vision, unable to relate what they know to the rest of their science.

A chap named Farrell was a part-time student in the department when I was there. He was an oddball, older than the other students, earning a living as an exterminator, using cyanide fumes to kill the roaches and bedbugs in the cheap rooming houses in Saint Paul. He was a radical— probably a communist. I don't think he knew Stauffer, since he had not had any courses from him, but he thought Stauffer was suspect—he looked like a "capitalist." And indeed Stauffer did resemble, in a way, the stereotype depicted by cartoonists—on the portly side, bald with a fringe of hair, wearing a vest and watch chain. Actually Stauffer was a very friendly person, considerate of his students' welfare and certainly unlike the legendary rapacious captains of high finance or industry.

At the time I entered Minnesota, in 1921, Dr. Emmons had become well known as an economic geologist. His major contribution had been his United States Geological Survey Bulletin on the secondary enrich- ment of ore deposits. This work was based mainly on field studies of sulfide ore deposits and the observation that relatively lean deposits were capped by markedly enriched zones. The grade of many ores, when followed to depth, declined, and many mines closed when they ran out of higher-grade ores as they mined deeper. But when I arrived at

Minnesota Emmons had left secondary enrichment to others and had become interested in the zonation of ore deposits. It had been known for some time that the geographic distribution of ores was commonly zoned with reference to a center—in many cases a pluton or stock—the presumed source of the ore-bearing solutions. With the help of part-time graduate student assistants, Emmons combed the world literature and plotted distributions on maps. He massed an extensive knowledge of the locations and kinds of ore deposits, and based on this knowledge he wrote his McGraw-Hill textbook *The Principles of Economic Geology*. Primarily dealing with ore deposits, the book was perhaps the only challenge to Lindgren's *Mineral Deposits*. But in the twenties the petroleum industry was mushrooming into the giant it has become today. Much of this growth came from the mass production of automobiles, leading to America's acceptance of the family car and its insatiable appetite for gasoline. Petroleum exploration was based on application of geology, and this in turn created a demand for geologists that the universities were hard pressed to supply. Emmons was dismayed that most of his students deserted ores for oil. Under pressure from the students he offered a course in petroleum geology, and, there being no suitable text for such a course, he wrote *Geology of Petroleum*, also published by McGraw-Hill. Based on an intensive search of the literature on petroleum, it was a monumental compilation. It provoked the remark from A. C. Lawson of Berkeley that Emmons was a remarkable fellow, for he had written a book on petroleum geology without ever seeing an oil well. Though not strictly correct, there was a large measure of truth in the assessment.

Emmons, though head of the department, always taught one section of beginning geology. He would appear before the class somewhat disheveled, having just come out of his workroom littered with maps, would open the textbook to the subject of the day, read three or four lines or perhaps a paragraph, and then, as some thought came to him, his face would light up with a broad grin and he would launch into a discourse, perhaps inspired by a specimen from the rock and ore collection piled high on the room-wide row of cases that served as a lecture desk. His lecture would be enlivened by something he had just read, or by a recollection of some earlier field experience, or by reference to a large geologic map of the United States that hung at the back of the room. He waxed enthusiastic as he talked, and his booming voice could be heard the length of the building. Despite his rather disorganized teaching, his enthusiasm won recruits; his direct introduction to geological phenomena in the field, even the first day, right on the campus, did something to his students. Many who meant to satisfy the university requirement for a course in science came to stay, switching majors even late in their college careers.

John Gruner, who taught mineralogy, was a German emigré. On arrival in this country, he first went to New Mexico, but he joined the Minnesota faculty in 1920. He took both his master's and his doctor's degrees at Minnesota.

Mineralogy was a required subject for students in the School of Mines as well as for geology majors, so Gruner had a large class. Essential to mineralogy is crystallography, and J. W. (as Gruner was called) included a good dose of the subject. Many of the mines students had difficulty with crystallography, and the mortality rate in the mineralogy course was high. As a result there were strong protests from Dean Appleby of the School of Mines. It was my impression that enrollment in the school was faltering and that the admission policy was bent a little to secure students. The dean didn't want to see too many flunk out because they couldn't pass mineralogy. So each year there was a tug-of-war—Gruner trying to uphold academic standards and the dean trying to prevent erosion of his student body.

Though he came to the States as a relatively young man, Gruner never quite lost his German accent. I was his student assistant. For the most part I worked on the mineral collections—dusting off specimens, writing new labels, and the like—for Minnesota, like many other colleges and university departments, maintained a somewhat neglected museum of minerals and rocks, and also fossils. The era of displays in glass cases had passed, and none of the faculty wanted to do museum work, yet they didn't have the courage to dismantle the whole operation.

Gruner was difficult at times, primarily because he was outspoken—he said whatever came to mind. His blunt and at times tactless manner caused friction. Despite some irritation I enjoyed my work with him and was his field assistant for two years—the only one, according to Miss Van Cleve, the departmental secretary, to last so long.

Gruner was a curious mineralogist in that, unlike most of his breed, he liked fieldwork and did a great deal of it. He was particularly interested in the Mesabi iron-bearing formation that gave rise to one of the world's greatest deposits of iron ore. He was also interested in the early Precambrian rocks of the border lakes area of Minnesota and was one of the first to work out their stratigraphy and structure—a truly pioneer study. In mineralogy he was one of the first to investigate the structure of crystals. With meager funds, he put together X-ray diffraction equipment that would be judged primitive by today's standards and worked out the structure of many minerals for the first time.

George Thiel was also a Minnesota product—born in Minnesota and educated wholly at Minnesota. Thiel started out in bacteriology, moved to geology and became instructor in 1921, got his Ph.D. in 1923, and eventually advanced to a professorship. He became department chairman in 1944 after Emmons's retirement. I had no courses from Thiel and hence never really knew him well, but I was impressed with his enthusiasm and his seemingly well-organized life. He put a lot of time and energy into his courses, especially the introductory course in geology. In fact he really made a career of teaching—not only the introductory course but also various educational ventures for the general public.

G. M. Schwartz was an assistant professor when I began my studies. Like Gruner and Thiel, he had a Minnesota doctor's degree, though he had taken his bachelor's and master's degrees at Wisconsin. The only two courses I had from him were on polished ores and structural geology. His course in structural geology was based on C. K. Leith's textbook, a not surprising choice considering his Wisconsin background. Schwartz was not a particularly good lecturer. The course followed the text closely; there was little illustrative material other than an occasional blackboard sketch, and no laboratory exercises. His course on ores was much better, since it was built around extended laboratory study of polished ores under the reflecting microscope. The techniques were new, the ore textures were fascinating, and working out paragenesis based on the fabric and grain boundaries was interesting.

Ira Allison was an instructor in geology when I entered Minnesota in 1921. He came from Chicago and, like Schwartz, took his Ph.D. at Minnesota, his thesis being a petrographic study of the Giants Range granite of northern Minnesota. Like other students of Grout, he had to make chemical analyses of the granite and its several phases. The trickiest part of such analyses is determining the alkalis. Unfortunately, Allison reversed the proportions of potassium and sodium, so he described the rock as a soda granite. The results were an embarrassment to all concerned, and a notice of the error had to be published (1929, *J. Geol.* 37:590). Allison taught a course in sedimentation based wholly on readings. There was no laboratory study of sedimentary materials or rocks and no field trips to see them in outcrop, which was a pity because the Twin Cities area had ample material. This lack of any field excursions in connection with the courses was a major defect of Minnesota. However, another student, Haymond Johnson, and I made an extended field trip to the Baraboo district of Wisconsin. Allison, who knew the area well from his Chicago background, was very helpful in planning the trip. He marked the classic localities on the topographic maps. So Johnson and I packed our blankets, filled a box with groceries, and took off in Johnson's not too reliable automobile. The car held together, and the trip was a memorable one. I saw more geology firsthand in those few days than I did in all my classes at Minnesota—the tilted Precambrian Baraboo quartzite with its cross-bedding, the famous Van Hise rock, the basal Cambrian conglomerates filling Precambrian valleys, the flat-lying

Cambrian sandstones, the abandoned water gaps in the Baraboo range, the terminal moraines, and a host of other features. Why, oh why, can't geology be taught where geology is and not in the lecture hall?

## THE NORTH COUNTRY

I graduated in the spring of 1924, at the end of my third year, as one could do if one accumulated enough grade points—calculated on course grades and credits. But I was not to attend my graduation ceremonies. I had been offered a job as a field assistant with the Minnesota Geological Survey at a salary of seventy-five dollars a month, and the Survey's field season began before commencement. I would receive my degree in absentia. The Minnesota Geological Survey and the Department of Geology were then one and the same. The departmental faculty became Survey employees in the summer months. Dr. Emmons, for example, was both head of the department and director of the Survey. My first assignment was as field assistant to Grout, and that is how I found myself, on 4 June 1924, in a canoe on Burntside Lake in northern Minnesota.

Grout was interested in the igneous and metamorphic rocks, and most rocks of this kind were in northern Minnesota—in Cook, Saint Louis, and Koochiching counties—north of Lake Superior and along the international boundary with Canada. Since much of this area was, and still is, without roads and accessible only by canoe, I was to be a member of a canoe party. I had never been in a canoe, had never made a portage, and knew nothing whatever about camping in the North Woods. With Frank Grout as my mentor I was to become a canoeman and woodsman, spending the next ten summers on my own in the country north of the border—a vast rocky area underlain by the world's oldest rocks, formed before the Cambrian period and the dawn of abundant life.

The first canoe trip was unforgettable—every part of it proved a novel experience. The trip began in Minneapolis, putting together my blankets and buying boots and clothes suitable for fieldwork. The blankets were folded and rolled up in a canvas tarpaulin tied with rope to form a bedroll—no sleeping bags then. We wore our regular clothes on departure, since we traveled by train to Duluth, from which point we were to proceed to Ely to outfit for fieldwork. I arrived at the Great Northern depot in Minneapolis with my baggage, including bedroll, for the 11 P.M. departure. The baggage agent refused to check my bedroll—to him it was not personal baggage. Certainly a bedroll didn't look like a suitcase. Despite our protests, he said that to him it was a tent, and that settled it. Grout was quite put out and made his displeasure known, but there was no recourse. Time was short, and the baggage agent had the last word. So I was obliged to stow my bedroll beneath the berth in the Pullman car. With us was R. J. Leonard, a gradute student in geology at the university, who was going along as cook for the party. Leonard was a World War I veteran, somewhat older and more mature than most of the students in the department at that time.

In the morning we were awakened by the porter, and as we pulled into Duluth I had my first look at this northern city. Named for Daniel Greysolen, Sieur Duluth, who established a trading post in 1679, it is a shoestring town, stretched out some twenty miles from Fond du Lac on the south to Lester Park in the northeast. It lies between a high rocky bluff and the waters of Lake Superior. In places the bluff is much too steep for roads and hence, for the benefit of those living high on its slopes, there was then what the Germans call a *Bergbahn*, or mountain railroad—actually a tram pulled by cables—that ran up the steep slope. There were two cars that ran on parallel tracks, balanced one against the other so that as one went up the other went down. A motorman, who sat in a control tower at the top of the hill, regulated their movement. In each car was a conductor who collected fares, and when the cars were clear he would telephone to the motorman at the top. From the summit we got a magnificent view of the azure waters of Lake Superior, of the city below, of the town of Superior, Wisconsin, of the flat country to the southeast, and of the estuarine Saint Louis River, the boundary between Minnesota and Wisconsin, with its iron-ore docks and steel mills.

Grout had several errands in Duluth, one to the Poirier Tent and Awning Company to have several packsacks repaired. After this was done we returned to the railway station and caught a train that wound its way slowly up the steep grade around the south end of the Duluth bluff to Short Line Park, where we disembarked. Grout had made an extensive study of the Duluth Gabbro, a body of crystalline igneous rock exposed here, and he was eager for us to see it. We then walked back along the track, where, exposed in a tunnel and many rock cuts, we saw not only the gabbro but also many lava flows of basaltic rock that lay above it. This was an exciting experience for me, for I had never seen lava flows before; my only acquaintance with either basalt or gabbro was in specimen trays in the laboratory. After several hours and nearly four miles of walking, we reached the city near Morgan Park. By now it was time to return to the station, pick up our baggage, and catch our train north.

Our train followed the lakeshore as far as Two Harbors, where we left Superior behind. As we did so, I caught my first glimpse of the north country, which was not at all what I thought it would be. No stately pines, only cutover land, littered with stumps and, in places, second-growth poplar brush. I saw for the first time the muskeg swamps—endless stretches of somber black spruce forming a pinnacled skyline. The whole scene had a desolate look. There were few habitations and no farms, only boulder-strewn stumpland without even the potential of being farmed. Quite a contrast to the lush fields of prosperous southern Minnesota.

After some time the train stopped at Allan Junction—a place where one track went on to the Mesabi Range and the other north to the Vermilion Range. The train stopped long enough for us to get off and order blueberry pie and coffee in the station restaurant.

Late in the afternoon we reached Ely, on the Vermilion Range—an iron-mining district. Ely was the largest city on the range. The Vermilion "Range," as I discovered, was no range at all, but most of the Lake Superior iron-bearing districts are referred to as such. A few did, indeed, boast a range of hills; most did not. The Vermilion Range, one of the smaller districts, was first explored for iron ore in 1875. The first ore shipment was in 1884, and production peaked at about two million tons a year in 1892. In 1924 there still were three active mines, all near Ely, that produced a little under one million tons that year. The range itself extended from Tower, near Vermilion Lake, to Winton, on Fall Lake, a distance of about twenty-two or twenty-three miles.

Ely had the look of a typical range town, an assortment of houses surrounded by wooden fences to keep out the cows—the principle being to fence the cow out, not in. Always prominent on the Minnesota ranges were the schools—oversize structures, lavishly furnished, that dominate the scene—schools built from the taxes on iron ore. We made for the Exchange Hotel, which, in contrast, was a boxlike frame building. The lobby was filled with rough-looking men smoking strong cigars or chewing tobacco, wearing boots and felt hats. It was furnished with overstuffed furniture, shiny brass spittoons, and a large potbellied stove, whose pipe went directly into the ceiling. The sills of the large windows facing the street were worn swaybacked by hobnailed boots. The lobby furniture, no doubt, faced the windows in summer and the stove in winter.

Our room, on the second floor, was sparsely furnished—iron bedsteads with squeaky springs and a dresser with a cracked mirror. On the dresser was a large china pitcher of water and a china washbasin. Under the bed was the usual china chamber pot. As the saying went, we had the makings of a baseball team—the pitcher and the catcher. Near the window was a large coil of heavy knotted rope—our fire escape. The windows had no counterweights—to keep them open one put a chair on the sill. In the center of the room was the pipe from the stove in the lobby—a fine hazard in the middle of the night. We did have electric lights—one naked bulb hanging from the ceiling with a pull string attached.

After a dinner of questionable merit in the hotel dining room, we had time for a stroll about town before dark—daylight lasts far into the evening in northern Minnesota in June. There were many prominent rocky knobs of greenstone. Grout showed us the pillow structure, a characteristic of submarine lavas, in the Ely greenstone, as it was called. These are very ancient lavas—much older than those we had seen at Duluth.

Early the next morning we went to Miller's—grocer and outfitter—where we left our "store clothes" in our suitcases and put on our boots and field clothes. I remember seeing all our groceries piled in the middle of a storeroom and sitting on the floor with Grout opening the containers and transferring the contents to cloth bags, which we tied shut. Everything had to go in a packsack. In due time the packs were ready, including one with the tent, kettles, frying pan, and reflector oven. We hired a truck, and our canoe, taken from Miller's storage shed, was loaded on, together with our packs and bedrolls. We scrambled aboard and were off.

After several miles' travel down a gravel road, surviving a good many jolts and bumps, we turned north on a lesser road for several miles more and came to Burntside Lodge on Burntside Lake. This newly built lodge was mainly for the benefit of fishermen who came up from the Twin Cities or Chicago for their holidays. The truck backed down to the dock; the canoe was launched and the packs were loaded. Grout handed me a paddle and told me to get in the bow; Leonard sat in the middle, and Grout took the stern. Grout said paddle—so for the first time in my life I was in a canoe, paddling.

Our canoe, I discovered, was rather different from most. It had no seats; one either sat on a bedroll or knelt, a posture I found very uncomfortable and hard on my knees. Moreover, this was a rather large canoe, covered not by canvas but by very thin overlapping strips of cedar. Its size and construction made it heavy, requiring two men on a portage. It was not so affectionately known as the Survey's battleship.

We paddled a couple of miles to an island campsite, and it was here that I learned from Grout about pitching the tent—including cutting the poles and lashing them into a framework. I also learned the details of setting up the camp kitchen, building a fire, and outdoor cooking. This is how I came to learn the art of canoeing—the Indian paddle stroke with that twist at the end that lets you paddle on one side only yet keep the canoe on a true course.

At the Burntside camp I also learned to use a reflector oven and bake

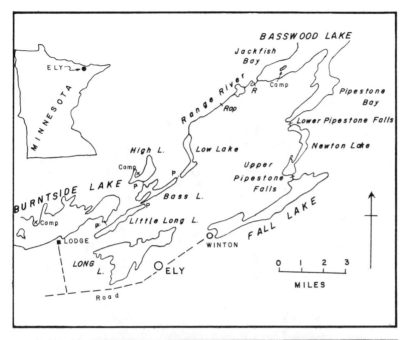

(*top*) Canoe route of 1924. (*bottom*) North Woods camp (J. Langwill and R. M. Grogan, 1934).

(*top*) Typical northern lake with rocky shore and islands. (*bottom*) Compassman (R. M. Grogan, 1934).

bannock. And it was here that we caught a lake trout, or landlocked salmon as it is often called, stuffed it with wild-rice dressing, and baked it. Leonard was soon initiated into camp cooking and took over that chore—including cleaning fish, a task I was happy to leave to him.

Everything was new—not only canoeing, camping, and cooking, but also the landscape—so novel, so different from anything in my experience. Burntside Lake was the first of the myriad lakes in the Canadian Shield that I had seen. Unlike the lakes of central and southern Minnesota and Wisconsin, with their sandy beaches and bays filled with lily pads and fringed by reeds and cattail marshes, Burntside Lake had rock shores, very deep water right up to the shore itself. The rocks themselves were in places rounded off, polished and scored by the glacial ice of the Pleistocene epoch; in other places the shore was clifflike. The surrounding rocky country was clothed with a mixture of evergreen and deciduous trees—not the oaks and maples of the south. There were a few giant pines, both red and white, remnants of the original forest gutted by the lumbermen. The woods were mostly a mixture of second-growth poplar, birch, and balsam—the fragrant Christmas trees of the market— and in places white and black spruce. The latter was the dominant tree of the muskeg swamps—very unlike the marshes of southern Wisconsin. Locally, as I came to discover, there were also alder thickets and, less commonly, cedar and tamarack swamps.

There were other discoveries too—the lichens that grow on the bare rock surfaces, with their many forms and colors, and the ubiquitous moss. Also new were the variety and size of the biting insects—an unwelcome discovery. Mosquitoes I had known, but the blackflies so prevalent on sunny June days and the pesky deerflies and dog flies were less familiar. And in 1924 we had no insect sprays or effective repellents. One could only wrap a bandana about one's face and neck, for wearing a net was out of the question in the bush and there was generally no need for one on the lakes.

Burntside Lake is an irregular body of water, generally elongated northeast-southwest, some eight miles long and about two miles wide. A sizable bay extends three or four miles to the north. The lake contains many islands, so there is no open sweep of water. Another surprise was the clarity of the water and its being drinkable—unheard of for any lake I had known.

The next morning Grout and I left Leonard in camp and started fieldwork. I was initiated into the role of compassman. The general plan is that the compassman runs the traverse line and the geologist maps and describes the rock outcroppings. The lines were generally run north-south or east-west. Direction is maintained by compass and distance by pacing—some two thousand paces per mile. The compassman plots his line and position in his notebook and calls out "tally one" after one hundred paces, "tally two" after two hundred paces, and so forth. The geologist, who wanders about looking for rock exposures, also plots the traverse as well as the rock exposures in his notebook. The compassman holds his tally point until he gets a confirmation call from the geologist, who may be out of sight but not out of hearing. The usual traverse is run on a rectangular course, so that at the end one is back at the starting point. We would pull the canoe ashore, run the traverse, and hope that our distances and directions were correct so that we would end up at the canoe.

The lines, set by compass bearing, should not deviate to one side or the other. Consequently the compassman went up rock ridges and down the other side, through briar patches, and across swamps. No obstacle was to be avoided and no detour made except for open water. And the pacing had to come out right no matter how difficult the going, how steep the slope, or how many fallen trees were encountered. All this while pursued by a horde of mosquitoes or blackflies.

Our first traverse was to check some outcroppings of rock mapped by John Gruner the summer before. For some reason we could not find these as Gruner had mapped them. Grout was puzzled and annoyed. Our traverse closed as it should, so I thought I could not be at fault. Then Grout asked for my compass. It was a Brunton compass, or pocket transit, as it is called, and Grout saw at once that it was adjusted for use in the Black Hills of South Dakota, where the magnetic declination is fourteen degrees—not the one degree of northern Minnesota. So instead of running true north I had been going northwest. After resetting the instrument to correct for the difference between true and magnetic north, we had no further problems. Such was my lesson on magnetic declination!

Our traverses varied in length, but we were always gone all day and commonly were on a traverse at lunchtime. When noon came Grout would build a fire, take out a small kettle he carried in his knapsack, open a can of condensed soup, and add some lake or, more often, swamp water. In a short time we had soup with some bannock baked the night before, topped off with a piece of chocolate.

We spent the most of the first week working out of the same camp, but then it came time to move. We packed the tent and our bedrolls, loaded the canoe, and paddled four or five miles to the east end of Burntside to our first portage. We turned the canoe over, and Grout got under it about a third of the way from the stern and placed it on his shoulders, while I took the prow on mine. The portage was less than a quarter-mile but was uphill all the way, and I was glad to reach the end at Little Long Lake. A second trip over the trail took care of the packsacks and bedrolls. The

(*top*) Portaging canoe (John Langwill and R. M. Grogan, 1934). (*bottom*) Portage (R. M. Grogan, 1934).

packsacks were heavy canvas affairs with both shoulder straps and a tumpline so the pack could be carried by either. The tumpline had a headband, so most of the weight was supported by the head and neck muscles. I found this an uncomfortable way to portage, though it is the only way used by the Indians; I preferred the straps even though they cut into my shoulders.

Little Long Lake was a narrow body of water, perhaps a quarter-mile wide and two miles long; hence a short paddle took us to the portage to Bass Lake, a little longer than the first but still less than a half-mile. On Bass Lake, an irregular small lake, we turned into a bay on the north side that led by way of a short portage to High Lake, itself a crescent-shaped lake a mile and a half long and not over a half-mile wide. Here at our second camp we were very much alone and saw no other campers or fishermen. The country around High Lake has all been logged off years ago, so that the forest was entirely second growth, chiefly poplar with a scattering of small birches and balsams.

I still recall vividly the oppressive stillness of the evenings after the wind had died down. The silence was broken only by the crackle of the campfire and the songs of the white-throated sparrow—a haunting melody, heard now close by, now far away. Each year, as I hear these songs, when the whitethroats migrate through, the mystery and magic of the North are momentarily recreated. Overhead were the night-hawks, soaring and wheeling about uttering their faint beep-beep. Periodically one would dive to capture an insect, for these birds are not hawks at all but weak-billed insectivores, relatives of the whippoorwill.

The birdlife in the North is abundant and varied. There were, of course, the many ducks and other water birds, the most striking being the loon. We heard the loons long before we saw them, for their cries were startling—at times a high-pitched mocking laughter, at other times very much like a person in distress, or again very mournful. The loon is a powerful swimmer that moves low in the water, with only its neck and head visible, and an extraordinary diver. They would dive in one place only to reappear a short time later on the other side of the lake. The wading birds were also plentiful, especially the long-legged blue herons standing motionless in a reedy bay awaiting an unwary frog. In the evening quiet we might hear the drumming of a grouse or partridge—a strange deep booming sound, slow at first, then more rapid, ending in a crescendo. Often on a traverse we would be startled as a grouse, which is very much like a bantam chicken, would spring to life in front of us, crying in anguish. She would flutter helplessly, feigning injury—a broken wing perhaps. As we approached she would retreat a little, leading us gradually away from her nest or giving her brood time to scatter and hide. Then she would take off with a great whir of wings and leave us standing baffled. Other times we would hear the scream of an eagle as it soared overhead. This was the fish eagle, or osprey, the largest bird of prey in the region, which lived on fish it caught in the northern lakes. And common too was the kingfisher, usually found along the shores, generally perched in an overhanging cedar tree, from which it would drop suddenly to snare an unwary minnow in the water below. When it was disturbed, the kingfisher's saucy call and flash of blue revealed its presence.

Wildlife of all kinds is plentiful in this region, though except for the white-tailed deer we did not see the larger game animals. We saw no moose or bears, though the latter are common. Nor did we see or hear wolves, which are in some people's minds associated with the North. We saw no beavers, though we later found signs of their activity. Chipmunks and squirrels were plentiful. The latter could be a nuisance, as a hole in one of my packsacks will testify. The red squirrel is up and about early, and once in a while one would jump from a tree to the ridgepole of our tent. I awakened one morning to hear one on the canvas. I could see his shadow, so I reached up and gave the tent a whack that sent him flying through space. The startled squirrel scampered up the nearest tree and set up a vociferous scolding. We saw an occasional porcupine and on one traverse flushed a rabbit. It sat still for a moment, and Grout threw his geologic pick at it. The pick would have been wide of the mark except that the rabbit jumped, and pick and rabbit collided in midair. No one was more surprised than Grout, who picked up the dead bunny and brought it back to camp. Leonard had the task of skinning it and preparing it for the pot. But it was a disappointment, since it was lean and tough—mostly sinew and gristle—no better than a goat I once ate in India.

After several days of arduous traversing and acquiring an assortment of mosquito and fly bites, I was glad to break camp and resume our canoe journey. We retraced our route to Bass Lake, then came to the portage to Low Lake.

Bass Lake and Low Lake occupy a long, narrow basin gouged out of the Precambrian crystalline rocks during the Ice Age. Both lakes are in the same rock basin, but they were separated by a ridge of glacial sand and gravel that served as a dam between them. As the glaciers receded the outlet of Bass Lake was established over a low point in the rim of the basin at its northeast end. The outlet channel was over bedrock, not the glacial dam. Low Lake was indeed much lower than Bass Lake—approximately sixty feet. The glacial dam held back the waters of Bass Lake. To make lumbering easier, the loggers had built a sluiceway connecting the two lakes that even in 1924 was a leaky affair and rotting away, allowing a trickle of water over the dam. The portage to Low Lake was short, less than a thousand feet and all downhill. But a year or two after we made the portage, the trickle of water became a torrent and the glacial dam was breached, creating a channel several hundred feet wide. Bass Lake was lowered fifty-five feet in less than ten hours by a catastrophic dam failure, apparently witnessed by no one! It is now a shrunken remnant of what it was, and the bay that led to High Lake is now a separate body of water, Dry Lake.

Low Lake, a rather small lake, drains out through Range River northeastward to Basswood Lake. The river itself was blocked in several places by beaver dams—apparently still maintained by beavers, since there were many fresh cuttings. The river trip was no more than four or five miles, but we had to drag or portage the canoe over or around the beaver dams and various rapids. I was glad when the waters of Jackfish Bay on Basswood Lake came into view.

By now it was time to camp, so Grout chose a small, narrow island in the middle of the bay, scarcely a hundred feet across and having only a few bushes and scattered small trees. Our canoe was on the western side, out of the water and upside down as usual; our tent and campfire were on the high part of the narrow island. As Leonard was preparing supper, a small summer storm developed west of us and moved across the water toward our camp. The squall hit with unusual violence, and a gust got under the canoe, picked it up, and hurled it into our fireplace, knocking the kettles off the fire and scattering the prunes. In my haste to avoid being hit, I jumped backward and collided with the tent, ripping the cloth. Fortunately the canoe stayed where it landed, or it might have smashed on the rocks of the eastern shore or even have been pitched into the water and floated away. As it was, it landed on one of the supports for our kettles, which punched a hole in the side below the waterline. The storm was short-lived and produced only a spatter of rain, so we soon set about putting things right. Leonard went around with a spoon collecting the prunes; Grout said nothing at all but produced a needle and thread from somewhere and set about mending the tent. After supper—still not saying much but obviously put out—Grout whittled a piece of wood to fit the hole in the canoe. He had trimmed the edges of the hole, which was an inch or two in diameter, beveling it a bit. The patch, carved to fit the contours of the bevel, was carefully inserted; he tacked a small piece of canvas over this and smeared on some canoe glue to make it watertight. It worked well, but I noticed that the next day Leonard kept a towel handy just in case the patch popped out.

The following day we resumed our travel, for we were by now homeward bound. Our route went through Basswood Lake—named, I presume, for the basswood or linden tree, a broadleaf species whose inner bark the Indians used to make baskets. Basswood Lake is an amoebalike body of considerable size, lying astride the international border. It stretches some sixteen miles northeast-southwest and has many large bays, of which Jackfish Bay is one, that extend into Minnesota and one large bay, North Bay, that projects into Canada. The international border follows an irregular course through the lake. This lake is a part of the chain of border lakes that formed the principal route of the French voyageurs from the Grand Portage on Lake Superior to Rainy Lake, Lake of the Woods, and Lake Winnepeg and the Northwest. So we traveled for a short distance on this famous route. But not for long, for we had scarcely left Jackfish Bay when we entered Pipestone Bay, which extended south and west to Pipestone Falls. A portage around this, and we found ourselves in Newton Lake, which in turn led, by a portage around upper Pipestone Falls, to Fall Lake, at whose southwest end was Winton, the end of our canoe trip.

Winton, situated at the site of a log hoist, was connected by road to Ely, some three or four miles distant. A call to Mr. Miller and a truck soon arrived to take us back to Ely. Our trip was over. Not a long trip to be sure, perhaps no more than thirty-five miles in all, but memorable for me. Despite the flies and mosquitoes, and in spite of wet feet, aching muscles, tough portages, and all the rest, I liked it. Captured by the magic of the North, I knew this was the place I wanted to be and that geology was the right choice.

Grout returned to Minneapolis, and I proceeded to Eveleth, Minnesota, on the great Mesabi Iron Range. Here I met Gruner, who was teaching the range field course. Every year the geology and mining majors spent two weeks on the Mesabi learning the elements of field geology. The course was nearly over, but I spent the last couple of days with the class mapping the Adams pit—one of the great open-pit iron mines that characterize the Mesabi Range.

The Minnesota Survey was preparing a new geological map of the state, and Gruner and I were assigned the task of examining the rock exposures along the Little Fork and Big Fork rivers in Koochiching County—rivers that drain north to the Rainy River. Koochiching County lies north of the Mesabi Range bordering on Canada, separated from it by Rainy Lake and the Rainy River. Much of the county is flat and muskeg-covered, with few rock exposures except along the course of the rivers we were to investigate. The plan was to launch our canoe well upstream, then follow the rivers down to their junction with the Rainy River. Unfortunately our start was in midsummer, so the rivers were low. I think we waded more than we rode down the boulder- and sandbar-filled channels. In other places we encountered logjams—logs being driven to the sawmills at Beaudette on the Rainy River that were stranded by the low water.

After the 1924 field season I returned to school in Minneapolis to complete a fourth year and obtain my master's degree, based on a study of phosphatized fossils and nodules in the local Platteville limestone.

The next field season, 1925, I was again assistant to Gruner, running his lines in the area between Eveleth and Virginia, Minnesota, where the basement—the formations that underlie the iron-bearing strata—was exposed. The Survey was interested in the quartz porphyries, a type of rock that was gold-bearing in the Porcupine district of Canada. We collected many samples to be assayed at the School of Mines in Minneapolis. But no gold.

It was three years before I returned to Minnesota in 1928 to complete the requirements for the Ph.D., which I received in absentia in 1930.

MINNESOTA IN RETROSPECT

How do I view Minnesota after fifty years? It is difficult to set aside all the nostalgia, all my warm feelings for the place and for the sympathetic and helpful teachers who opened the door to a lifelong career. I am indeed a sentimental alumnus. Objectivity comes hard.

Minnesota had, by any objective measure, a strong faculty. It had Grout—by all odds one of the best teachers of petrology in the country, rivaled only by Buddington at Princeton and Waters at Stanford. Gruner was also a scientist of stature who was elected president of the Mineralogical Society and later received that society's Roebling Medal. He certainly was one of the foremost mineralogists of his time. Emmons was known for his work on ores, but also for his successful textbooks on ore deposits and petroleum geology. Many of Emmons's students became well-known mining geologists; he himself received the Penrose Medal from the Society of Economic Geologists.

Minnesota fell short in several respects. There was no geology club or departmental forum for presentation of research by either students or faculty. The value of oral presentations by graduate students before their peers and under scrutiny of the whole faculty is not to be underestimated. They may be painful for the listeners, but the experience is needed if one is to become an effective speaker. Such a forum also gives the students a chance to hear and meet visiting geologists.

Although most research at Minnesota was then field-based, fieldwork, other than the formal field courses, played no part in the course program. This was a great contrast to Berkeley, where extended field trips were a part of the teaching program. Only Emmons, in the beginning course, used the field for teaching, and he did so very effectively. There is no reason excursions to the Duluth area, to the Saint Croix Dalles, or even to the Baraboo region of Wisconsin could not have been an integral part of the curriculum. The field is the proper place to teach geology—any kind of geology.

Minnesota has a good track record, and many of its graduates attained recognition in the profession. Several were elected to the National Academy of Sciences—an honor denied its faculty, though in my judgment two were of Academy stature. Some of its graduates became prominent in industry—in exploration for ores and petroleum. Among these were A. I. Levorsen, Anton Gray, Harrison Schmidt, Ira H. Cram, T. M. Broderick, Donald M. Davidson, and Philip J. Shenon. Minnesota also made its contribution to the United States Geological Survey and the academic world, including such graduates as C. P. Berkey, Thomas S. Lovering, Charles Park, Jr., Samuel S. Goldich, and John W. Gruner. I am justly proud of my own Minnesota degree and my public-school education. It is interesting that all my education was in public schools and all my teaching in private schools—Oberlin, Chicago, and Hopkins.

# 3

## Oberlin: Interlude at a Small College (1925–27)

I had just finished my master's degree in geology at the University of Minnesota and was flat broke. I needed a job. I would have taken any job—any port in a storm, as the sailors say—exploring for oil in South America or mapping Alaska for the United States Geological Survey. It turned out that I went to Oberlin, where I had been offered an instructorship in geology at $150 a month—$1,800 a year. I was delighted, so in 1925 I joined Professor George Hubbard to make the Department of Geology a two-man operation.

What kind of place was this Oberlin? Although I had passed through Ohio once on my way to Washington during World War I, I had never been to Oberlin. So when I stepped off the train and was greeted by Professor Hubbard, I had my first look at the town, the college, and the region. After my summer of fieldwork in northern Minnesota, a region of rockbound lakes and pine forests, the contrast could not have been greater. I was dismayed by the flatness of northern Ohio, the sparse patches of woods, the farms set one next to the other. As a geologist I could not imagine a less promising area.

Oberlin itself was a contrast to most Minnesota towns. It was so flat that, as I found out later, many streets became canals after a heavy rain. The streets were paved with brick, the sidewalks made of sandstone; many large houses were brick capped by slate roofs; others were frame with spoolwork and gingerbread trim, products of the Victorian architectural reign of terror. Oberlin was a town of large trees and

This chapter is modified from a version that appeared in *Oberlin Alumni Magazine* in 1981 (vol. 77, no. 2).

extensive lawns. I had not been there an hour before I was aware of its large black population—another contrast to the homogeneous Scandinavian communities in Minnesota. I was impressed also by the myriad bicycles and by the size and number of bicycle racks everywhere, including a monstrous one in front of the Carnegie Library. Bicycles were not just for the young. I saw riders of all ages—housewives going to market, men carrying their lunch pails to work, and, not least impressive, Professor Cowdery and his wife, who rode to the college every morning at a stately pace. I soon joined the throng, bought a bicycle, and mastered the art of riding it. I frequently rode off on weekend field trips to hunt for fossils, and I learned that the rutted, unpaved country roads (of which there still were a good many) were hazardous to cyclists. I had more than one nasty spill.

The college was a diverse group of buildings arrayed on the three sides of Tappan Square. The square itself was graced by stately elms, the largest and most historic being at its southeast corner. Then, as now, there were a cluster of stores across the street from this historic elm.

The students lived in various college-owned and private residence halls—converted private mansions. These not only resembled the sorority and fraternity houses at other colleges, lacking only the Greek letters, they also functioned the same way, but without the exclusive, snobbish character of those institutions. For the most part each residence house had its own dining and kitchen facilities. In some cases these were large enough to accommodate walk-in boarders. Some, like Talcott, were for the exclusive use of women; others, like Baldwin, had coeducational dining. There being no financial barriers, the students dining together came from all socioeconomic groups. Seating at meals was determined by lot; table assignments were changed weekly. Meals prepared in the house kitchen were served by student waiters at an appointed time. The house chaplain, a student, said grace, the men held the chairs for the women, and some learned table manners for the first time. The Oberlin houses, except perhaps the Men's Building, were not so large as to have an "institutional" flavor; one felt like a member of an extended family, not like an inmate.

Professor Hubbard was able to find a room for me at a private home and arranged for me to take my meals at Baldwin. So I not only joined the Oberlin faculty, but also became a member of the student population. Since I was only twenty-one I fit in readily enough.

My status at Oberlin was indeed ambiguous. I was, of course, a member of the faculty—a full-time instructor in geology. I taught classes, conducted examinations, gave out grades, and attended faculty meetings. But my whole social life was with the students. I was the same age, ate with them, partipated in student activities, and even took a freshman course in French and a course in descriptive geometry. I needed a reading knowledge of French for my doctor's degree, which I planned to get. The French course led to some confusion. My classmates assumed I was a freshman, and I came very near being hazed for not wearing the little green cap that upperclassmen demanded of all first-year men. My assertion that I was faculty was received with disbelief. You can imagine the embarrassment of my classmates when they spotted me sitting with the faculty on the platform during daily chapel services.

The students at Baldwin eventually became aware of my faculty status, but that did not seem a barrier to my participation in the life of the place. It did, however, pose a challenge to two girls who lived in the old Fairchild residence across Elm Street and came to Baldwin for meals—a challenge to get a date with a faculty member. So by devious methods known only to girls, I became the not unwilling target of their efforts. In fact, before the year was out I was engaged to one of them, though I became disengaged the following year.

This dual existence—as a member of the faculty and for all practical purposes also a member of the student body—gave me a special vantage point for observing the Oberlin scene. In 1925 student conduct was closely regulated. No student cars were permitted. The girls had to reside in college or college-approved houses. Freshmen women were due in their rooms by 8:00, sophomores by 8:30, and upperclasswomen by 9:40. Lights out at 10:00 for all. Evening study in the library required signing out and signing in. No smoking was a campuswide rule, and of course there was no liquor.

The men were much less restricted and were free to come and go, though cars were forbidden. One could go to nearby Elyria or on to Cleveland, since the electric interurban system so prevalent in the early part of the century had not yet succumbed to buses and private cars, though the signs of the end had appeared. These electric cars, railbound, linked nearly all the major cities of Ohio. But male students usually hitchhiked, a practice more widespread and safer then than now. I joined the army of hitchhikers and saw a good deal of Ohio beyond the reach of my bicycle.

Attendance at chapel was mandatory—every noon, five days a week. The students sat in the regular pews, with the faculty on the platform facing them. Faculty seating was by seniority and rank, the elder statesmen in the front and newcomers like myself in the rear. Sitting erect at the organ was Professor Andrews, who accompanied the hymns and played an "amen" for the prayers. Speakers were varied, some from the faculty, many from the seminary, and a few from outside.

Recreation was limited to what Oberlin could provide—a stroll to the arboretum on a Sunday, a movie at the Apollo, college-sponsored intramural sports, intercollegiate events, student and artist recitals, and some social affairs put on by the residence halls. Library dates were an Oberlin tradition. You could escort your girl friend to and from the library weekday evenings. The library was strictly for study, but at least you could have a hand-in-hand stroll back—provided you didn't miss the 10:00 curfew for women.

I became acquainted with the science faculty, since we met periodically to discuss academic matters. There were Budington, Rogers, and Lynds Jones in Zoology; Holmes, Chapin, and McCollough in Chemistry; Taylor in Physics; Grover, Nichols, and George Jones in Botany, and Stetson, with his neat bow tie, in Psychology. The general faculty met frequently, and their sessions were interminable. When I first arrived, these meetings were presided over by Henry Churchill King, who even then was declining in vigor and health. At that time the faculty was the college as far as academic matters were concerned. Faculty governance demanded many hours of committee service. As a very junior member I escaped most of these responsibilities.

Geology at Oberlin had a long and honorable tradition. In the early years geology and theology were entwined in the persons of G. F. Wright and A. A. Wright. Both were graduates of the college; both had received degrees from the seminary. After an interlude of service in the Civil War and as pastor in several rural churches, G. Frederick Wright returned to the seminary, in 1881, as professor in the Department of Harmony of Science and Revelation. He was a highly respected geologist greatly interested in the Ice Age, an interest that took him to Greenland, where he was shipwrecked, and to Alaska. He was one of the founders of the Geological Society of America. A. A. Wright studied at Columbia, and in 1874 he was appointed professor of geology and natural science in the college. After Zoology and Botany became separate departments, he taught geology until his death in 1905. Five years later George David Hubbard joined the faculty as professor of geology, a post he retained until he retired in 1936.

The Department of Geology occupied an old two-story frame house, enlarged by an addition in the rear. It was situated on the west side of Professor Street, just north of Severance Laboratory. The Geology Department had been the smallest of the science departments. It was a one-man affair, and Professor Hubbard was that man. He *was* the department, a jack-of-all-trades: teacher of geology, geography, mineralogy, petrology, and paleontology as well as department head and keeper of the house. I considered him an old man when I arrived in 1925; he was fifty-four, which from my present vantage point does not seem like much. Perhaps it was his mustache and goatee and near-bald head with a fringe of white hair. Hubbard was short and somewhat stocky and

George David Hubbard, professor of geology, Oberlin College. Photo courtesy of
Oberlin College Archives.

walked with a peculiar gait—like the country boy that in fact he was. He
was a storehouse of information about the college, about people, and
about places. He knew just about everybody—faculty colleagues, former students, and the geological fraternity, particularly in Ohio. Hubbard belonged to the generation in which thrift was still a virtue. He
saved wrappings and string and straightened nails to use again. Though
by no means niggardly, he would be unhappy in this throwaway generation. He was, in fact, very generous and solicitous toward anyone in
need.

Hubbard had an uneven educational career. He received his earlier
science training at the University of Illinois—in geology and paleontology—later studied physiography with Nathaniel Southgate Shaler and
William Morris Davis at Harvard, and finally enrolled at Cornell where,
under the tutelage of R. S. Tarr, he received his Ph.D. in geography—
the first such degree granted in the United States. He taught at several
colleges before he came to Oberlin, where he stayed until he retired after
twenty-six years of service. The major event in his life was his trip to
China, which he was fond of telling about.

Hubbard had set up the geology program at Oberlin. Basic to it was
the beginning course, a two-semester course in physical and historical

geology that many Oberlin students took to satisfy the college's science requirement. I am sure many did so to avoid what seemed to them to be the more demanding courses in chemistry and physics. Perhaps the prospect of field trips was also alluring. But if they expected to get off easily they soon discovered their mistake, for the geology course was on a par with courses in all the other sciences—four classes a week and two afternoons of laboratory, plus Saturday field trips. Two afternoons a week is a lot of time, and Hubbard had put together a series of laboratory exercises on the elements of crystallography, including work with crystal models to study their symmetry and classification, exercises in determinative mineralogy using blowpipes and other techniques, and determination and classification of rocks by study of hand specimens—about six weeks on each subject. In the second semester the class studied fossils, geologic maps, and cross sections.

Saturday field trips were an integral part of the course. Almost the first day, Hubbard took his class on a walking tour of Plum Creek in Oberlin to see the landforms produced by stream erosion. More extended excursions took the class to the Black River valley in Elyria and the valley of the Rocky River near Cleveland to study stream erosion and valley development. To study the work of groundwater they went to Bellevue to see sinkholes and to Castalia to see the big spring ("Blue Hole"). A field trip to Lake Erie illustrated shore processes and deposits. The seemingly featureless lake plain between Oberlin and the lake disclosed subtle landforms, the ridge roads (Butternut Ridge, Middle Ridge, and North Ridge) following the beaches of the now-vanished glacial Lake Whittelsey and other predecessors of Lake Erie. Field excursions during the second term concentrated on bedrock geology and involved study of natural and man-made rock exposures of the Paleozoic strata of northern Ohio—from the Silurian to the Carboniferous. Each student had to write an integrated report on the geology of northern Ohio based on half a dozen day-long field trips. There were trips to the limestone quarries near Fremont, to the valleys of the Huron and Vermilion rivers to study the black Devonian shales, to the sandstone quarries at Berea, and to the exposures of the Pottsville formation near Strongsville. The first course in geology was indeed a solid science course. My arrival changed little; Hubbard did the lecturing, I took over the laboratories and assisted on field trips.

Geology majors were few, but the half-dozen or so needed more advanced courses. I supplied most of these, teaching both petrology and paleontology. In the latter I was one lesson ahead of the students, an education for me as well as them. Two of the geology majors, Don Baker and Walt Chappell, became my field assistants while I was on leave of absence from Oberlin, working on my doctoral thesis in northwestern

Ontario. Some, like Walt Chappell and Kitty Chase, went on to get their Ph.D.s; others, like Chuck Wilder, Granville Quakenbush, and Wynne Hastings, pursued geological careers without further study.

If the first-year course in geology was the backbone of Oberlin's program in geology, the field course was the pièce de résistance for the geology majors. It was in this course that they learned what the science was all about. An account of geology at Oberlin in the mid-1920s would be incomplete without mention of the field course.

The field course was taught for six (or was it eight?) weeks during the summer, alternately in Vermont and in southwestern Virginia. In the summer of 1926 it was scheduled for Virginia. Despite a good initial show of interest, there were only three registrations as the date of departure approached—really only two. J. Elliott Fisher and Wynne K. Hastings were bona fide students, and I was the third registrant. Hubbard was on the verge of canceling the course when Lester Longman signed on as cook and part-time student. We spent a busy week sorting field equipment and supplies—plane table and alidade, transit, surveyor's chain and tape, aneroid barometer, and sundry camp equipment—tents, cots, stove, and kitchen gear—packing all this in wooden boxes to be shipped by rail to Ripplemead, on the New River in southwestern Virginia. Several weeks later we left Oberlin, caught the Big Four at Wellington, changed to the Norfolk and Western in Cincinnati, and after an overnight in the Pullman arrived at Ripplemead, a flag stop of half a dozen houses.

Professor Hubbard found our freight, bought some lumber, and hired a wagon and team. We piled the freight, the lumber, and our luggage into the wagon, climbed aboard, and took off. We crossed the New River and rode several miles west to a road that turned north up the valley of Stony Creek. After a mile or two we reached Kimballton—the site of a quarry and limekiln. The road was unpaved and rough, and after a jolting ride we stopped at a small Appalachian valley farm where, after negotiations with the farmer, we unloaded the wagon and pitched camp in his orchard alongside the road.

Pitching camp proved a two-day chore. We had to unpack the tents, select suitable sites, then struggle to set the tents up. The result was a veritable village—an army squad tent for the four of us, a tent for Professor Hubbard, a tent to house the kitchen supplies, a "library" tent containing books, instruments, and field equipment, and a dining fly, to provide cover for the table we built from the lumber we had purchased. There was also a small tent to conceal the latrine.

Fieldwork soon got under way. Since the region was inadequately mapped, our first task was to make a topographic map of the area. To do this we had to establish a number of triangulation points, then lay out and measure a baseline. Next we had to learn the rudiments of plane

surveying. These tasks alternated with trips to study the rock formations—to become familiar with them before we could begin geologic
mapping. The first week was busy and somewhat strenuous; the days
were hot and sticky. No doubt the natives were astonished to see us
roaming the hills, lugging our plane table or transit, and especially to see
Professor Hubbard, who, to protect his bald head from the sun, wore a
handkerchief knotted at the four corners like a beret.

At one place, we came upon an abandoned farmstead and found a
number of trees with black sweet cherries; we stopped and ate our fill.
Professor Hubbard was not one to let a crop go to waste, so the next day
we returned with kettles and pails and picked them full. Hubbard
suggested that Longman pit and cook them for later, so he set to work
early the next day and pitted cherries all day without completing the job.
That night I was awakened by voices and caught snatches of conversation about train schedules. The next morning we found Les Longman
gone. The cherries had been the last straw.

This left us without a cook, so Professor Hubbard put in a hurried call
to Mrs. Hubbard, and two days later she and Marjorie, their teenage
daughter, joined the party. We had to put up still another tent to
accommodate the new arrivals.

We worked very hard, from early morning to dusk. Our only day off
was Sunday, when Wynne and I would slip off and walk two or three
miles down to the New River for a swim—our weekly bath. The river
was muddy and swift; hidden rocks made for poor swimming, but at
least we got wet and cool. I don't think Professor Hubbard liked our
performance; I believe he expected us to remain in camp for Sunday
worship, for there were a good many hymnbooks packed in one of the
boxes.

We varied our routine by taking a few longer excursions—out of the
valley of Stony Creek. We walked to the rail station some four or five
miles distant, then went by train. Once Professor Hubbard hired a car to
drive us to Mountain Lake. On the way we had trouble with the steep
grades, so several of us had to get out and push. Another excursion was
on the branch rail line that ran past our camp to the limekiln at Kimballton and beyond to Paint Bank. On weekdays a mixed passenger/freight
train went up in the morning and back in the evening. We boarded the
trailing passenger car, but halfway to our destination a boxcar broke a
flange and derailed. After several hours the train crew got the car back on
the track and pushed it to a siding, and we finally got back to camp late at
night.

At the close of the season the camp was dismantled and packed into
boxes for shipment to Oberlin. The farmer whose land we camped on
invited us all for a farewell dinner. The dining-room table was loaded
with food, the screenless windows were wide open, and the flies were

legion. The children stood by with long-handled moplike contraptions, sticks with paper streamers on the end, to shoo the flies away. Late that afternoon Wynne's parents, Dr. and Mrs. Hastings of Cleveland, arrived to pick him up; they graciously offered me a ride back to Oberlin. Wynne and I had become good friends, and the next summer we left for the newly discovered goldfields of northwestern Ontario.

My career at Oberlin came to an end the following year when I took a leave of absence to continue graduate studies, and then I was offered a job at the University of Chicago as instructor in geology. I had intended to return to Oberlin, but John Gruner, professor of mineralogy at Minnesota, took me aside and said that nobody refused an offer from Chicago, which was indeed the leading school in the Midwest. To be invited to join the Chicago faculty was an honor not to be lightly dismissed. I accepted the Chicago offer and wrote Oberlin a letter of resignation. When Fred Foreman, a fellow student at Minnesota, heard I had resigned my post, he applied for the job and was appointed my successor. Eventually, when Professor Hubbard retired, he became head of the Geology Department, a position he held until his retirement many years later.

Oberlin gave me not only a job but also an opportunity. I had a chance to teach, which I found both challenging and rewarding; teaching became my life's work. Moreover, I found that one learned more as a teacher than as a student, especially if one had to teach some less familiar aspects of geology. And northern Ohio, which seemed so unpromising at first sight, had an intriguing geological story to tell—a story closely and effectively integrated with classwork. Finally, as a bonus, I found a wife, for in 1930 Dorothy Bracken, a geology major, and I were married.

How do I look at my two years at Oberlin a half-century later and after a career of teaching in two graduate schools—Chicago and Johns Hopkins? What is the nature and value of teaching at a small liberal arts college like Oberlin? There is a tendency in the educational world to look down on undergraduate college teaching. Many regard such an appointment as a way station en route to a post in a graduate school. Like "housewife," the "college teacher" is a put-down. To me this view is badly misguided. College teaching provides a real opportunity. One can make a difference—open a door—give the student a new direction and a new goal. It is truly rewarding to watch students "turned on" so they move on to graduate school and to a lifelong career. The undergraduate college is where this happens; the graduate school comes too late.

I never regretted my Oberlin sojourn, and I could have been happy indeed to make college teaching my life's work. But fate decreed otherwise, and I moved on.

# 4

## Canoe Voyage:
## A Young Man's Odyssey
## (1927)

During the summer of 1924, canoeing the rivers and lakes along the Canadian border as student assistant to Gruner and Grout, I acquired a great desire to cross over and explore the Canadian side. At that time much of the North had not been mapped. Aerial surveying was just beginning, and many areas were still unknown; one could discover unnamed lakes not shown on maps. Moreover, the Canadian North had an aura of romance, owing perhaps to the stories of Robert W. Service on wolves and northern lights and also to the tales of the voyageurs and the fur trade, the Hudson's Bay Company, and of course prospecting and gold. My chance came when I finished teaching at Oberlin.

Wynne Hastings had just finished his college work at Oberlin and wanted to get out of the classroom, away from books, and take a break before settling down to a job. He wanted to go to Alaska—to get as far away as possible—and he suggested I join him. I persuaded him to give up the Alaskan venture and try the lake country of northwestern Ontario—to join forces with me and make a canoe voyage into the northland to Red Lake, where there had been a major gold strike the winter before. We would join the gold rush, making a canoe voyage into what was then very nearly uninhabited wilderness.

And so we made the long drive in Wynne's Model T Ford from Oberlin to Chicago, Minneapolis, and eventually Duluth, where we purchased tent, packsacks and other camping gear. From there we drove to Ranier on the American shore of Rainy Lake, where we rented a canoe from Erikson, bought provisions, stowed them in the canoe, and embarked.

Frank Grout and his assistant were then working on Rainy Lake, checking Lawson's report on the Coutchiching mica schists and the

Keewatin greenstones. So after leaving Ranier we sought out their camp and, with their help, set up our tent. After the evening meal Grout gave us a quick look at the geology of the area, especially those outcrops that had a critical bearing on the Coutchiching problem.

The next day we set forth on our long canoe trip north. I had just turned twenty-three, and this was my first trip "on my own." I had learned something of the art of canoeing and camping from my experience with Grout, but though Wynne had canoed a little he had no experience in the North—never in a truly wilderness area.

The canoe trip proved a turning point in my career. I never returned to Oberlin, and I spent many years in the North. The trip was undertaken with no scientific goals or serious purpose, though I had promised Grout I would collect granites and other plutonic rocks, since he was interested in the chemical composition of the Canadian Shield and needed samples from more remote northern places. In the course of the trip I discovered, on the shores of Abram Lake, those outcrops of ancient Archean conglomerates—hitherto unmapped—that became the subject of my doctor's thesis. Completing the thesis did not end my involvement in the area; it was only the beginning. For nearly a decade the Archean in northwestern Ontario was the subject of my research, and our Red Lake trip led to a lifetime study of Precambrian geology. What follows is an account of that journey.

## The North

We waved good-bye to our hosts and turned our canoe northward. We were off on our voyage into the wilderness—destination Red Lake, some three hundred miles distant, the site of the greatest gold rush since the Klondike. The year was 1927, the date June 25, the day bright and clear. The wind had not yet risen, and the surface of Rainy Lake was like glass.

Rainy Lake (Lac la Pluie) is part of the boundary waters between the United States and Canada, on the main canoe route of the early fur traders. The diminishing fur supply from the Lake Superior region and the drain of furs from the west and north to the British on Hudson Bay led to the encircling effort in 1728 by Pierre Gaultier de Varennes, Sieur de La Vérendrye, a fur trader of Three Rivers. He moved in from Nipigon and the Grand Portage, swinging north of the unfriendly Sioux, to establish control of the Manitoba basin in 1731–34, thereby intersecting the flow of furs down to York Factory at the mouth of the Nelson River. The chief route for the French was over the nine-mile Grand Portage, which bypassed the many rapids and falls on the Pigeon River, down a chain of lakes that mark the present boundary between Minnesota and Ontario, through Rainy Lake and Lake of the Woods, to

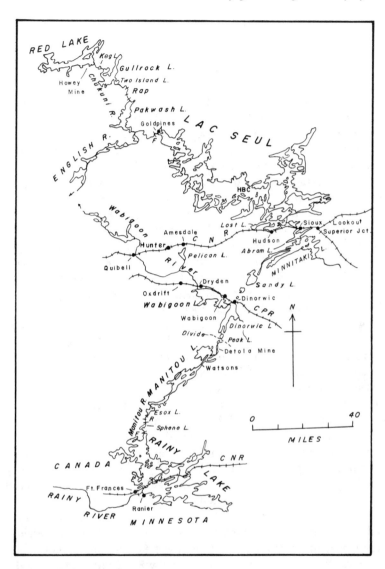

Route to Red Lake, 1927.

the northern parts of Manitoba and Saskatchewan. The French voyageurs made an astonishing canoe journey of more than fifteen hundred miles of rivers, lakes and portages to bring the furs to Lake Superior, where they were transhipped to Montreal. Their legacy is the legends of their incredible feats of paddle and portage and the names they gave to the areas they traversed—Lac la Pluie (Rainy Lake), Lac du Bois (Lake of the Woods), Lac la Croix, and Lac Seul among many.

Our voyage, though it totaled some six hundred miles, was miniscule by comparison, yet we had some of the same sense of adventure and excitement as we pushed north. We too traveled by canoe, battled the waves, ran the rapids, carried our packs on the portage trails, camped on the shores of the same lakes, and explored the wilderness—for much of it remained, not pristine perhaps, but still uninhabited and roadless.

Rainy Lake itself is one of the larger lakes along the boundary. It stretches nearly forty miles eastward from its outlet at Coutchiching Falls and some thirty miles northward to where the Manitou River plunges over the Devils Cascade into the head of Manitou Sound. It has a very irregular shoreline, several large, irregular bays, and myriad islands. The largest part of the lake lies north of the Canadian National track, which crosses on a series of small islands connected by a bridge and causeways. The lake south of the track is international waters, the south shore being part of Minnesota; north of the track the lake is wholly in Canada. Like Lake of the Woods, Rainy Lake was then accessible both by rail and by road, hence there were a fair number of summer cottages and power boats. The lake was not so exploited, however, as to be fully settled. Most islands and most of the mainland were still uninhabited, and settlement seemed to be concentrated in and near the outlet—at Ranier on the Minnesota side and at Fort Frances on the Canadian side. Fort Frances was the head of navigation on the Rainy River when, years ago, stern wheel steamboats traveled from Rat Portage (Kenora) on Lake of the Woods to dock below Coutchiching Falls.

As we started north across the lake, we passed Pithers Point, on the Canadian side, where once stood Fort Saint Pierre, built by La Vérendrye in 1731. On the Minnesota side once was a fur trading post of John Jacob Astor, the rival of the French. After we left Pithers Point and passed under the railway bridge into the northern part of the lake, the sawmills on the Canadian shore and the town of Ranier in Minnesota were lost to sight. The steady rhythm of the paddles carried us farther and farther north. We were on our own now, and we had a chance to look the country over.

Rainy Lake is but one of many thousands—yes, tens of thousands—of lakes, many smaller, some larger, that characterize this region. These lakes occupy rock basins in a vast area of granite and crystalline rocks known to geologists as the Canadian or Precambrian Shield. The Shield covers nearly a third of the whole continent and stretches from Labrador on the east to Manitoba and Saskatchewan on the west. It is a vast rocky area indeed, the basins filled with lakes or muskeg swamps, with intervening rocky hills covered with moss and clothed with a dominantly evergreen forest. Where the forest has burned—and with it the moss cover—the rocks stand naked. The rock is mainly massive granite, usually pink. Common also is greenstone, a dark lava rock with its surface splotched with patches of lichens.

Such were our observations as we paddled north. The day had an unusual quality . The winds were fickle—starting up from this direction or that, then dropping off to a dead calm, so that the few white puffs of cloud were reflected in the water. We felt suspended in space; time seemed to stand still. The only sound was the swish of the paddles or the distant cry of gulls. The surface of the lake was disturbed only by the wake of the canoe or the ripples of fish that jumped here and there. Here we were, silent, each with his own thoughts.

Our plan was to travel north on Rainy Lake, up the Manitou River to the Manitou country, then over a low divide to the Wabigoon drainage, down the Wabigoon River to the English River, and up the English to the Chukuni, which we would follow upstream to Red Lake. We were out to travel. The voyageurs were not much on our minds when we started. We were two college-age chaps on a lark—a canoe voyage to the goldfields of Red Lake. We would find our own way through the maze of lakes and portages with map and compass, out of touch for days. What adventures lay ahead?

THE CANOE

The innumerable lakes, linked by short stretches of river marked by falls and rapids, form a limitless system of waterways. This was our highway, and the canoe was our vehicle. The canoe we inherit from the Indian—a craft born of the woods, made of birch bark on a spruce frame, sealed with pine pitch. Such canoes had all but disappeared and had been replaced by a carefully crafted frame covered with canvas protected by paint and half a dozen coats of marine varnish. The all-metal "tinny" canoes had not yet been invented. The handcrafted canoe is a thing of beauty, eminently suited to its task. It moves silently through the water as an extension of the canoeman, responsive to his slightest touch. If handled and loaded properly it is remarkably stable and will weather heavy seas, yet is light enough to be carried on the portage trail. It will even shelter a man and his packs if need be. It deserves respect and loving care, for without it there would be no return from the wilderness. Our canoe was an eighteen-foot Old Town, made in Maine, that could carry two men, three packs, and two bedrolls with ease. We carried an extra paddle in case we lost or broke one.

## Our Camp

As the afternoon wore on we began to look for a campsite. We chose a small island near the entrance to Manitou Sound, an arm of Rainy Lake that leads to the Devils Cascade and the Manitou River. The site provided a smooth rock shelf, behind which was a level tent site among the pines. After a quick look around, we tossed out the packs and bedrolls, pulled the canoe out, and turned it bottom up. Since Wynne was new at the game, I showed him all the steps in setting up camp—camping in the North being much different from camping as most people know it. First a level tent site in a safe spot—not where a storm could bring a tree crashing down on tent or canoe. Next cutting tent poles—a straight sapling or two provided the five poles needed, the longest being the ridgepole. We spread out our tent—a seven-by-nine wall tent—and tied it to the ridgepole so it hung like a sheet hangs on a clothesline. The other poles were tied at one end in pairs and spread like an inverted V, one pair at each end of the tent to support the ridgepole. Ropes were tied from each pair of end poles to trees or stakes to steady the whole structure. The sides of the tent were then opened out and tied to boulders, trees, or whatever was available. Our tent was thus supported by the pole framework, made to order at each campsite. Next we tossed in our bedrolls, each wrapped in a tarpaulin that served as a ground cloth, since the tent itself had none. The bedrolls contained our blankets, and wrapped inside were our clothes and toilet articles. No sleeping bags, no air mattresses. If we had time and wanted more comfort, we could collect balsam boughs to put under the tarpaulins. The front of the tent was closed by mosquito netting, sewn in, with pleats so we could lift it up to crawl under. No zippers in 1927. Tent stakes, if needed, were cut at each site in the same manner as the poles, but since this region is so rocky, we could seldom drive stakes. More often the tent ropes were tied to large boulders or nearby trees.

Our tent up and ready for the night, we turned to making a campfire. First a fireplace in a safe spot—on bare rock. We cut a long pole of green wood from which to hang our nested kettles. This pole was balanced over a large boulder, one end weighted down with heavy rocks. The other end tilted up. The kettles could be hooked over the free end and moved up or down to vary their distance above the flame. The fire itself was started by lighting birch bark—a remarkable substance that never failed to burn vigorously, even in the rain. To this was added kindling, then split wood. No Coleman stove to be sure, but a workable arrangement. Our frying pan was an old-fashioned sheet-metal skillet with a metal handle, which we had cut off and replaced with a metal loop. A sapling inserted in the loop provided a six-foot handle. No more singed hair or smoke in the eyes. To move the kettles up or down our kettle pole and to put them on or take them off, we fashioned "kettlehooks"—sticks a couple feet long with stout side branches cut off short. No need to touch the hot wire handle or risk flame or smoke. A pail of water from the lake, and we are ready to start supper.

A quick search of the provision pack brought out the ingredients. Since we had not yet had to portage and were fresh from town, we still had white bread, steak, eggs, and a few other perishables. But tomorrow we would be down to our staple bill of fare. Our supplies did *not* include canned goods, which are much too heavy, nor did we have the dehydrated foods of today. Instead our larder consisted of such items as flour, cornmeal, oatmeal, rice, dry lima beans, elbow macaroni, dried apples, peaches, and prunes, sugar, salt, tea, cocoa and coffee, a side of lean bacon (unsliced of course), cheese, rye wafers, peanut butter, jam, and dried whole milk (Klim). We did have tinned butter and chocolate bars—our two luxuries. Supplies adequate for two or even three weeks could be carried. We counted on fish and possibly blueberries to supplement our diet.

Wynne noted with interest that nearly all our supplies had been transferred from the original containers to cloth bags. Less weight, more readily packed, and less likely to jab one in the back on a portage. There were exceptions to be sure. Jam, peanut butter, and such remained in their original containers. It became a bit of a game to identify the contents of each sack by feel—to distinguish flour, oatmeal, and sugar, for example.

As soon as the meal was finished, we washed our tin cups and plates at the lakeshore, drew a fresh pail of water, and cut and split some firewood to store in the tent in case it rained during the night. Our chores done, we sat by the campfire resting our aching muscles—we had paddled twenty-two miles that day—and watched the sun sink below the horizon. We soon turned to the tent after dousing the last glowing embers of the fire—a very necessary precaution. There is nothing more alarming than to be awakened in the night by the tent flapping in a fresh wind and to see sparks flying into the woods from a fire you thought was out. We straightened out our blankets by candlelight and killed any mosquitoes that had come in, for there were no such insect repellents as we have now. We turned in for the night wondering what the next day would bring—for we would have our first portage and start up the Manitou River.

Canoe Travel

*Sunday, June 26: Manitou River*

We woke the next morning rested from the first day's paddle. Since we had paddled without our shirts, our backs were a bit pink and tender—a tenderness we were shortly to regret as we made our first portage.

The fire was soon burning brightly, the cereal cooking, and the coffee water boiling. We were eager to get on, so we made short work of breakfast. Bedrolls were reassembled, the tent was struck, folded, and put into its packsack. The kettles were cleaned and nested and placed in a special bag that isolated their sooty exteriors from the other contents of the pack. A quick check for anything overlooked and an extra pail of water on the campfire, and we were off.

The day was fair and our paddle to the Devils Cascade a short one. We could hear the cascades before we saw them, for here the Manitou River drops nearly fifty feet over rock ledges into the head of Manitou Sound. It was a popular fishing spot, and several motorboats were drifting slowly about in the sudsy, turbulent waters below the cascades. The portage trail was easy to spot. We unloaded and beached the canoe. Since we had three packs and two bedrolls as well as the canoe, we had to make two trips over the portage. Each of us carried a packsack with a bedroll on top. Our packs were heavy, since we were fully stocked with provisions, and though the portage was short the trail was steep. Though the morning was cool, we were perspiring when we returned for the other pack and the canoe. To carry the canoe, we lashed the paddles to the center and forward thwarts so that when the canoe was turned upside down the flat blades of the paddles rested on our shoulders. The canoe was light enough to be carried by one person, but it was an awkward load and it took a special know-how to swing it up on one's shoulders and set it down again. On a long portage one might find a canoe rest—a pole nailed between two trees—on which to lean the canoe for a moment's breather. On the longer portages we usually made the carry in two or more stages, setting down our first load after a short carry and returning for the second load, which we then carried beyond the first, thus getting a bit of rest while returning to pick up the first load. Unlike the voyageurs, who were said to trot across the longest portage, we were glad to proceed more slowly in this leapfrog way.

A very short stretch of river led to Sphene Lake—a lake of irregular form, presumably named for the mineral sphene. Lake names in this region of uncounted lakes fascinated us. Most, especially the smaller ones, were unnamed. The largest carried French names or their English translations; a great many had Indian names, though many if not most of these were known by other names. This caused considerable confusion, because we used the names shown on our maps, which were sometimes unfamiliar to the local inhabitants. To add to our confusion, the name shown on one map might be different on another. Manitou was the name of both the river we were ascending and also the lake it came from and the region around the lake. It was the Indian name for the Great Spirit, and the region was a sacred one.

Just beyond Sphene Lake we came to Whitehorse Rapids—really a falls over some bold granite ledges. The portage was just a "liftover" of no more than two or three canoe lengths. The upstream end, however, was just above the lip of the falls, and it was a ticklish job to skirt a rock promontory that jutted out into the river at this point without getting caught in the swift current and sucked backward over the falls. We discovered that the water was at an abnormally high stage so part of the portage trail was under water, and also that the portages were adjusted to low water rather than high water. This was dramatically shown about a mile upstream from Whitehorse, where we came to a stretch of rapids requiring a longer portage. The portage was steep and the trail poor, in places over boulders, in places wet and mucky. The upstream end was under water. Here we loaded our canoe as usual and cast off, working away from the flooded willows and alders toward midstream. To our dismay, we found we were drifting downstream in spite of our efforts to paddle upstream. The sound of the rapids and a quick backward glance at the mists arising from the tumult below spurred us to greater effort. Wynne dug in and pulled hard on his paddle. I did likewise, and little by little we inched forward, for I was able to swing the canoe a bit closer to the edge of the stream, where the drag of the banks reduced the speed of the current. It seemed for a moment that our voyage was about to end in disaster.

We shortly came to two more rapids requiring portaging. At the head of the uppermost one was a dam built for storing water, to be released during a log drive to ensure an adequate flow to carry the logs down the Manitou River to Rainy Lake and thence to the sawmills at Fort Frances. The dam consisted of rock fill on the sides and a sluice with sluice gates made of logs in the center. The gates would be opened for the drive, the logs guided into the sluice and thence downstream.

Above the dam we entered Cedar Narrows, leaving behind the Manitou River with its rapids and falls and, of course, all the motorboats of Rainy Lake. The country along the river we had come through was largely clothed by second-growth timber, dominantly poplar mixed with balsam and a little birch. Here and there, as just above Whitehorse Rapids, one would see an occasional mature white pine—a reminder of what had once been.

After we passed through Cedar Narrows we entered Pickerel Lake (Esox Lake on the newer maps). This lake, the largest since Rainy Lake, was an irregular body of water marked by much standing dead timber along its shores and islands. Such dead trees usually are caused by a rise in water level and flooding of the woods, in this case apparently owing to the dam at the outlet. This event must have happened some years ago, since the trees were now stark naked, with few or no branches and of course no foliage whatever. On top of one of these, a giant beheaded pine, was an osprey's nest—a large affair, built of sticks, that overhung its standard. The osprey, or fish eagle, is a large bird fairly common in this region; it catches fish live as it swoops from a soaring flight down to the surface of the lake. The osprey returns year after year to the same nest. We passed this landmark and paddled several more miles before finding a suitable island campsite. We had traveled no more than twelve or fifteen miles, but we had made five portages. We had ascended the Manitou, gaining over one hundred feet in elevation, and were ready to call it a day. Our second camp, pitched more efficiently, was now a wilderness camp—no more passing motor boats, no more habitations— the silence broken only by the cry of a loon, the songs of white-throated sparrows at sundown, and the wheeling and plunging of nighthawks in the evening sky.

*Monday, June 27: The Third Day*

We woke to find the weather holding fair. After breaking camp and making a short paddle, we entered the narrows between Pickerel Lake and Manitou Lake. Although the map showed rapids at this point, we found only a swift current that we could negotiate under paddle. We now entered Manitou Lake, a long, irregular, but generally narrow body of water, stretching some thirty-five miles to the northeast. Here one seemed always to be in a small landlocked body of water, but this illusion was repeatedly shattered as the rockbound shores parted to present a new vista. Each island we skirted, each point we rounded, brought a fresh view. In the calm of the early morning the rocky shores, here and there splotched with orange lichens, formed a kaleidoscopic reflection in the water.

The country surrounding the Lower Manitou was then covered with pine and spruce—more presentable than the poplar bush of the Manitou River. We took in the unending panorama; rounding each point was an adventure. We surprised a deer that bounded away flashing its white tail as it leaped into the forest, or we startled a great blue heron wading in the reeds back in a bay. This large bird with its stiltlike legs would spread its great wings and silently flap away. Once we saw a moose, shoulder-deep

Wynne K. Hastings and canoe, Manitou Lake, northwestern Ontario, 1927.

in the water, browsing on underwater vegetation. The moose would put its head under from time to time, then raise it again to get a breath and look around. Since we were downwind, we could approach closely enough to see the cloud of flies hovering about its head. Upon discovering our presence, the moose lumbered awkwardly ashore and crashed through the underbrush to disappear in the forest.

Hours passed quickly, and the miles melted away. By midafternoon we reached the main body of the lake, an open sheet of water large enough to present a problem if the winds are not favorable. Lucky for us, the breeze was light and at our backs. We followed the south shore, a more or less straight exposed coast flanked by rocky cliffs, above which were pine-clad hills. A paddle of about eight miles brought us to the narrow, tortuous waters of Manitou Straits, which connect Lower Manitou and Upper Manitou lakes. As we were leaving the main lake we passed several bare, rocky islets with their load of herring gulls. At our approach the gulls dispersed with cries of alarm. These rather large, generally all-white birds are scavengers, eating any fish floating belly-up. They congregate and nest on the nearly treeless rocky islets that emerge reeflike from the larger lakes. These barren rocks are often soiled with guano and have an unpleasant odor.

We sight another canoe—a rare event—almost cause for alarm—an invasion of our privacy! Indian, prospector, or just another pair of adventurers? We stop, exchange information on the route ahead, and pass on into solitude once more.

We entered the Manitou Straits after a brief stop for lunch. The prospect of rough water, which never materialized, was now behind us, so we felt less impelled to hurry. The aspect of the country had changed somewhat. There were the same rocky shores, but the forest cover was more like that of the Manitou River, largely poplar and balsam—second growth. No doubt this area was once logged and perhaps burned over, to be partially reclaimed by the poplar bush. The forest of the Lower Manitou was largely evergreen—in places large white and red pines—the source of the logs for the sawmills at Fort Frances. In other places the trees were mostly white spruce and balsam. Where the country has been denuded by recent forest fires there remain only the bare, rocky hills, blackened stumps, gaunt charred tree trunks—some standing, others lying prone—with here and there a new growth of pin cherries and small poplars wherever a crevice or low spot is capable of retaining soil and moisture. The original forest was a parklike stand of giant pines. The forest floor was then moss, knee-deep and spongy, damp and verdant, covering the rock surface like a deep-pile carpet. Since it was all organic, it too was consumed by the forest fire, leaving acres of solid granite without enough soil to pot a geranium. How would one reforest such a rocky desert?

As we paddled we caught glimpses of the muskegs that marked the head of each passing bay. The low areas that are not lake-filled are occupied by the forested swamp or muskeg of the North. Most common is black spruce, which gives the muskeg its somber dark color and pinnacled skyline. Less common is tamarack, the deciduous needle-bearing tree, or more rarely white cedar. Around the edges of the muskeg are alder bushes. The swamp floor is wet, with pools of tea-colored water, but mostly the surface is covered with spongy sphagnum moss. One can walk in such a muskeg swamp without getting in over one's boot tops, but it is very tiring—like walking on a feather bed. In places the muskeg is open, with only a scattering of stunted black spruce and small, shrublike Labrador tea. The waters of the muskeg are very acid, so trees are dwarfed. The muskeg is a replacement of a former lake that has been invaded and filled by organic matter, forming a considerable deposit of peat. The vegetation grows from the shore inward, gradually closing in until only a small pond of open water remains. It too will disappear in time. The advancing fringe of vegetation may actually float on the surface of the residual lake, forming a quaking bog. A portage that ends in a quaking bog is an eerie experience! The prospect of breaking through the floating mat into the water below is chilling.

Having paddled about twenty-five miles, we were ready to make camp. We soon did so on a pretty island in the narrow waters of the Manitou Straits. The breeze had died and a great silence fell over the land. The plaintive song of the whitethroat, the occasional splash of a fish, or the crackle of our campfire were all that could be heard.

## MANITOU AND GOLD

*Tuesday, June 28: The Fourth Day*

The next morning we slept late. Three long days of paddle and portage—some sixty-five or seventy miles from our start, exercising little-used muscles—plus a bit too much sun—had left us lame and sore.

We had a leisurely breakfast, struck camp, loaded our canoe, and resumed our journey. After about an hour's paddle we rounded a point. What a surprise! There on a low, sandy point of land was a two-story frame house, once painted, and a few outbuildings, all enclosed by a picket fence—a most incongruous touch of civilization in a wilderness of lake, rock, and forest. As we approached several dogs began to bark furiously, and an old man appeared and slowly walked down to his dock, motioning to us to pull in. Thus we made the acquaintance of Rattlesnake Bill Watson.

Since visitors so seldom passed Bill's place, he insisted we stop in for "tea." We tied up our canoe, opened the gate, and followed Bill into his house, where we met his wife Alice. Bill took off his hat and sat in his rocking chair while Mrs. Watson put on the kettle. Bill was an old man by any standard, with white hair—a little sparse on top—a full white beard, a wrinkled visage, and blue eyes that, as Wynne later remarked, had the glitter of gold in them. For Watson was indeed a prospector and an incurable optimist. He had several claims nearby. His trousers were held up by a rope, his shoes were battered, and his shirt, missing a button or two, was partly open. He was a native of Scotland, born in 1849, the year gold was discovered in California, He came to Canada as a lad and ran away from home to join the Union army with a Massachusetts regiment. The war ended before he saw any action, and when he returned to Canada he went west to Alberta, where he discovered the hot springs at Banff, now a famous resort and national park. Bill came upon the springs while working his claim in the Canadian Rockies. The Canadian government had for a long while tried to buy the property from him, but since he had opened a health resort at the springs and the place was headed for a boom, he refused to sell at the price the government offered. Then a crippled old man came to Bill and told him he wanted to buy the property so he would have some way to make a living. Bill's kind heart forced him to part with his holdings for five thousand dollars, a fraction of what the government had offered. The feeble old man who had won his sympathy turned out to be a government agent. This now-famous recreational center and health spa was just one of the many fortunes that had slipped through Watson's fingers.

We asked about his name—Rattlesnake Bill. He said he had been bitten by a rattlesnake during his days in the West. No antivenin was available, and no fewer than six doctors considered him beyond help. Nonetheless he survived, and the name Rattlesnake Bill stuck.

Mrs. Watson, some twenty years his junior, in her late fifties, was hale and hearty. She wore a man's shirt and trousers, long before they became fashionable. She gave us fresh-baked bread with plenty of tea and thimbleberry jam. Mrs. Watson did most of the chores, including looking after the cow and the thirty-three dogs, which had the run of the yard and house. She tended the garden, kept house, and looked after Bill. The nearest settlement was Wabigoon, some thirty-five miles distant, past many lakes and portages. The Watsons' supplies were brought in once a year by sleigh over the ice and winter portages. What a grocery order that must have been. It was said that Mrs. Watson was a mail-order bride, having been a schoolteacher somewhere in eastern Canada.

Our talk turned to the Manitou region, which, as we learned, had once been the site of a mining boom. Watson had lived here for the past forty years, having come in when gold was first discovered shortly before 1894. This discovery precipitated a gold rush, and Watson was among the first to arrive. Between 1895 and 1912 at least twenty mines were opened up around the Manitou lakes, but by 1912 mining had practically ceased and only three mines had produced any gold. The promise of the area had faded—except in the mind of Bill Watson.

Bill had an unending supply of stories on Manitou gold and mining. There was the story, for example, of the Swede Boys. I include it here as best I can reconstruct it from Bill's account.

## THE SWEDE BOYS' CLAIM

In 1893 two unshaven men made their way up a small creek in a canoe, pushing, pulling, and poling their craft along the tortuous course of a small stream as it wriggled through the muskeg. "Damn this country anyway. Good enough for the Indians maybe, but not fer white men. We'd a done better to have stayed at Wabigoon." It was Nels, the younger of the two, who spoke, the one with fairer complexion, sandy hair, blue eyes, and high cheekbones, betokening his Swedish ancestry. He paddled the bow and for a moment was engrossed in avoiding a rat-root snag. His companion Ole was darker and older. His hair was a bit thin on top, and a taggy fringe surrounded the crown of his head. The younger man spoke again as he brushed the flies from face. "Do you suppose that Indian told you right? This is the only creek coming out of that lake. We've gone upcurrent through eight lakes, over the divide, and followed down the flowage to the lake with the picture rocks. This inlet looks blind to me." The older man, a bit impatiently, answered, "Can't trust an Indian too far, but what'd we be doing in Wabigoon? Drinkin' at Tony's Café, like as not." For a moment neither spoke. Then Nels remarked, "Sounds like shallows ahead; another beaver dam likely," then added, "Hell of a fine showing though—that rock sample—plastered full of leaf gold. Never seen a thing like it, 'cept at the Mikado."

Straining every muscle, the two worked along a while longer and at last came to a bit of a pool below a cascade over granite ledges. There was a faint portage trail on the right of the rapid, to which they easily made their way. In a brief moment they pulled the canoe alongside a flat rock, threw several dirty packsacks and a couple of duffel bags out into a heap, and lifted the canoe out onto solid ground. The two stood there a moment, mopped their brows, and gazed at the sinking sun. "We'll have to get along to camp 'fore long. Tain't but an hour till sundown." The younger man didn't answer directly but presently remarked, as he swung pack and duffel onto his back, "Fine moose country this." "Huh, fine granite country too," replied the other; "looks like we're on a wild-goose chase, right?" The branches of the shrubs parted; the two pushed through and were gone. In half an hour they were back, sweaty and tired. "Well Ole, that's a damn poor portage—'bout as good as a game trail, my way a thinkin'." "Well don't start that again. Find a better one if you can. Leastwise it comes to water at the far end. Better than end on a mountain like yourn did over on Flying Loon Lake," replied Ole as he swung the canoe easily onto his shoulders. They sloshed along over boulders and logs, at times mired up to their knees, until they finally emerged on a lake, now quiet in the evening calm and reflecting the growing pink of the sky. Only a few minutes' respite and they were off to the nearest island, where there seemed to be a possibility of a tent site.

"Greenstone, by golly, Nels," exclaimed the older man before they touched the shore. "Surefire," replied Nels as he stepped out and began to unload. "Likely enough looking, too."

Before twilight had settled the campfire began to blaze, and within an hour Ole had fixed a supper of bacon, bannock, and coffee while Nels put up the none-too-white tent in a group of jack pines. Darkness fell not long after. Thus the two who had left Wabigoon a week before arrived at an unnamed lake on a quest for the lode from which the Indian, Kabaguski, had taken his sample. Old Kabaguski had since died, but the details of his story were as fresh in Ole's mind as when he heard them the winter before in the lumber camp near Rat Portage, now called Kenora. Ole was cook then and had befriended Kabaguski when the Indian, after a run of bad luck with his traps, had stumbled into the cookshack with a bullet in his foot. The mishap had occurred a week before, and it was too late. Complications set in, and the Indian didn't last a fortnight. But before he died he told Ole how to find the lode from which two small samples of gold-bearing rock had come. Nels was a harness-maker by trade, Minnesota born, but had drifted northward and become more or less a floater, finding employment now and then in the lumber camps caring for the horses, mending harness, and doing other odd jobs. Ole had first come into the region as a cook during the construction of the Canadian Pacific a few years before. Both had an eye for "mineral," however, particularly since the discoveries were now coming thick and fast. First the Huronian mine in Mors Township, then the Sultana and the Mikado on Lake of the Woods, then the Foley mine on Shoal Lake, and now the Manitou was opening.

For the past week they had been traveling from one rock-rimmed lake to another over portage trails.

Breakfast came with the rising sun of a late summer day. A little before the coffee water boiled, Ole knelt with a glass to his eye, hat tilted back, studying a bit of rock. When Nels paddled in with the morning catch of pike, Ole tossed him a chip. "Give a look, Nels. Am I crazy, or are my eyes getting poor?" Nels looked the chip over. "Gold, no doubt of it, peppered full. Fer God's sake, where did it come from?" "Float," responded Ole. "Carried in here—saw the chippings around the camp, not so old either. Found 'em by the old pine over there. Winter camp—Indians." "The old fellow was right then; must've been here he put the bullet in his foot," remarked Nels. Breakfast was a perfunctory affair. The two soon paddled off, leaving their camp intact, followed the left shore a mile or two, then turned in at an inlet on the left side, passing into what appeared to be a blind bay.

Hours passed, and it was almost dark when the canoe reappeared and made directly for the camp.

Two weeks later this item appeared in a Port Arthur newspaper: "Ole Jannsen and Nels Wetclainen have filed on three claims on a lake fourteen miles east of Manitou Straits, according to Mr. John Williamson, the recorder. Martin Mayer, assayer and surveyor, reported the samples to be exceptionally rich." But the "Swede Boys," as they were generally known, wouldn't disclose to anyone the exact route to the claims, and since they were in unsurveyed country there wasn't much to be learned at the recorder's office.

Ten days later Ole and Nels quietly left Port Arthur, outfitted again at Wabigoon and disappeared into the bush. This time they took picks, shovels, drills, and other tools. Some time later the two put in an appearance at Port Arthur. They created quite a sensation by depositing at the bank a bag of about 120 ounces of coarse gold.

Winter was setting in, so Ole took up lodgings in Port Arthur while Nels made a trip to Minneapolis. Ole caught pneumonia in March of that year and died without giving any information—true to his partner to the last. Nels returned in the spring, withdrew what remained of their account at the bank, and took into his confidence a chap named Colleen. Colleen, a gaunt middle-aged Swede, was a fisherman at Nipigon but had spent the winter in Fort William with his brother. The two took the train to Wabigoon, now in the height of a boom, for the Manitou had become the scene of a frenzied gold rush. They purchased an outfit from Jonathan Walsh, who had opened a store and ran a hotel. After some time they presumably reached the claims and worked them during the early part of the summer. About the middle of July they reappeared at Wabigoon, well supplied with gold. They had, they said, extracted it from the ore with spring pole, mortar, and amalgam pan. The richness of the ore was easy to guess, since they could have hand-crushed only a ton or two at the most with their crude mill. They went to Port Arthur and invested their money in a small hand mill, which was to be shipped from Liverpool. Some delay ensued, and before the mill arrived winter had set in. They were not overanxious, however, since the summer's workings had yielded enough not only to finance the hand mill but to keep them well through the winter. Colleen decided to make a trip back to the old country to visit his relatives, for it had been twenty-one years since he had seen his parents. Spring came and he had not returned. The mill, meanwhile, had been misdirected and had gone to some point in British Columbia. Consequently Nels Wetclainen signed up to drive logs down the Rainy River to the mills at Baudette. During the drive he slipped and was caught between two boom logs. They took him on the tug to Rat Portage, and he was sent to Winnepeg, where he spent a long time in a hospital. A head injury had impaired his memory so that he could not recall his past experiences or even his name. In the meantime Colleen returned and, unable to find Nels, promptly went back to Sweden to raise capital to continue the mining venture. He was fairly successful, but misfortune followed in the closing of a bank where the funds were deposited. Colleen then resumed his fishing to make ends meet for the time being. He also married again—his first wife had died long before—and his family responsibilities tied him down for a few years.

To his son he imparted all the details of his past ventures as well as the story of the original discovery as told him by the unfortunate Nels. Age forced Colleen to retire. His son Hakon carried on the fishing and also married and had a family. His father died without resuming his development of the claims. Young Colleen, though he inherited them, did not follow up his father's interest until his family was more or less able to shift for itself. Then he undertook the task of tracing Nels as rightful part owner of the claims and the only person likely to know the exact location. He had little luck at first but eventually traced him to Winnepeg, where he found him active and at work at the harness trade though he was now old and had a number of nearly grown sons. His memory was still clouded by the blow on the head in his Rainy River accident. So Colleen the younger got no aid from this quarter.

He therefore resolved to set out according to oral directions given by his father. The expedition was not successful, however, though it was said he located the island camp from which the prospectors had worked the deposit. As proof he had several chips of the float that had first verified Kabaguski's story.

Colleen then lived at Wabigoon, planning yet another venture into the Manitou region to find the Swede Boys' location. The boom on the Manitou has since been extinguished. The closing of the Laurentian mine in 1907 was really the end. Wabigoon is today nearly a "ghost town," with boarded-up buildings. Tony's Café with its false front is patronized only by an occasional porcupine.

There is but one thing further. Some years later a party from Fort Frances, on a pleasure trip by canoe, mistook a game trail for a portage and ended up at a little lake not then shown on the map. In an effort to find a route out of this lake they were led into a bay that, though it seemed to lead nowhere, proved a good deal larger than anticipated. Oncoming darkness forced them to camp. Concerned with rediscovering their route and returning to the fort, they did not pay much attention to details of the camp's location. One did, however, bring back a pick with its handle rotted away, which he found at the water's edge near a pile of broken rock. They retraced their route with much difficulty and returned safely to Fort Frances. The pick was seen by an old-time prospector at Fort Frances, who declared it was unlike any then used in the region but resembled the Hudson Bay pick used forty or fifty years earlier. It occurred to the prospector then that the souvenir might be the clue to the lost Swede Boys' claim. The owner of the pick proposed to revisit the locality, but the press of his Chicago business made it impossible to do so.

The claims, of course, are now crown land once more, since the assessment work has not been done for years and since they were never surveyed in the first place. So they are any man's find. But time has passed, and they must be overgrown with brush, back in their natural state. And time has also permitted many versions of the story of the Swede Boys' venture. I cannot—nor could any man, except the younger Colleen himself—vouch for the truth of the details I have recorded here.

We had become so engrossed in Bill's tales that before we knew it the morning had slipped by and it was well past noon. We took our leave and promised to stop again on our return from Red Lake. So we took off and continued through Upper Manitou waters, finally reaching the end of Manitou Straits, and in doing so we passed the opening into Upper Manitou Lake (or Anzhekuming Lake, as the map has it). A small creek led to Power Lake, a mere pond with a single islet. From Power Lake we made a short carry to Selby Lake, also very small. Since it was by now quite late, we camped on the liftover between Selby Lake and Kabagukski Lake, otherwise known as Mud Lake. Our campsite was a novel one, a low, rocky rise with a lake on each side. As dusk approached the mosquitoes got bad, so we lost no time in setting up camp, preparing supper, and turning in.

## Detola

*Wednesday, June 29*

The following morning we made an early start, since we had many portages ahead, including one a mile long. Kabagukski or Mud Lake is a riverlike body, some three miles long and not much over a quarter-mile wide at the widest place. Though it is fairly shallow, especially at the north end, its shores rise steeply. About a mile from our camp we spied the headframe of the old Detola mine on the west shore. The Detola is one of the many "mines" in the Manitou region—a gaunt relict of the frenzied gold rush of the 1890s and early 1900s. It now stands deserted and forlorn—a silent monument to the lost hopes of men, to money, sweat, and tears. We got out at the ruins of an old dock to explore. A large rock pile extends out from the headframe. A rusty track with rotting ties runs along the top; several small derailed mine cars are nearby. Poplar growth had sprung up between the rails. The shaft itself had been boarded over, but the planks had mostly rotted away. We

Shaft house of Detola mine (Ed Espenshade, Scott Griffith, and Gordon Rittenhouse, 1932).

stepped gingerly to the edge and peered down. It was too dark to see so we tossed in a stone, which rattled its way down the shaft to land with a resounding splash.

The Detola was abandoned in 1911. All the buildings and equipment were just as they had been left. Some of the smaller articles may have been carried off, but much remained untouched. According to Bill Watson, the machinery cost half a million dollars, and none of it was ever used because there was no gold there in the first place. Prospectors had salted the claims before they showed them to buyers; the samples showing free gold had been taken from Watson's claims and placed at various points on the Detola property. The claims were then purchased by a corporation of American and German stockholders, who hired John Bachich as superintendent. Because he suspected there might be no ore on the property, he was dismissed in 1909. Dryden Smith was hired to take his place, but there were no profitable results, and in 1911 the whole project was given up and the miners left in a hurry.

There were three main buildings. Close to the shore was the boarding house; on the first floor were the office and living quarters, including kitchen and mess hall. Stove, dishes, tables, and chairs cluttered the kitchen; in the office were the safe—still locked—desk, stationery, and files and records of all kinds. On the second floor was the dormitory, the beds were still there and even some clothing.

A little farther back from the lake was the stamp mill, which was to treat the ore that never was found. The building is of sheet metal and was in very good condition. It was of considerable height and the top could be seen from quite a distance, either up or down the lake. Slowly, however, all the buildings and their contents were disappearing into the encroaching bush.

We left the place, reflecting on the men who worked there—worked in vain—and on the lost hopes and dreams of the stockholders whose savings were invested. In the Detola was embodied the history of the whole Manitou district—a dream that never materialized and lives on only in the mind of Rattlesnake Bill.

We resumed our voyage and in less than a half-hour arrived at the portage to Sasakwei Lake. This portage, which proved one of the longest on our trip to Red Lake, followed the course of a small stream that connected Sasakwei Lake to Kabagukski Lake. Although level for the most part, it was swampy, much of it through muskeg. We had to make our carry in three or four stages, and we were plagued by mosquitoes, which were most annoying to the person carrying the canoe. Since it takes both hands to balance the canoe properly, you cannot dislodge mosquitoes that light on your arms or face—even the bridge of your nose. The portage ended in an expanded portion of the creek, blocked by

Wynne K. Hastings and canoe, beaver pond on Sasakwei Creek, northwestern Ontario, 1927.

an old beaver dam. The pond thus created widened the creek and flooded the adjacent area. There we stood facing a forest of poles—all killed years ago by the backwater above the old dam. We could see no signs of recent activity; presumably the beavers had all been trapped. We loaded the canoe and looked for the creek channel, lost somewhere in the forest of dead trees. After maneuvering around many stumps and fallen tree trunks we got into the channel, which led us on a twisting course to Sasakwei Lake. We were glad to be on open water once more and to catch a breeze that blew away the pesky mosquitoes. A short paddle took us across this small lake to the portage to Peak Lake. This carry took us over the divide into the Wabigoon drainage—waters flowing north, not south or southwest to Rainy Lake. Peak Lake, a couple of miles long, led by a short portage around Minnehaha Falls into Minnehaha Lake, also very small. Here we left the Manitou country by a sluggish stream from Minnehaha Lake to Stanawan Lake and thence to Dinorwic or Little Wabigoon Lake. The landscape changed dramatically. It was of a different aspect, wholly unlike anything we had seen since leaving Rainy Lake.

## Pioneer Life

The creek leading to Stanawan Lake and beyond, wide and sluggish, was choked with aquatic plants and fringed by lily pads. On either side were extensive marshes with acres and acres of cattail rushes reminiscent of the marshes of southern Wisconsin, in marked contrast to the muskeg swamps we had seen so far. They were a haven for a vast number of water birds; each bend in the creek brought new surprises—here a pair of mallards with a flotilla of ducklings, there teals and grebes. At the edge of the stream were the wading birds—the long-legged blue herons, the nervous sandpipers. Among the rushes one could glimpse an occasional bittern and see and hear innumerable redwing blackbirds. Overhead the terns swooped this way and that. As the channel opened up and we came to the main lake, we saw a small island, a low, treeless piece of ground scarcely a hundred feet in diameter and no more than a few feet above lake level. A cloud of terns flew up as we approached. It was evidently a nesting colony. Wynne stepped ashore and counted over a hundred nests all filled with eggs. He suggested we throw all the eggs out and come back the next day so we could have fresh eggs for breakfast. Suggestion not heeded!

Time to look for a campsite. We chose an island a bit farther out in the lake, but as we approached we saw that, unlike the islands in the Manitou country, this one had steep clay banks. wave-eroded and overhanging in places. Deposited on the Precambrian rock surface, here exposed beneath the clay cover, was a blanket of clay that at this point was no more than ten feet thick but, as we were to discover, was much thicker elsewhere. We were in fact entering a "clay belt"—an extensive area where the Precambrian basement was mantled with clay deposited by an ancient glacial lake, one coextensive perhaps with glacial Lake Agassiz. As we saw when we landed, the clays were strikingly banded, layers of light-colored silt alternating with very fine dark clay; the whole bank was composed of these layers. Each pair, no more than a half-inch thick, represented one year's deposit, the silt being formed in the summer and the dark clay settling out in winter when the glacial lake was covered with ice. These "varves" are a record of seasons past, recording annual sedimentation much as the rings of a tree record annual growth.

The clifflike embankment presented something of an obstacle to landing and making camp, but Wynne found a place where, with the aid of exposed tree roots, he could scramble up. I tossed up the packs and eventually we had all our gear, including the canoe, on top. We found a suitable level spot to pitch tent, build a fire, and make everything secure for the night. It proved awkward, however, to have to shinny up and down for water—water that was somewhat murky with suspended clay, produced no doubt by wave erosion of the clay banks that surround the lake.

*Thursday, June 30: Dinorwic to Dryden*

We were awakened early by a sharp thunderclap. In a few minutes we heard rain coming across the lake and shortly were engulfed in a heavy shower. It was brief, however, and the sky soon cleared—a prelude to a sunny and unusually warm day. While I was preparing breakfast, Wynne disappeared in the woods behind the tent and reappeared in a few minutes carrying a human skull. He had found a box containing a skeleton. "What shall I do with it?" he asked. "Throw it in the lake," was my response, and so he did. So today, if you visit this island and look in the right place, you will find a headless skeleton. As we learned afterward, we were on an Indian reservation and the island where we camped was an Indian graveyard. The Ojibway Indians commonly place their dead in boxlike structures on *top* of the ground. We were later to see other such "burial" grounds, usually small islands, often displaying poles from which flutter flags or banners.

After breaking camp and negotiating the clay cliff a second time, we paddled north toward Wabigoon, passing many similar eroded banks, some clifflike, with trees being undermined and toppling into the lake. My guess was that the water level of the lake had been raised, probably by a dam, so that the shores were undergoing rapid erosion, which also explained the cloudy waters of the lake. This surmise proved to be correct, for Dinorwic Lake is freely connected to Wabigoon Lake, which displays the same features and at whose outlet, at Dryden, are a pulp mill and dam.

We followed the western shore and noted that we were indeed in an Indian reservation, for there were many small clearings with log cabins and other shacks. There were no Indians, so presumably we were looking at their winter habitations. Before noon we passed through the narrows between Dinorwic Lake and Wabigoon Lake, and we soon caught a glimpse of the town of Wabigoon. Wabigoon is now almost a ghost town; it consists of a dozen or so houses scattered about, various boarded-up stores, a railway station and water tank, and a wharf and boathouse. We wondered which of the several now-abandoned false fronts was Tony's Café. The sound of a pickup truck rattling through town reminded us that this was the first outpost of civilization since Ranier on Rainy Lake, about one hundred miles to the south. We weren't impressed.

The Wabigoon clay belt is a smaller edition of the great clay belt of eastern Ontario. Like the latter, it is an island of settlement and agriculture in the vastly greater inhospitable rocky Shield. The Wabigoon clay belt extends westward nearly forty miles to Vermilion Bay on Eagle Lake. It had been surveyed and subdivided into 160-acre homesteads and opened to settlement. Dryden, the largest town in this area, with a population of perhaps a thousand, had a pulp mill and was the trading center for the region. Dirt or gravel roads connected Dryden with Wabigoon on the east and Vermilion Bay on the west, and side roads provided access to the various bush farms. The road system, however, led nowhere at this time, for it was then not possible to reach the "outside" by car. The Trans Canada Highway had not yet been built; the Canadian Pacific Railroad, completed in 1885, was the only link between this area of settlement and the rest of the world.

On Wabigoon Lake our course turned more westward. The north shore was fringed by settlement; the south shore was wild and foreboding. Wabigoon Lake is a large body of water and, because most of its many islands are small and afford little protection, it can kick up a rough sea in high winds. Fortunately for us the weather was fair. The thundershower of early morning had given way to generally clear skies with light and variable southeasterly winds. We passed an occasional clearing and saw a few houses, some grazing cows, and an occasional motorboat; since we were anxious to get to Dryden and pick up fresh supplies, we did not stop but paddled steadily westward. It was now late in the day—we had come about twenty-five miles—so we did not go to town that evening but pitched our tent where the river leaves Wabigoon Lake, some two miles upstream from Dryden.

*Friday, July 1: Dominion Day*

We paddled downstream to Dryden, a bustling place full of mill workers, lumberjacks, settlers and their families, and a great number of Indians with assorted children and dogs. We discovered that the reason for all the activity was Dominion Day—July 1—the Canadian equivalent of our Fourth of July, so everybody was in town for the celebration. And of course every place of business as well as the postoffice was closed. We were stymied—couldn't send our mail or buy supplies—so we had no choice but to stay and celebrate too. We decided to splurge. Instead of going back to our regular camp fare, we would try a little café we had seen on the main street—eat at a table, with real china dishes with a tablecloth. The cafe—the only one in town—was a pretty ordinary affair with a lunch counter and a row of tables. It was well patronized, mainly by rough-looking men wearing boots and work clothes. We found an empty table and began studying the dog-eared and grease-stained handwritten menu. While thus engaged I became aware that someone at the next table was speaking to us in Latin. Wynne and I were something of a novelty, a pair of strangers who could not have driven in by car, and, despite our clothes and boots, no less presentable than the others in the café. But our Latin-speaking friend had correctly sized us up as a couple of college kids "out to see the country." Unlike his companions, he was loquacious, inquisitive, and a person with an uncommonly sharp mind—an anomaly himself in the midst of the generally illiterate crowd of lumberjacks, settlers, and mill workers. It turned out he was the younger son of a British evangelist, the Reverend Charles Haddon Spurgeon, who had attained worldwide fame—the Billy Sunday (or Billy Graham) of his day. As the son of a minister, our Jack Spurgeon was entitled to a free university education and had therefore gone to Oxford, where he had learned both Latin and Greek. But, like a great many younger sons, he saw his future in the colonies rather than the mother country, so he left England and cast his lot with Canada. Apparently he drifted about; as a good cook, he always found ready employment in the lumber camps. He neither smoked nor chewed nor drank, but he did play cards. And he played them exceedingly well, for he was always, as he said, able to "make expenses." It didn't take Jack Spurgeon long to get all the details of our story—where we came from, our travel plans, and our destination. He didn't approve of our plans to continue down the Wabigoon River—the river was too high, the banks were flooded, there would be logjams in places, the rapids were bad. Not very encouraging news! But he had an alternate plan: we could probably find someone with a car who would take us to a crossing of the Wabigoon River about ten miles west of Dryden, below the mill and dam, where we could canoe downstream a short distance to the junction with Pelican Creek, thence up the creek to Pelican Lake, thence up Twenty-Mile Creek to a landing from which we could portage a half-mile to Amesdale, on the Canadian National Railway. From Amesdale a local train would take us east some thirty miles to Hudson, from which we could canoe the waterways to Lac Seul and the English River, then follow our original plans and go up the Chukuni to Red Lake. The plan sounded sensible in view of the condition of the Wabigoon River. We asked if he could get us a car and driver; he assured us he could. So he disappeared and returned shortly to inform us a young engineer at the mill would provide the car. The only problem was that nothing could be done immediately, since the family had other plans for Dominion Day and he could not make the trip until after supper.

We did learn a good deal from Jack Spurgeon about life in the North—about the lumber camps and about the life of the homesteader. Spurgeon himself had a homestead that touched Pelican Lake with a cabin, newly built, on the lake itself. He gave us the key and invited us to use it, leaving the key under the doormat when we left. He asked us not to wear our hobnailed boots inside, since the floors were newly varnished. Spurgeon told us something about the settlers' struggle for a living. Many were World War I veterans who were offered homesteads by the Canadian government—a war bonus as it were. Many took up homesteads because they couldn't readjust to normal life after the trauma of trench warfare in Europe. They escaped to the North Woods where pressures were less and often married Indian squaws and fathered large families. One of Spurgeon's companions in the café, John, was such a person. He had ridden his horse ten miles out of his way, in mud almost to the horse's flanks, to avoid passing the door of a man with whom he had a quarrel—he could not cope with a confrontation.

We decided to see the goings-on in Dryden, so we paid our bill and sallied forth. The most interesting events were held along the waterfront. There was logrolling, where a pair of seasoned lumber jacks stood balanced on a huge pine log in the river, each trying to roll it over beneath his feet and dunk his adversary before he lost his own footing. There were also canoe races, the most interesting being the one for squaws, an event accompanied by much laughter and shouting from the mixed crowd of Indians and others on the bank. On land there were log-chopping and log-sawing contests. It was a pleasure to watch an axman wield the large double-bitted ax and cut neatly through a large pine log, never missing his mark by more than a quarter of an inch.

By evening the sky had clouded over and an east wind sprang up—an almost sure sign of rain. And before long the rains began—gentle at first and then harder. Between showers we returned to camp, packed our wet tent, loaded the canoe, and paddled in to the dock at Dryden. As arranged, the young engineer, Erickson appeared in the company of Jack Spurgeon. We transferred our packs and loose gear to the back of his car, put the canoe on top, and secured it with the tent ropes. We soon discovered that the Model A Ford has less carrying capacity than our canoe. We shook hands with Spurgeon, then Wynne and I climbed into the crowded front seat with the driver. The rain began falling again as we drove off.

First we followed a gravel road west toward Oxdrift; in the waning light we had our first land view of the clay belt. The road passed farms and fields—on the whole a rather depressing sight. The settlers' houses were simple frame structures or log cabins or in some cases tar-paper shacks, usually standing naked and forlorn in clearings in the forest, in some cases surrounded by stumpland or hayfields. The dark, somber forest had been pushed back, leaving the dwellings exposed to winter's blasts with not so much as a tree or shrub to give shelter. There might be a small outbuilding or two, but always present was the huge stack of firewood—the year's supply of fuel. As the dark descended we would see feeble light from a kerosene lamp within. The life of the homesteader was hard—backbreaking work cutting pulpwood, the first cash crop. Then the equally hard labor of removing stumps. The first field crop was usually hay, a mixture of timothy and clover. Horses were still king—they were used in the lumber camps—so there was a good demand for hay. A small garden and a few chickens helped sustain life. The home-steader paid his taxes with his labor, mainly road work for the govern-ment. Even the Trans-Canada Highway, built a few years later, was constructed by hundreds of men with pick and shovel and teams of horses drawing scoops—none of the great earth-moving equipment used in modern road building.

We reached Oxdrift just as it became totally dark. Oxdrift was a crossroads, a store with a gas pump, and half a dozen houses. Here we turned north on a dirt road—wet, slippery clay. Although the country was generally level, we encountered several creeks flowing in swampy lower ground. The car first slithered downgrade to the swollen creek, then struggled to go upgrade. Generally Wynne and I got out to push and tried to avoid, as far as possible, the spatter from the spinning wheels. Slipping, sweating, and swearing, we made it to the top again, our boots plastered with sticky clay. The engine boiled from the upgrade effort, and at one point I had to clamber down the road embankment to the swamp to get water—all in the dark of course.

Finally, after what seemed hours, and after a long downgrade, we reached the crossing of the Wabigoon River. The headlights of the car revealed the scene—a swollen river, bank-full and more, with a wooden bridge that had been lifted off its abutments and tied with a large hawser to keep it from floating down stream. A plank had been laid from the abutment to the bridge, which had drifted a bit askew. We unloaded our packs and covered them from the rain, which by now was a steady drizzle, helped Erickson turn around, paid our fare, and watched the tail lights of his car disappear over the hill. It was now very late, dark—no moon—and wet, and the only sound was the gurgling of the black river water, the croak of frogs, and the hum of mosquitoes. We couldn't help thinking there must be a better place to be.

Jack Spurgeon had said that a settler named Johnson lived a quarter-mile beyond the bridge and might put us up for the night, so we decided to carry our canoe and packs to the other side of the river and look for Mr. Johnson's place. We hoisted our packs and groped our way over the narrow, slippery plank, across the bridge, and over another plank to "dry" land on the other side. Then we fetched the canoe, which we placed upside down over our packs. We sloshed along the road until Johnson's house loomed out of the dark. No lights and no sounds. We stepped up on the porch and knocked on the door. No response. We knocked again, louder. We heard muffled voices, then saw a gleam of light. The door opened a crack, and a half-dressed, black-bearded giant with a very deep voice asked our business. We stated our request. The door closed; more voices, then it reopened a bit and, yes, we could stay overnight. We explained that we had to go back for our packs and would return shortly. We returned, stowed our gear on the porch, and fumbled with our mud-encased boots so we could enter in stocking feet. Mrs. Johnson had routed her two near-grown sons out of their bed to make way for two mud-spattered strangers from the night. We lost no time climbing into the still-warm bed. We also discovered why the seemingly inhospitable closing the door in our faces when we first arrived: to keep out the horde of mosquitoes that also wanted in. Thus ended Dominion Day.

*Saturday, July 2: To Amesdale*

We woke to the sound of wood-chopping and Mrs. Johnson stirring about her kitchen. We shared breakfast with the Johnsons, who apologized because their sugar supply was about exhausted. We promptly pulled our sugar sack from our pack. Surprise and delight—fine granulated cane sugar! The Johnsons had had only the coarse beet sugar used in this region. We packed up and asked about our bill for the night's lodging. The Johnsons would accept nothing, but we did not think this right so we gave them an American silver dollar. They had never seen this coin before but were delighted and vowed to keep it as a souvenir.

The rain had stopped; the sun and blue sky were a welcome sight. We carried our packs and canoe back to the Wabigoon and were soon afloat, and carried by the swift current to the mouth of Pelican Creek (now called Rugby Creek). In an hour or two we reached the falls at the outlet of Pelican Lake (Rugby Lake). A short portage and a short paddle brought us to Spurgeon's cabin, on the west shore, so we stopped for lunch and spread the tent out to dry. The cabin was new, made of peeled cedar logs chinked with sphagnum moss, with a roof of asphalt shingles. The inside was neat and tidy; Jack Spurgeon was indeed a meticulous person. We left the key as instructed, and after a paddle of six or seven miles we came to the place where Twenty-Mile Creek entered the lake. Then began a slow paddle up the twists and turns of the surprisingly swift muskeg stream. It was late afternoon when we came to a half-submerged rowboat tied up at a path. This must be the trail to Amesdale. As we were getting out to reconnoiter, we heard a train whistle and surmised that we were indeed close to our destination. A scramble up the path disclosed an open field. We walked across, through a small patch of woods, and emerged in another field, on the far side of which was the railroad track and Amesdale. All we could see was a one-story log house and outbuilding, which proved to be the residence, store, and postoffice combined of Mr. and Mrs. Ames. As it was now late and there was no good campsite in view, we entered the store/postoffice section and asked Mrs. Ames about the prospect of supper and staying overnight. We struck a bargain, then hurried back to our canoe and began to portage all our rig from the swampy landing to the Ameses'. It was rapidly getting dark, and we wanted to complete the carry before the evening onslaught of mosquitoes.

After a dinner of fried potatoes and bacon and what else I don't remember, we were shown out to the bunkhouse—a log building with no door. There were double-deck bunks filled with straw. Wynne took the upper, I had the lower. We spread our blankets and soon fell asleep. The night was clear and cold, and during the night I awoke to feel something warm and furry at my feet. It was one of the large dogs I had seen wandering about. I gave the dog a shove with my foot and told him to take his fleas elsewhere.

*Sunday, July 3: Amesdale*

At supper the night before we had found that train service east to Hudson was available only three days a week. The train, a mixed freight and passenger local, ran west on Monday. The next local train east was Tuesday afternoon. The prospect of three days in Amesdale was not a welcome one. Clearly our exchequer would not stand the bill, so early Sunday morning we walked a quarter-mile down the track to the railroad station, where we hoped to persuade the agent to flag down the limited,

Amesdale, Ontario, 1927.

which had daily service east. At the station we found there was no agent, only a section foreman living with his large family in a house nearby. The foreman, an Italian, told us in broken English that there was an agent at Hunter, some six miles west. We decided to move all our gear into the station, walk to Hunter, and hope to secure a ride east that afternoon. The agent at Hunter telegraphed our request to Winnepeg, but the dispatcher there would not grant approval without an OK from the superintendent, and since this was Sunday the superintendent was not in. We could only tramp the six miles back to Amesdale, place our baggage and canoe on the station platform, and hope the superintendent had been reached and had given his approval. At midafternoon we heard the whistle and saw the train round the curve. It roared into Amesdale and out again, showering us with cinders, without so much as slowing down. So went Sunday.

There being no good campsites about, we moved into the empty waiting room of the station and slept on the bare boards.

### *Monday, July 4: Independence Day and Quibell*

We concocted a plan. The local went west on Monday, so why not hitch a ride to Quibell, where we should have mail waiting for us, according to our original travel plans, then return east with the train the next day, pick up our things in Amesdale, and go on to Hudson. Better than sitting around the station for two days. We didn't intend to pay for the ride, of course, since we felt no love for the Canadian National, which had passed us up on Sunday. We thought a free ride was just the way to even up. Besides, we had had unplanned expenses during the past week and wanted to conserve our depleted funds.

The train pulled into Amesdale, belching smoke from its tired old steam engine, dropped an empty flatcar on a siding to be loaded with ties or pulpwood, reassembled, and started west. As it picked up speed we scrambled aboard another flatcar, taking care to pick one forward of a boxcar—to keep us out of sight of the trailing passenger car. But we were discovered, and as soon as we reached Hunter an irate conductor appeared and ordered us off, threatening dire consequences if we reboarded the train. We stood on the track watching the train disappear around the curve until nothing remained but a drifting cloud of smoke. Not to be defeated, we decided to hike the rest of the way—some sixteen miles—down the track to Quibell, which we did, venting our frustration by making uncomplimentary remarks about the conductor, the Canadian National and things in general. The only incidents were stepping aside to let the eastbound limited pass in midafternoon and seeing a doe and her fawn cross the track. Nearly five hours later, near suppertime—

our legs nearly as tired as our arms were after the first day's paddle up
Rainy Lake—we crossed the Wabigoon River on a high trestle about a
mile east of Quibell. The river here was entrenched in a deep gorge
swirling over rocks. ledges, and falls below. Shortly beyond we saw the
town, a small place of half a dozen houses, railroad station, store, school,
and two-story boxlike hotel. The postoffice had closed for the day, so our
mail, if any, would have to wait. We obtained a room on the second floor
of the old hotel—probably the first guests in months. I was afflicted with
one of my migraine headaches and nausea, so I passed up supper and
went to bed while Wynne sat up visiting with the proprietor, who no
doubt was glad to have company. Thus ended our Fourth of July.

*Tuesday, July 5: Eastbound by Rail*

We woke up in good shape. The day was fair and, with the thought of
getting into our canoe and away from it all once more, our spirits rose.
Also to receive mail from home and friends added a new outlook on life,
which had seemed so depressing the day before. We had a look around
Quibell—which did not take long. Not only was Quibell on the track,
but it was the end of a gravel road to Vermilion Bay of Eagle Lake, which
in turn connected with Dryden and Wabigoon. It was a bit more wooded
here than around most of these northern towns—if, indeed, they could
be called such.

We waited impatiently for the train, which was due early in the
afternoon. Eventually it arrived, with the same train crew on board. The
conductor soon spotted us, and we saw him talking to the station agent,
with occasional glances in our direction. We got aboard—with tickets
this time—and took our places in the passenger car. Our fellow travelers
were a mix of booted woodsmen and Indians, most with packsacks and
nondescript bundles. The train started; the conductor appeared and
promptly collected our tickets, saying nothing. We stopped at every
siding to break the train, add a car of pulpwood or ties, or drop an empty
car. We also had to take to a siding to let the limited roar by. At Amesdale
we hopped off, hustled our canoe from the station platform to the
baggage car, tossed our packs aboard, and resumed our seats for the ride
to Hudson, some thirty miles east.

## RED LAKE STAMPEDE

As the train rattled along toward Hudson our thoughts turned to resuming our canoe voyage and to our ultimate destination. What would Red
Lake be like? We had read accounts of the discovery of gold in the fall of
1925 and the rush the news had precipitated. It was said to be the biggest

rush since the Klondike. The most intrepid came by dog team and toboggan; the others waited till the ice broke up and came by canoe or, for the first time, by air. The float plane had become available for travel to the most inaccessible areas; every lake was an airfield. And the Erickson brothers of Sioux Lookout had adapted toboggans into skis that could be fitted on the plane to replace the pontoons. So except for a short time during breakup in the spring and freeze-up in the fall, planes became year-round transportation in the Canadian North—at least for those who could afford it.

The first discovery of gold in the Canadian Shield was made in the Lake of the Woods area about 1885, when the new Canadian Pacific track provided ready access. This discovery led to the first gold rush, which quickly spead to the nearby Manitou area. Wabigoon and Rat Portage (now Kenora) were the jumping-off points. From these travel was by boat and canoe in summer and dog team or horse-drawn sleigh in winter. Wabigoon was the Dawson City of the Manitou—a boom town of false fronts, hotels, and questionable hangers-on.

With the discovery of the Klondike in 1896 the boom in the Manitou country faded, and by 1910 or 1911 it became history without producing much gold. The Klondike rush was a frenzied affair. Twenty-seven thousand people surged north, many knowing little or nothing about prospecting or mining, most knowing even less about the woods or how to cope with the harsh winter—a replay of California in 1849. The Klondike waned, and interest shifted to eastern Ontario with the discoveries at Porcupine and Kirkland Lake in 1908 and 1910. The latter areas led to significant and continuing gold production from several large mines. But in 1925, word that the Howey brothers had discovered gold at Red Lake started a new rush. Some twenty thousand were said to have made the trek, one way or another, in the following year.

Such were our reflections as the train crawled eastward toward Hudson. Was Red Lake another Dawson City with its riotous living? It was indeed a frontier, some 150 miles north of the railroad track. Hudson was the principal point of departure—the only place for transshipment of heavy freight. As the engineer applied the brakes, we pressed our noses against the windows to get a glimpse of our destination and were not a little touched by the gold fever ourselves. We were about to join the throng that disembarked from Wabigoon for the Manitou, that struggled over Chilkoot Pass to the Yukon, or that had left Hudson for Red Lake and GOLD.

The railroad skirted the south shore of Lost Lake, a rather large lake shored by granite outcroppings. Between the track and the water's edge were docks and warehouses. We saw at once the signs of activity. Several barges or scows tied up at the docks, which were piled high with oil drums, lumber , crates, and boxes —all freight for the goldfields. Several seaplanes rode at anchor. There was an assortment of large powerboats in the water and freight canoes on the dock. Nearby were other warehouses constructed from fresh-cut lumber, all bulging with still more freight.

Rail freight, especially heavy machinery, was here transferred to scows or barges to go by an uninterrupted but devious water route to Lac Seul and thence to Goldpines, a settlement at the outlet some one hundred miles from Hudson. From there the freight was broken up and loaded into large freight canoes for the trip down the English River and up the Chukuni to Red Lake, about fifty miles farther. The river travel was interrupted in several places by rapids and falls. In winter the frieght left Hudson in sleighs, several of which would be linked together and pulled over the ice by a tractor. Most of the heavy equipment moved this way. Not uncommonly, the tractor or a heavy-laden sleigh would break through the ice.

Hudson was otherwise a small place, strewn along the Canadian National tracks. Most of the settlement was on the uphill side of the track, opposite the waterfront development. The hills in back of the town had largely burned off and were unsightly.

We made short work of unloading our canoe and baggage, then carried them across the tracks to the dock. After loading the canoe and making a quick check to see that we had left nothing behind, we maneuvered past the scows and set off for the North once more. What a relief to feel the motion of the canoe, to be under way after the misadventures of Amesdale. We had no regrets at leaving and were glad to see the Hudson waterfront and its clutter recede from view.

Lost Lake is a clear-water lake. We had left the clay belt and its settlements behind and now passed shores of solid granite—no more clay banks and no more murky water. The lake itself is largely in the Lac Seul Indian Reservation, a point driven home as we passed a small island burial site with its tattered banners fluttering in the wind. We made for an island, selected a camping spot out of sight of Hudson, and pitched our tent. The clean shelf of granite provided a suitable dock. We were back to our tent, our campfire, the sound of the wind in the pines, the lapping of the waves on the rocks. Civilization be damned!

*Wednesday, July 6: Lac Seul*

The maps we had were rather poor, and the waterway from Lost Lake to Lac Seul was rather complex and circuitous. To follow the barge route would add many miles to our journey. We were sure the Indians would have a shorter way. After studying the situation we decided on a shortcut: a portage from Lost Lake to Grassy Bay of Lac Seul, thence by another portage to Canoe Lake, and down Canoe River into the main part of Lac Seul. The portage to Grassy Bay was not particularly difficult, though it was nearly a mile long. Canoe Lake was soon traversed and then, to our relief, we negotiated Canoe River without further obstacles and reached Lac Seul.

Lac Seul, also called Lonely Lake, is one of the largest lakes in this part of the Shield. It forms an irregular sprawling crescent from the outlet at Goldpines eastward nearly one hundred miles to the Root River inlet. Farther east lies Lake Saint Joseph, of comparable size. Between the two is a height of land, Lac Seul draining southwestward by the English River and Lake Saint Joseph flowing eastward down the Albany to James Bay. Both were on the fur traders' route, the Pine Ridge Post and the Lac Seul Post of the Hudson's Bay Company being on Lac Seul and the famous Osnaburgh House being on Saint Joseph.

As we came into Lac Seul, we spied the Lac Seul Post on the north shore some three or four miles distant. The post itself was a cluster of neatly kept white buildings in a large cleared, grassy area. The neatly clipped grass was in fact a three-hole golf course. Since the Hudson's Bay Company employed Scotsmen as post managers or factors, it was not surprising that, where possible, golf should be there also. Nearby was a small Anglican church and the rector's house. The Lac Seul Post was no longer as remote as it had once been. The traffic to Red Lake passed its door, and it was not unusual to see scows towed by diesel-powered tugs and other craft. It was only a few years back, before the railroad reached Lost Lake in 1910, that this was indeed a lonely lake and lonely outpost, though an important point in the fur trade of the North. Most of the furs went down the great rivers to the company's York Factory and Moose Factory posts on Hudson Bay, but, as noted, the French intercepted this profitable business and carried the furs from the Northwest to the English River and Rainy River route to Grand Portage and Lake Superior. Lac Seul, from its name, must have been in the area of the French fur trade.

Despite its great size, Lac Seul does not appear so large because of its highly irregular shoreline, many narrows, and multitude of islands. There is no large, unbroken sweep of water. It is large enough in places, however, to give one trouble when there are strong headwinds, and there are places, too, where a wind can get a heavy sea rolling.

We passed the Hudson's Bay post and headed westward, where from time to time we encountered motor-powered craft, reminiscent of Rainy Lake. But unlike the pleasure boats of the latter, these were carrying freight to Red Lake. The only canoes under paddle, other than ours, were those of the Indians. And even the Indians, if they could afford it, would have a canoe with an outboard motor, often of unreliable vintage, commonly with one or more other canoes in tow, filled with women, children, and dogs. We camped somewhere near Pine Island.

Two long days of paddling blessed with good weather and light winds, through Poplar Narrows, Shanty Narrows, and past the Goose Islands, brought us to Goldpines at the outlet of Lac Seul. The old maps show Goldpines as the site of the Pine Ridge Post of the Hudson's Bay Company. Instead of such a post, we found that a small settlement had sprung up—a place alive with activity and new construction. It was the terminus of the barge navigation on Lac Seul, for between here and Red Lake stood the Ear Falls, both Upper and Lower, and beyond them several falls and rapids on the Chunkuni River. From Goldpines the barge freight, broken into smaller loads, had to make the river trip in large freight canoes.

Goldpines reflected the gold fever even more. There were docks and freight-laden scows along the waterfront and new construction every-where—cabins of freshly peeled logs, and sheds and other buildings of newly cut lumber. There were an assortment of winterized tents—pitched on wooden platforms and equipped with stoves and stovepipes—and a conglomerate population of boatmen, storekeepers, and Indians, together with innumerable Indian children and dogs, all in apparent disarray. The larger boats were tied to the docks; canoes were pulled up here and there along the half-mile of sandy shore. In back of the town was the forest. As we neared the dock we heard voices and barking dogs and caught a whiff of wood smoke. It was getting late in the day, so we took a quick look around, bought a loaf of fresh bread at an exorbitant price, and decided that an offshore island, free of dogs and Indians, would make a better campsite. The nearest island had been preempted by a large Indian encampment, but another mile away was a secluded spot that met our needs. Occasional sounds of outboard motors, of an incoming or outgoing seaplane, or of dogs barking reached our ears, but we soon fell asleep.

### *Saturday, July 9: Ear Falls and the English River*

After breaking camp we made for the river outlet. The English River is a very large stream—much larger than the Manitou River—and at this place the current was swift. The banks were under water, the waters flowing through the willows and other shrubs. We had a very fast ride indeed and wondered how we would make the return trip. The water was much too swift to paddle against, and the flooded banks would prevent lining upcurrent—that is, walking the shore with a tow line attached to the canoe. Were we making a one-way trip? We also became concerned about spotting the portage landing in time to put ashore before being swept over Ear Falls. The Upper and Lower falls are close together and add up to a drop of twenty-nine feet. We recalled our experience on the Manitou River, but now the stakes were higher—the river was bigger and swifter.

The distance from Lac Seul to the Ear Falls is no more than two miles at most. We were pondering the situation when we were swept around a bend. The falls were very near, as the thundering sound and rising mists testified, but our fears about missing the portage proved groundless, since it was a veritable roadway. The landing was obvious—there was even a dock. On the banks were several beached canoes. Clearly a lot of traffic went over this portage. The falls we didn't see, but the roar of the falling waters left no doubt of their awesome size.

The going on the portage was not as easy as we first thought it would be. Though wide and roadlike, with corduroy in places, there had been so much traffic that in spots the ground was churned to a mire up to our shoe tops. Apparently some boats and large canoes had been skidded across on rollers, and perhaps some freight had been ferried over with horse and wagon. This was a very different kind of portage from the faint and narrow trails in the Manitou country, some of which may not have been traveled for years. The carry was not long and was downhill all the way (and of course uphill all the way back). A freight canoe beached at the lower end gave us our first close look at large canoes. They are built with frame and canvas cover like an ordinary canoe but are much larger, with a square stern for an outboard motor and no seats. They will carry two thousand pounds or in some cases twice as much (two tons!).

The English River below the falls was a narrow, lakelike waterway with rockbound shores and promontories. The narrower parts were swift; giant eddies formed in the slack water below each narrows. However, we encountered no rapids or falls requiring portaging before we reached the confluence with the Chukuni, some twelve miles below Ear Falls. We made the trip with ease and in very good time. The Chukuni River was considerably smaller and less swift, but still a river to be reckoned with. Seven or eight miles up the Chukuni, wider and more lakelike than the English River, brought us to Pakwash Lake, about ten miles long and up to four miles wide. The lake contains only a few small scattered islands and had a bad reputation, for it was said to be rather shallow, so that the waves tended to be steep and closely spaced, making canoeing hazardous in rough weather. The lake was benign when we entered, and it didn't take us long to paddle north to a point on the east shore, where we made camp.

*Sunday, July 10: Windbound*

We were awakened by the tent flapping and waves pounding on the rocky ledges. Since it was daylight we got up, made a fire, and cooked breakfast. The wind increased in strength, and it soon became evident that we were windbound. The wind was from the southwest, and it was clear that if we had camped on the west shore we could have traveled, but we were not unhappy to have a day of rest, for we had paddled, without interruption except for two portages, for the past four days and were now well over a hundred miles from Hudson. It was Sunday and a day of rest indeed.

Our enforced delay gave us a chance to wash our rather smelly clothes and to cook something more than we normally had time for. So we began the day with pancakes. Experience had shown that our frying pan did very well with bacon and fish but poorly with flapjacks, which often burned on the outside and were underdone on the inside. A better griddle was a smooth, flat slab of rock an inch or two thick, supported by two large rocks. You build a fire under this an hour ahead of time, and when the upper surface reaches the right temperature you pour on the batter, made from a prepared mix. In a short time the steady, even heat will cook the cakes to perfection. Melted brown sugar makes an excellent syrup. At noontime we decided to bake cornbread in our reflector oven, a collapsible shiny sheet metal affair. When opened it resembles a V-shaped hopper tilted ninety degrees. The oven is open toward the fire, resting on one edge and supported in the rear by two folding legs. A pan slides in horizontally on two brackets, bisecting the hopper, and a batter of cornmeal, flour, powdered milk, and baking powder, mixed to the right consistency with water, is poured into the pan. The fire is specially constructed. A large green backlog is cut; against it, firewood is arranged upright to produce a sheet of flame. The oven is placed in front of the fire so that the radiant heat is reflected down and up from the two sloping walls of the V-shaped oven—hence *reflector* oven. Temperature is adjusted by moving the oven closer to or farther from the fire.

The day passed quickly. Except for a couple of freight canoes, there was very little lake traffic.

*Monday, July 11: Chukuni River*

The next morning the wind had blown itself out, but taking no chances on its rising again, we ate a hurried breakfast and broke camp. We were eager to get to Red Lake. The map showed Snake Falls, a six-foot drop at the point where the Chukuni River enters Pakwash Lake. We arrived to find no trace of the falls; apparently the high water on Pakwash had obliterated them. It was not high enough, however, to do the same with

Author on portage, Chukuni River, northwestern Ontario, 1927.

other falls and rapids farther upstream. There were three portages, none of them very long, before we reached Two Island Lake, about twelve to fifteen miles from Pakwash. These portages, like that around the Ear Falls, were in reality corduroy roads. There usually was a freight canoe on the bank at one end or the other.

Two Island Lake was a very small lake with two very small islands. A short stretch of river brought us to Gullrock Lake, a granite-shored lake about the same size as Pakwash but much more irregular and with many islands. It was surrounded by verdant hills of fir and spruce. Here we camped.

### *Tuesday, July 12: Red Lake*

From Gullrock we went through a narrows into Keg Lake, a much smaller body of water, and thence by a short stretch of river into Red

Lake. We had made it! Seventeen days, four of them spent in enforced delays at Dryden and Amesdale, thirteen on the lakes and rivers, some three hundred miles more or less, from Rainy Lake without getting lost, overturning the canoe, or suffering a major mishap. Mecca at last!

Red Lake is rather large, some thirty miles from its western extremity, Pipestone Bay, to East Bay at the northeastern end. It has a very irregular shore with many deep bays and has one very large island—McKenzie Island—and many smaller ones. There is relatively little open water.

We soon saw signs of mining activity, for on the south shore, to our left as we entered the lake, was the Howey gold mine, the original discovery which has become one of Canada's great gold producers. When we saw it it consisted of a clearing, a cluster of buildings, and a headframe, being still in an early stage of development. As usual, the mining operations intruded rudely into the wilderness. Trees were cut down and in places were burned off leaving naked rock. The moss had been burned or stripped off, and test pits and trenches left major scars on the landscape. Such is progress.

Unlike the Klondike, where gold occurs in stream sands and gravels, or placers, the gold of Red Lake occurs in veins—usually quartz veins. Hence it is necessary to trench to uncover and follow these veins. Whereas with placer gold one has only to shovel up the sands and swish them around in a miner's pan or run them through a sluice to recover the precious metal, a prospector in this region must blast the vein, crush the loosened rock in a mortar, then pan or sluice the finely crushed material. At the old Detola mine there was a stamp mill to crush the ore fine enough for separation of the gold. The richer ores ran a little more than forty dollars a ton and the price of gold then was only twenty dollars an ounce, but there would be no more than two ounces of gold in a ton of such ore. In these quartz veins, moreover, a brassy mineral, pyrite, is often mistaken for gold. It is aptly called fool's gold. It takes the keen eye of the prospector to discover the minute flecks of gold and distinguish them from their false counterpart.

The Howey mine had a cluster of buildings and other characteristic features. Most obvious was the headframe over the shaft, with its great wheels over which ran cables to raise and lower the man-carrying cage and ore-carrying skip that went up and down the shaft. The cables ran from the top of the headframe to the nearby hoist, where they were wound or unwound from a large drum powered by a steam engine. The other buildings included cookshack and mess hall, bunkhouse, assay and office shed, and a "dry" where the miners changed into their underground work clothes. There might also be a machine shop and blacksmith shop. Always present was the ever-growing rock pile and—

something we didn't see at the old Detola mine in the Manitou—the long rows of neatly stacked mine timbers, used to shore up the walls and "ceilings" of the mine workings. Should the mine pay out, a mill would be built to process the ore. Many are the gold claims, but only a few become mines and fewer still pay dividends. The Howey mine, still in a state of development in 1927, produced its first gold in 1930 and has since become a large producing mine.

In 1927 there was no town of Red Lake and of course no road leading to it. All freight was brought in by water in summer and over the ice in winter, except items that could be carried by air. With the building of the road, all that has changed. When we saw Red Lake it was as yet largely undeveloped, but prospectors' camps were numerous. Since most of the original explorations and discoveries were made from canoes, along the lakeshores, it is along the shores that we saw such camps, some with log cabins, others with tents, many pitched on wooden platforms and equipped with stoves for winter use. In places the forest was stripped off and the rocks laid bare—naked hills of dark greenstone crossed by large white veins of quartz. In places we saw a thin veil of white smoke rising above the bush and heard the clink of steel against rock and the occasional blast of dynamite and its aftermath of falling fragments.

We turned north from the Howey property and west up the channel between McKenzie Island and the mainland. Near the north end of the island we passed the McKenzie–Red Lake property, another mine under development that also became a gold producer, its headframe visible from the lake. We could hear the mine whistle and the sound of the skip. All this activity reminded us of the old Detola mine of the Manitou, now a silent monument to similar activity long past. All mines, like all lives, have a finite existence and are destined to end—to rust and weather away—to disappear as the brush reclaims its own and heals the scars of man's desecration.

We continued into the northeastern part of Red Lake, near the entrance to East Bay, where we found a suitable island campsite. The lake here had fewer camps, and its shores were still green and largely unscarred by mining. It was late afternoon, when we had the camp in order, that we decided to try our luck at fishing. Heretofore we had risen early and traveled late, leaving little time to fish, though fish were plentiful. As usual we trolled. We had no rod and reel, only a strong line, a few sinkers, a leader, and a spoon hook—a silvery spoon that spun as we trolled, attached to a three-pronged feathered hook of the largest size. We would unwind some fifty feet of line and paddle slowly along. The line would be tied to the fisherman's leg so it would come loose should it be snagged by a reef or submerged log. At a tug on the line we would

McKenzie–Red Lake mine, Red Lake, Ontario, about 1933. Photo courtesy of the Ontario Department of Mines.

stop, pull it in hand over hand, and swing the fish over the gunwale. Quick action with a pocketknife put an end to the wild thrashing about in the canoe. Our tackle was so big that we caught only the largest fish, usually nothing less than twenty-four inches long, and the line was strong enough to haul them in without a net. Not very sporting, perhaps, but an effective way to ensure a change of diet. We had no means of weighing our fish, but we could measure their length. Our record was a forty-two-inch northern pike caught in Pickerel Arm of Minnitaki Lake on our return trip. It probably weighed eighteen to twenty pounds.

Red Lake turned out to be a good lake for walleyed pike, and we had just pulled in two nice fish when we saw a canoe put out from shore and paddle toward us. The game warden perhaps? We had no fishing licenses, so we watched the lone canoeman approach with some trepidation. In our haste to get under way we had left Rainy Lake without fishing licenses or even the usual immigration formalities. We were illegal aliens as well. "Any luck?" the canoeman asked as he came alongside. "Not much," we replied as we held up our catch, "Just a couple of walleyes." "B'Jesus you boys must be from the States." Such was our introduction to Joe Prena, trapper and prospector. Joe explained that in Canada these fish are called pickerel—a term that in the States refers to a very different fish, the northern pike, which in Canada is called a jackfish. We had given ourselves away. Joe soon heard the details of our trip. He had a cabin on East Bay and suggested we come over that evening. We promised we would, and he told us how to find his place.

So we spent that evening and several others at Joe's cabin and heard many stories about his life as a trapper, how he left his wife when he found she was unfaithful and took to the North Woods. He was more trapper than prospector, but he was able to fill us in on the Red Lake story. Joe was like many others we met, who had a claim or two somewhere no matter what their regular occupation was. Joe told us that by the previous fall the area had been staked solid. "No more open ground for miles around. Now they've gone up the Woman River to Woman and Birch lakes," Joe remarked. "Suppose you find a likely showing," we asked, "then how do you go about staking a claim?" Joe explained that the whole matter was regulated by the government. In the first place you had to buy a miner's license for five dollars, which entitled you to stake nine claims in one mining division. A claim was a square tract of land a quarter-mile (1,320 feet) on a side, or about forty acres in area. The claim was marked by placing a squared post at each corner, marked in a proper manner. Once the claim was recorded, the appropriate metal tag was added. The claim boundaries, which were supposed to run north-south and east-west, were marked by cut lines, or more commonly by blazes—ax marks—on trees along the line. To hold the claims some "assessment work" must be performed—two hundred days of such work over a five-year period. This work might consist of test pitting and trenching to trace the vein and obtain samples for assaying. If the development warranted further work the claims might be optioned to a syndicate or mining company, which would do diamond drilling to test the extension in depth and further sample the vein. Should all this prove favorable, a shaft might be sunk and mining begun. As we were to discover, in 1927 few of the Red Lake claims had reached this stage of development. The Howey property was one that had.

Joe wanted to move to the States, where he opined things were better, prices lower, and wages higher. But it was clear that he was better adapted to the independent life of the northern bush than to the workaday world of the city.

Before we left Red Lake Joe promised to write to us, which he did once. What an effort his letter must have been for this rough but kindhearted and generous woodsman. Joe told us, among other things, about a canoe party we had passed on the way to Red Lake, under paddle, a man and a boy from the States. Joe said they had drowned, swept over a big falls on the English River on their way home.

We spent the next several days cruising around. Once, when we heard sounds of activity back from the shore, we landed and pushed our way inland. As we broke out of the underbrush into the open, we startled several prospectors working on a trench. Thin bluish smoke from a smudge to keep down the blackflies filled the air. The miners looked up, when Wynne appeared in his Oberlin College sweater with "1926" emblazoned across the front one of the men stopped, brushed away the flies, and said, "Looks like you're one year too late!"

We returned to the canoe, paddled along the shore, and saw a point of land with a large tent above which was a sign "Bank of Canada." Another tent nearby was marked "Stock Broker." These were the beginnings of the town of Red Lake, near the southeast part of the lake where mining development was concentrated. Here also were a dock and a log building marked "Western Canada Airways, Ltd." A seaplane was riding an anchor, and drums of gasoline were stored ashore.

We were not alone on Red Lake. The roar of a plane taking off, the whine of an outboard, or the muffled sound of a distant blast, replacing the silence usually broken only by the cries of gulls or loons, reminded us that progress had come to Red Lake.

*A Week Later: Homeward Bound*

Since I planned to leave for graduate school in California about mid-August, it became clear that we would soon have to leave Red Lake, for it was now late July. We had no intention of returning by way of Amesdale and Dryden, as we had had enough of both. We planned instead to retrace our route to Lost Lake and from there ascend the English River by way of Sioux Lookout on the Canadian National route and thence paddle upstream through Abram and Minnitaki lakes. From Minnitaki we would portage over a divide into Sandy Lake and thence proceed to Dinorwic Lake by way of Little and Wee Sandy lakes, a route that involved several long portages. From Dinorwic Lake we would retrace our path to Ranier on Rainy Lake—our starting point.

So we reluctantly broke camp, bid good-bye to Joe Prena, and were homeward bound. No gold perhaps, but richer for the experience. By late afternoon we reached Gullrock Lake, where we stopped on a rocky point for lunch. A group of prospectors in several canoes joined us. We had barely introduced ourselves when we heard a shot that echoed back and forth across the water. In a very few moments another canoe joined the group. I saw a rifle leaning against a thwart. The occupants seemed suspicious, but upon being reassured by the others that we were not game wardens, they went around a point and shortly returned with a deer. Obviously the shot we heard had reached its mark. The deer was a doe, but she had a dry udder so there was no fawn to wander motherless.

The party butchered the animal then and there. I had built a small fire, so I added some green leaves for a smudge to keep down the blackflies, which seemed especially bad, as they often are before a rain. The sky was overcast, the air unusually mild, and the lake very calm. In less time than it takes to tell, we departed with a sizable chunk of venison cut from the hindquarters. We soon made camp, built a fire, and dined on venison steaks. Before we had finished it began to sprinkle, and within a short time a gentle rain was falling.

## English River and Lac Seul Once More

The next day was bright and clear; the rain was over, and we were ready to tackle the Chukuni, retracing our route to the English River. We made it through Pakwash Lake without getting hung up by strong winds and soon reached the English River. Now it was upcurrent, and a swift current it was, especially at the narrowest places. After making slow progress, we discovered we could do better by taking advantage of the back eddies generated at each narrows. The rapid flow through a narrows entrains some of the more placid waters below and creates a compensating backflow near the shore, thus forming a very large eddy. We found we could ride these countercurrents upstream. We did, however, have to reenter the swift current carefully at each narrows, then paddle vigorously and seek the next back eddy to carry us upstream once more.

Above Ear Falls the story was different. Here there were no back eddies, only an incredibly strong current. As we stood at the portage landing watching the water sweep past and wondering how to cope with it, we were hailed from a canoe that had just cast off and was about to start upriver. We were offered a tow, since the square-stern canoe had an outboard motor. We accepted with unseemly haste, made fast a towline, and cast off. Both canoes, ours and our benefactor's, began drifting downcurrent toward the thundering falls. Our host gave a pull on the starting rope. The engine coughed and sputtered out. Another try, same result. A glance at the approaching mist arising from the tumult below increased our anxiety. The canoeman also saw it and gave a mighty pull on the rope. The engine started. He quickly pointed the bow upstream; the tow rope tightened with a jerk and became taut as a fiddle string. Our backward drift halted, and as he opened the throttle we slowly began to creep upcurrent. In due time and much to our relief, we emerged from the river into the wide expanse of Lac Seul and the man untied the towline. We pulled in the rope, waved a grateful thanks, and paddled off. Since it was by now very late in the day, we passed the island with the Indian encampment and sought our old site a mile beyond. As the quiet of the evening settled in, we heard the monotonous sound of drums and the chanting of the Indians. Their powwow lasted far into the night.

## THE RAILROAD EPOCH

### Sioux Lookout

In the morning we broke camp, loaded the canoe, and settled down to the long paddle on Lac Seul. It took us three days to reach Canoe Lake and Grassy Bay and portage over into Lost Lake. Our trip was uneventful. We had a following wind, not too strong to create a problem. However, the dog flies were very bad at times. This fly looks much like a housefly but is not so innocuous. Unlike blackflies and mosquitoes, the scourge of the North, which are left behind when one is afloat, the dog flies follow relentlessly. They alight undetected on your ankles and deliver sharp jabs. The North has an assortment of other flying pests. In addition to the dog flies and the blackflies and mosquitoes, there are brown-spotted deerflies that circle one's head looking for a vulnerable spot. The largest fly of all is the moose fly, which much resembles what we call a horsefly at home. They are not so numerous, but one is sure to show up if you go swimming. They prefer the middle of your back—an unreachable spot—and they can deliver a moose-sized bite. The smallest of the flies is what the Indians call the "no-see-um," a minute fly barely visible to the unaided eye. Though very small, they can raise quite a welt. They are particularly bad at sundown, and they can pass through the mosquito bar.

When we reached Lost Lake we sought our old campsite. It had not been occupied since we had left, so we were able to set up quickly using the same tent poles and building our fire with ready-cut firewood. There too was my geologic pick—just where I had left it.

On leaving Lost Lake we followed the English River to Pelican Falls, a drop of twelve feet from Pelican Lake. The portage here also was roadlike. There was even a broad-gauge track with a flatcar drawn by a team of horses—a sort of marine railroad—to carry freight from Sioux Lookout on Pelican Lake enroute to Goldpines and Red Lake. We declined the service and carried our packs and canoe as usual over the short portage to Pelican Lake.

Pelican Lake, above the falls, is similar to Lost Lake, though smaller. The northern part has granite shores, and the surrounding hills are covered mainly by second-growth poplar and balsam. Rounding a point, we passed a large frame building—a residential school for Indian boys.

Since it was a warm, sunny day, the dock and water were alive with boys out for a swim. All were totally naked, and, owing to modesty or to uncertainty about our sex, they covered their private parts with their hands. It was amusing to see nearly fifty boys, large and small, all in the same posture.

A two-mile paddle brought us to the main part of the lake. Southeast of us was the track of the Canadian National Railway and the bridge across the narrows. We also saw the high greenstone knob on the west shore and the lookout tower of the Ontario Forestry Branch. This prominent landmark is the Sioux Lookout for which the nearby town was named. It is a bold rocky knob that gives a commanding view of the surrounding country and was the spot where the local Indians posted a sentry to warn of the approach of the hostile Sioux, who made forays from their southern homeland.

We went under the bridge and through the narrows into the southern part of Pelican Lake. There on the eastern shore to our left lay Sioux Lookout, the largest town in the region. As we headed for a small beach, we passed Folger's sawmill with its "log pond"—an area enclosed by a boom and filled with floating logs. On shore were piles of neatly stacked newly cut lumber. The mill itself was marked by the usual large waste burner, shaped like a silo, with a hemispherical screen cap and a plume of white wood smoke. Puffs of steam and the sound of the saws greeted us as we passed. The beach toward which we headed was the lower part of town, the town itself being mainly on higher ground on the other side of the railroad tracks. As we approached the beach we could see several boathouses, a number of boats tied to a long dock, several children in swimming, a few stray dogs, and several canoes and rowboats pulled up on the sand. We landed on the beach and, since we were now back in "civilization" and wanted to pick up our mail and some fresh supplies, we looked about for a safe place to leave our packs and canoe paddles. There was a row of houses back of the beach, partially hidden in the trees, so we approached one and asked permission to store our things. We were told to go around back, where we found a large workshop that turned out to be that of the Erickson brothers, famous for their toboggans and airplane skis. The Ericksons let us leave our gear in their shop.

Sioux Lookout was a division point on the Canadian National Railroad, and except for the sawmill was strictly a railroad town. Here were the roundhouse, car shops, a freight yard, an imposing red-brick station, a large switching yard, and beyond it a pole yard for creosoting poles and ties. A few miles farther east, at Superior Junction, a branch line led to Fort William and Port Arthur on Lake Superior. So it was at Sioux Lookout that the freight was broken up and reassembled for shipment either to the lake or eastward or westward along the main line. Here also was a large red-brick structure, the Railroad YMCA, that functioned as a hotel for the train crews.

The railroad that gave life to the town was the main line of the Canadian National Railways—a truly transcontinental railroad running from Nova Scotia to British Columbia. The line itself had been completed in 1910. Its construction was the last major epoch of railroad building in North America, and an epoch it was. The line started under private auspices as the Grand Trunk Pacific, built to compete with the Canadian Pacific, which had been completed in 1896. The trial lines, of which there were several before actual building began, were said to have been surveyed in the dead of winter. The survey parties slept in tents and traversed the route on snowshoes. Imagine tenting out, looking through a transit, and taking notes at fifty to sixty below zero. And much of the route was many, many miles from any outpost of civilization.

Construction, with all the deep rock cuts, muskeg, and river crossings, proved more expensive than anticipated. The Grand Trunk was faced with bankruptcy. Had the venture failed, several banks would have gone under and precipitated a financial crisis. So in the end the government had to bail out the enterprise. Thus Canada came to have a government-owned railroad, from coast to coast, competing with the privately owned Canadian Pacific. Moreover, the Lake Superior branch was immediately constructed to carry wheat—the major item of freight—down to the ships at Port Arthur. The main line extending east, far north of Lake Superior, remained without much traffic. To make matters worse, the Canadians later built a line from the prairie province of Saskatchewan to Churchill on Hudson Bay to carry the grain to vessels on the bay for shipment to Europe—a further short circuit and further diversion of freight from the main line.

When we arrived in 1927, only seventeen years after the construction of the railway, Sioux Lookout still seemed new. There was no road to the outside, but the town was full of trucks, and even some passenger cars, though the only road then open went no farther than Frog Rapids, three miles from town. It was some years before this road was extended to Dinorwic to connect with the Trans-Canada Highway, which had not yet been built.

Sioux Lookout had the general aspect of the new towns in the North, with its wide, treeless unpaved streets. Most of the people lived hillward of the main street. The houses were frame or tar-paper or even made of logs, nearly all with gardens alongside or even in front, and all with huge piles of stacked firewood.

We arrived uptown just in time to see the eastbound limited pull in. The train stopped for a half-hour while the steam locomotive was detached and replaced by another. The wheel bearings of the cars were inspected and baggage and express were offloaded and replaced by boxes of iced fish, baskets of blueberries, and personal baggage. Most of the passengers disembarked to stretch their legs and take a bit of air, mingling with the local population, who had turned out en masse to greet the train. A motley crowd it was—the coach passengers, many toting packsacks, the well-dressed first-class passengers, the railroad service crew and the uniformed conductor, the station agent and baggage handlers, various Indians, and a multitude of children and dogs all mingled in agitated confusion. In due time the engineer on the new locomotive was handed his orders by the agent, the conductor gave the signal, and the train began to move, the engine wheels thrashing furiously as the train picked up speed. In a few moments, the train disappeared from sight; only a faint whistle and lingering cloud of smoke told of its having been here. The crowd dispersed its noise and confusion replaced by the sound of the chattering telegraph in the station.

Sioux Lookout was indeed a railroad town, for the railroad gave it life. But time marches on, for now the diesel locomotive has replaced the steam engine and the ritual of changing engines is no longer necessary. So the roundhouse and shops are closed, and much of the glamour is gone. The limited still arrives, but it hesitates only slightly, then is gone. And the pine has run out. Folger's mill is closed; only the foundations remain. But this was yet to be, and in 1927 Sioux Lookout was at its height.

We were exhausted by the time we returned to the canoe. The crowds, the excitement, the train seemed overwhelming after the slower pace of canoe travel. We were glad to shove off, to be on the water again. As we pulled away from Sioux Lookout, we passed the Patricia Airways seaplane base and found ourselves in the takeoff path of a departing plane. We could do nothing but hope the pilot saw us; whether he did we never knew, but though he didn't alter his course he lifted off just in time and passed a few feet over our heads with an ear-splitting roar and a spray-laden propeller wash. As we rounded a point, Frog Rapids, between Pelican Lake and Abram Lake, came into view. The road from Sioux Lookout is carried over Frog Rapids on a wooden bridge, only to become a stump-filled swath through the forest beyond this point. The rapids are just a narrows with a swift current—by paddling close to the shore and avoiding the faster current in the center, we passed into Abram Lake.

Abram Lake is an elongate body of water stretching about ten miles northeast–southwest. We entered the lake about midpoint. Directly across was a chain of islands and beyond that a bay, at the far end of which was Abram Chutes, a rapids between Minnitaki and Abram lakes.

We headed that way. Halfway there, however, near the islands, we found our way barred by thousands of floating logs, encircled by a boom, that filled the lake in front of us. The boom, moving very slowly, was towed by a gator (alligator), bound for Folger's mill at Sioux Lookout no doubt. Even standing up in the canoe we could see no open water. The logs seemed to extend from shore to shore. To get a better look and plan our course of action, we paddled to the nearest island, its closest end a huge "whaleback" outcropping of rock. I scrambled up to the highest point to search for a safe route free of logs. The rock surface was a smooth pavement scoured and striated by the movement of the ice of the glacial period. The rock itself was a magnificent conglomerate—of a darkish hue with embedded cobbles and boulders of light-pink granite. A spectacular sight. I was so engrossed that I forgot what I had come to look for. Here was an ancient sedimentary deposit—a gravel, a record of a torrent that had tumbled and rolled these boulders along some ancient stream. One of the most ancient rocks in North America, recording the flow of water and the wearing down of granite hills of even greater antiquity—a deposit, as we now know, nearly three billion years old. Think of it, 3,000,000,000 years old! I resolved then and there that this rock would be the subject of my doctoral thesis. I returned to begin my study of it the very next year.

Having discovered not only the conglomerate but also a passage around the logs, I returned to the canoe. We soon reached Abram Chutes, where the drop was too great and the water too swift to paddle against. Fortunately for us, the loggers had built a docklike structure alongside the swift water. We landed, attached a towline to the canoe and pulled it up the rapids, reboarded, and paddled off into Minnitaki Lake. By now it was evening, so we made for the nearest island to camp.

THE LAST OF THE PINE

*Minnitaki*

Minnitaki is a large lake, running about thirty miles southwest–northeast, more or less parallel to Abram Lake. The east end has several rather large irregular, island-filled bays. We had entered Northeast Bay. The name Minnitaki is not Ojibwa; it is generally attributed to the Sioux Indians, akin to other Sioux names like Minnesota and Minnehaha. Abram and Pelican lakes were about the northern limit of the dreaded forays of the warlike Sioux. Our course took us along the northern shore, past Troutfish and Lyons bays, and through a narrow inlet into Pickerel Arm, a very narrow, eighteen-mile-long riverlike bay. We camped on a beautiful pine-covered islet near the end of Pickerel Arm.

(*top*) Logs enclosed in boom for transport to sawmill. Abram Lake, Ontario, about 1935. Photo by R. M. Grogan. (*bottom*) Archean Abram conglomerate near Sioux Lookout, Ontario, 1929.

Our thoughts turned to the logging of pine and the log drives. We had seen logging dams on the Manitou, abandoned logging camps, and the gator at Sioux Lookout with its boom and logs in tow. Logging had all but ceased in Minnesota and Wisconsin. We were seeing the end of pine in the North.

In this lake country logging was divided into three phases—the winter cutting in the logging camps, the spring and summer drive to bring the logs to the mill, and the sawing of logs into lumber. We had not seen the cutting, but we had passed many abandoned camps, some recent but most in advanced decay. The latter were usually a cluster of log buildings, with doors ajar, window panes broken, and perhaps the roof collapsed. The clearing surrounding the buildings would be overgrown with brambles—often a good patch of raspberries—with some pin cherries and the usual small poplars. Inside the buildings were overturned benches, a rusty stove; outside one might find an abandoned washtub, a bit of heavy chain—monuments to an era at an end. When the camp was operating, there had been men who cut the pines with two-man crosscut saws, axmen who felled trees with their double-bitted axes, and teamsters who drove sleighs loaded with logs—cut in fifteen- to eighteen-foot lengths—to the river or lake, where they were piled on the ice to await the spring breakup and drive.

In Minnesota and Wisconsin the logs usually floated down rivers to the sawmills. But in this lake country they were moved, as we saw them by the gator. The free-floating logs were enclosed in a boom made of somewhat larger logs connected by a few chain links. The gator itself was a bargelike craft with steam engine and winch. A steel cable and anchor were carried forward in a skiff, the anchor was dropped, and the gator slowly wound in the cable, pulling itself forward along with the boom and enclosed logs. The progress took many days. Attached to the boom and moving with it was the wanigan, essentially a houseboat where the crew ate and slept. When the logs reached the outlet of the lake they were sent loose down the river. As we saw on the Manitou River, a log dam was often built at the head of the river to impound water for the drive. At the critical moment the sluice gate was opened and the drive began. Lumberjacks with their peaveys guided the logs into the sluice. Others along the stream kept them from coming ashore or getting stuck on rocks and creating a logjam. A lumberjack's job was risky. He had to walk from one floating log to another without losing his balance. If the river ended in another lake, a boom was swung across the inlet to collect the logs as they came down the river, then they in turn were towed by a gator until they reached their destination—the sawmill. Travel across large lakes was slow and might be delayed by unfavorable winds.

At the mill the logs were stored in a "log pond," an area enclosed by a boom anchored to pilings. The logs were fed one by one to an endless chain studded with hooks—the bull chain—which took them up an incline to the saws. The lumberjacks had to guide the logs to this conveyor system. This work continued as long as the logs lasted—with luck, until the freezeup and the next winter's cut of pine.

The mills were steam powered, though the large circular saws might be electrically driven from power generated on the spot. Each entering log was placed on a moving carriage, clamped securely, and moved toward the saw. The logs were first squared up, and the slabbing produced was fed to a waste burner—the large silolike stack we saw at Folger's mill. The logs were seized by giant clawlike arms operated by steam, held firmly while being cut, then flipped over ninety degrees to be cut again.

We had seen the aftermath of logging—the cutover land, the slash, the few large, defective pines remaining, or the all-too-often burned-over area with its denuded rocky hills, charred stumps, and gaunt trunks, some lying prone with their charred roots reaching toward the sky. These areas were soon invaded by the pink-blooming fireweed and later by second-growth bush, mainly aspen or poplar with a scattering of birch and balsam. This was the legacy of the era of pine, even then drawing to a close in northwestern Ontario.

SANDY LAKES EPISODE

From Minnitaki Lake we made the Blackface portage, of some thirty chains (a chain equals sixty-six feet), to Sandy Lake—Sandybeach on the new maps. It was our plan to cross Sandy Lake, make a two and half mile portage to Little Sandy and another portage of some two miles to Wee Sandy Lake, then to make the half-mile carry to McKenzie Creek, which leads to Dinorwic Lake. Sandy, or Big Sandy Lake as it is known locally, is a rather large open lake, nearly six miles by direct line to the portage leading to Little Sandy. It has almost no islands and had a bad reputation. Like Pakwash Lake, it is shallow, so that strong winds can stir up a dangerous sea—steep, closely spaced waves. We were fortunate and skirted the southeast shore. The shores of the lake were peculiar—unlike any we had seen elsewhere. Although there were a few rock outcroppings, most of the shore was a terracelike accumulation of cobbles and boulders. The slope to the water's edge was steep and would be a hazardous place to land a canoe in a rough sea. It seemed to me that the water level of the lake must have dropped ten feet or so, leaving the rampart of cobbles and boulders exposed.

As we approached the portage landing we could see an old dock, a shack, and a large boat pulled up on shore. As we got closer we saw a man bending over the boat, apparently working on its inboard engine. The shack was a one-story frame structure with its siding nailed on vertically—a style of construction common in the backwoods of Georgia but never seen in the North. A porch with a sagging roof sheltered an old bicycle. The man was so intent on his chore that he had neither seen or heard us land. When we called out he looked up very much startled and shaken, and his coal-black face turned gray. We thus met Hazelwood, the only black man we had seen on all our trip. Hazelwood, wearing a cap tilted to one side of his head, a blue denim shirt, rumpled baggy trousers of an uncertain color, and rather dilapidated shoes, recovered from his fright and shook hands with us. He had a large scar on one side of his face, caused, we later surmised, by a razor slash. He lived alone and had a license to fish commercially on Sandy Lake. He was tinkering with the engine of his boat trying to put it right so he could set out his nets. He had not, he told us, fished for a number of years. We asked how he would get fish to market. He pointed to a partly overgrown narrow dirt road that led to Dinorwic on the railroad, a distance of some nine miles. A team and wagon could make the round trip in a day. He himself used his bicycle to go to town once or twice a month.

Hazelwood, we afterward learned, had appeared unannounced in Dinorwic one day, having ridden a freight into town. When asked his name he hesitated, then his eyes fell on the potbellied cast-iron stove in the railway station. The brand of the stove, "Hazelwood," was cast in the stove top, so he said "Hazelwood" and became known as the man who got his name from a stove. He claimed to be Canadian born, from somewhere down east, but there was speculation that he had been in a razor duel, killed a man, and perhaps found the woods of northwestern Ontario better for his health. To us, at least, the style of his house was reminiscent of the South, and his vivid scar gave some credence to the notion that he had fled the States to escape retribution or jail.

We asked about the canoe portage to Little Sandy Lake. Hazelwood was astonished, then he laughed. If there ever had been one, it was long since overgrown. Nobody had made such a portage in all the twenty years he had lived there. So there we were stranded on Sandy Lake, faced with a nine-mile portage. Hazelwood thought a few moments, then told us we could portage down the road a mile and a half, then follow his trapline over to Little Sandy Lake. He volunteered to show us the way. Since this seemed the only practical solution, we took his suggestion. The road was fair going—at least it was open and not completely overgrown. The trapline, however, was barely discernible and would require considerable brushing out before we could get a canoe through. So we spent the rest of the day carrying packs and canoe down the road, clearing out a trail from the road to Little Sandy Lake, and finally getting all our things to the shore of Little Sandy. It was a relief to get in the canoe, away from the flies and mosquitoes, and paddle off to a small point near the southwest end of the lake, where we camped. It was much too late to find the portage and make the carry to Wee Sandy. Now we were really alone—surrounded by woods and bottled up. Was there any trail to Wee Sandy, or would we spend all the next day cutting one?

Little Sandy Lake (Hartman Lake) was indeed a small lake, no more than a mile and a half across in any direction. We were eager to get out of our imprisonment, so early the next day we made for the presumed portage trail. We found a trail of sorts, but to make sure it was not one of those elusive game trails that lead nowhere, we followed it. It went south, which was good, and sure enough it did indeed end at Wee Sandy Lake. It was not ideal, but with some ax work it would serve as a portage. We rested a while at Wee Sandy where across from us, not much over a half mile distant, we saw a white house in a clearing. We returned to Little Sandy, ate a bite, then began the arduous task of toting packs and canoe over the two miles of poorly marked trail. In places we had to do a good deal of brushing out. We did find a spring of ice-cold water about halfway across—most unusual in the northern bush. The country here, as the names of the lakes suggest, was very sandy, with few rock exposures and a great deal of glacial drift. The cold spring water was much appreciated, since the day was warm, the flies were bad, and we had had only tepid lake water to drink. After several hours of leapfrogging our packs and canoe, we reached Wee Sandy Lake. We had made three round trips—one to reconnoiter and two to carry—some twelve miles in all, four with full loads. So we arrived on Wee Sandy pretty well beat and bitten. By now it was past midafternoon. A half-hour under paddle, and we landed at a small dock near the house we had seen.

The house was a neat log structure, a story and a half, chinked with plaster. The front, completely covered with plaster and whitewashed, was graced by a full-width porch. Curtains and geraniums testified to a feminine touch. A couple of outbuildings, a fenced garden, and the ubiquitous pile of firewood completed the scene. Except for a cow tethered nearby, we saw no sign of life. But not for long. We were discovered, and furious barking ensued. A dog bounded out. He was a setter of some kind and not too unfriendly, but his alarm brought out Jack Ovunstone, whose homestead we had invaded. Jack took in our woebegone appearance and our canoe and packs and asked how we came to be there. We explained that we had portaged from Big Sandy by way of Little Sandy. Jack was astonished and called his wife to come out and see the boys who had arrived. Jack had short-cropped curly hair tinged with gray, a stern chin, and twinkling blue eyes and always had a pipe in his mouth. He came from New York State but had spent most of his life in the North as forest ranger, trapper, and now homesteader. He was a typical pioneer in this new North and a thorough gentleman. Mrs. Ovunstone was Canadian born, from the prairie provinces—Saskatchewan, I believe. She was an excellent housekeeper and their log house was as neat as anyplace I have seen. John and Fannie, the children, were typical of this hardy pioneer stock. John took after his father and was engaged in putting up his own place on Little Sandy Lake. It was his trail we had used in making our portage. Nothing would do but to come in and have tea. We hesitated, seedy as we were, but the invitation was so genuine and our resistance so low that we yielded. It took a few minutes for the pot to boil. Mrs. Ovunstone spread a white tablecloth and put out two dishes of strawberries—wild strawberries—and a pitcher of cream—real cream. It was almost too much. I knew how many mosquito bites those wild strawberries represented.

The Ovunstones heard many of the details of our travels, from Rainy Lake to Dryden, to Amesdale and Hudson and Lac Seul, and to Red Lake and back. They laughed at our account of meeting Hazelwood and filled us in on the details of his arrival in Dinorwic and his career before and since, both known and surmised. Before we knew it time had slipped away and evening was fast approaching. Jack offered to show us the shortest path to Dinorwic.

So we bid a grateful good-bye and shouldered our packs. Jack guided us along a footpath to Dinorwic, going a bit slowly because of a leg injury he had suffered some weeks before. Dinorwic, about a half-mile away, was a station on the Canadian Pacific, a place formerly known as Wabigoon Tank, and appeared to be not much more than a station, a Hudson's Bay Company store, and half a dozen cabins and shacks. We portaged our gear across the track, then had to negotiate a barbed-wire fence that kept back some cows and cross a pasture to a landing on McKenzie Creek. We said good-bye to Jack, with many thanks, loaded the canoe, and set off as quickly as we could, since it was almost dark and mosquitoes from the reedy banks of the stream were getting bad. We made haste slowly as the creek wriggled its leisurely way to Dinorwic Lake. Owing to the lateness of the hour, we camped on the first small island we saw. By now the mosquitoes were nearly unbearable. We got the tent up, and a sloppy job it was. We were too tired to do more and were all but devoured by the millions of mosquitoes with their menacing hum. Though we had had nothing to eat since noon except the tea and strawberries we did not have the courage to leave the tent even for a drink of water, let alone to cook a meal. In the morning the mosquito netting across the front of the tent was black with mosquitoes waiting for us to come out. We wasted no time rolling up the tent and fleeing this accursed place to find an open breezy point where we could build a fire and make breakfast.

We were back on Dinorwic Lake, or Little Wabigoon Lake as it is known thereabouts, with its clouded water, caving clay banks, and bays with drowned muskegs and their forest of dead trees—not a pleasant lake. It was, as I noted earlier, in the middle of the Wabigoon Lake Indian Reserve.

On our voyage out we had passed through this reserve and had also been in the Lac Seul Reservation on Lost Lake, but in neither place had we seen many Indians. Most of those we saw were in such places as Hudson, Goldpines, and Sioux Lookout. These Indians all belonged to the Ojibwa tribes (or Chippewa as they are called in Wisconsin). To the north were the Cree and to the south the warlike Sioux, only a few scattered remnants of whom remained in the Dakotas. The Ojibwa, then more numerous than the Sioux, were nomads who lived by hunting and fishing.

Those we saw were for the most part a sorry lot. They had been placed on reservations, land of little value. We did not see a single Indian farm. Apparently they wintered over in log cabins or shacks on the reservations and in summer traveled about, often camping in tents on the fringes of towns or settlements. They still hunted and fished, and we were told they were not subject to any game laws and could shoot without limit at all seasons.

The government did provide schools and for some an annual treaty payment of five dollars each. Otherwise they were left to shift for themselves. Few if any had regular employment; they did some trapping, but the fur trade had greatly declined. In all our travels, we saw no fresh beaver cuttings, and beaver pelts, once the mainstay of the fur trade, had all but vanished. The Indians were employed from time to time at odd jobs such as cutting pulpwood or railroad ties. They might pick wild blueberries in season and ship them out by rail to the eastern markets.

There had been much intermarrying between Indians and whites; usually a homesteader or trapper would marry an Indian woman. Hence there were many children of mixed blood. Poverty, alcoholism, and poor health afflicted large numbers. The Indians' own culture was disintegrating, and they had not been assimilated into white society.

We were glad to leave Dinorwic Lake behind and soon found ourselves in the winding, reedy channel, hemmed in by cattail marshes, that leads to Stanawan and Minnehaha lakes. Here again we were overwhelmed by the abundance of birdlife—soaring gulls and terns, wading herons and bitterns, grebes, and a multitude of teals and other ducks.

## Rainy Lake and Finis

We were homeward bound. Familiarity with the route, especially the portages, sped our journey back through the beautiful Manitou, down the Manitou River to Rainy Lake, down Rainy Lake, and under the railroad bridge to Sand Bay, with Pithers Point on our right and Ranier, Minnesota, in full view some three miles away. A strong north wind was blowing, so we made good time, going mostly from island to island or from one sheltered point to another to avoid the open lake. But now that the end was in sight we made a beeline across Sand Bay. This turned out not to be the best course. As we left the protected north shore, the waves grew larger and larger, and by the time we were halfway across they were menacing indeed. It seemed we would not be able to handle anything larger, but it was too late to change our minds though even larger waves lay ahead. We continued and it was all we could do to keep from shipping water. Fortunately our packs were light, since our grub-stake was nearly exhausted, so we rode high in the water. As we neared the Ranier dock we saw people watching us battle the waves, no doubt expecting us to go under at any moment. But we rode it out and came in with surprisingly little water in the canoe. We were back. As we came alongside the dock Wynne sprang out and steadied the bucking canoe while I tossed up the packs. In a moment the canoe was out and the trip over. We shook hands. "Damned good trip," said Wynne, perhaps his longest speech of the whole voyage. It was finished!

The voyage had ended. The memories of the unpleasant episodes—stranded in Amesdale, mired knee-deep on a portage, plagued by flies and mosquitoes—were already fast receding. Instead we recalled the moments of incredible beauty—sunsets over the water, star-studded skies, the sights and sounds of a nocturnal thunderstorm with its awesome lightning and giant thunderheads, the sound of the rapids and the waves and the wind in the pines, the scents of balsam and wood smoke, the magic of early morning with the sunlight on the mists from the lake, the total silence at times so intense one could hear his blood coursing—all treasures beyond price.

# 5

## California and the King's Seminar (1927–28)

I had been at Oberlin nearly two years. Even when I came I had planned to resume graduate studies and work for my doctor's degree, so in the spring of 1927 I applied at several schools—Chicago, Wisconsin, Yale, and California (Berkeley). I thought I should go somewhere other than Minnesota, to broaden my education. Though I had saved some money from my Oberlin salary, I needed financial aid, so I applied for a fellowship at each of the schools. I had selected Wisconsin and Chicago as the strongest schools in geology in the Midwest and California and Yale as outstanding schools on the west and east coasts.

I was accepted and offered financial aid at all four. Chicago offered me $400 but not tuition, which would have left nothing for expenses, so I turned Chicago down. Of the others California was most attractive—a $750 fellowship and the assurance that I could get a waiver of out-of-state tuition. But above all Andy Lawson was there, so I accepted the California offer.

Since California started the fall term in August, Wynne Hastings and I had made our Canadian trip in June and July. Upon returning from the North, I packed my bags and took the train west. I had to borrow $100 from my mother's sister, my Aunt Irene, to launch this venture.

The rail trip from Minneapolis to California, via Omaha, took several days and nights. It was my first trip west, my first look at the Rocky Mountains and the Great Basin, and my first time to California. The only western mountains I had seen were the Black Hills of South Dakota, an isolated cluster I had visited as a small boy about 1913 or 1914.

My first view of California was very disappointing. We had crossed the Sierra Nevada during the night, and when I woke next morning we were in the Sacramento Valley—level as far as the eye would see. Since it was August, no rain had fallen for many weeks—months—so the vegetation was burned yellow and brown. As we approached the Coast Ranges and hills began to appear, these too were bare and brown and generally treeless. So this was the promised land! I began to wonder why I had left the well-watered green of the East and come here to school. The train approached Suisun Straits, where it slowed to a crawl, then stopped. The reason for the stop became evident as soon as the train moved again; very slowly the cars were being shunted onto a car ferry to cross the straits. The whole procedure took quite a while, but finally we were across and the train was reassembled and on its way to Oakland. I detrained in Berkeley and made my way to the campus.

Berkeley is between San Francisco Bay on the west and the Berkeley Hills on the east. The university itself nestles close to the Berkeley Hills—in reality a part of the Coast Ranges. The highest peak was old Baldy, rising about nineteen hundred feet above sea level. The Hills themselves were cut by several sharp valleys or "canyons" that drained toward the Bay. Just in back of the campus was Strawberry Canyon, which I came to know well, since it was used as a field training area for the geologists. The Berkeley Hills, like many of the Coast Ranges, were largely bare, the shrubs and trees being mainly confined to the canyons. The largest trees, common in the town and in places in the canyons, were eucalyptus—trees native to Australia but that thrived in this part of California. They are dirty trees, constantly shedding bark and other debris. Palm trees there were also, though not many, and most looked spare or maimed.

My first task was to find a place to live. I obtained a list of boarding and rooming houses that took in students and soon found a place close by—a few steps to Telegraph Avenue and not much more to the campus. The place was a large frame house—an elegant mansion in its heyday but now in need of paint. It was run by an Italian woman. She and her family lived on the first floor, and the second-floor rooms were let to students. I think this was her first business venture, necessary to support her and her family. The three children were out of school age; the oldest, a boy in high school, seemed to be the man of the house. Once, to my surprise, the husband and father made his appearance. I hadn't known he existed. He was a mild and ineffectual person who seemed to have little to do with the management of the place. I can't remember much about the table fare; it must have been adequate. I was introduced to macaroni salad and to artichokes—things we never had at home.

There were about five or six other roomers, all undergraduates and, except one, all freshmen. The exception was a chap named Krieger who was in his last year of civil engineering. He had completed all his required courses and was filling out his last year with electives. I soon discovered he was studying Plato's *Republic* and enjoying it very much. One of the students left about midyear—ostensibly because his wrist-watch had been stolen, but Krieger surmised he had been pledged and wanted to move into the fraternity house. I had a small room at the front of the house overlooking the street. This was to be my workplace during my year at Berkeley.

## GEOLOGY AT BERKELEY

I reported to the department to introduce myself and register for the ensuing term. Professor G. D. Louderback, the chairman at that time, functioned as advisor to graduate students. Although he had my Minnesota transcript showing courses taken, he ignored it and proceeded to lay out a course of study that duplicated and overlapped what I already had. I had studied structural geology with Schwartz. No matter, I would take structural geology with Taliaferro. I had had hand-specimen and thin-section petrography from Grout: no matter, I would take the subject again. I resented the implication that Minnesota courses and credits were second rate and that only at California could I get a quality education. As it turned out, I discovered the wisdom of this action; the same course taught by a different person from a different perspective and in different surroundings was in fact a different course. My registration completed, I applied for tuition remission, which was granted a few days later.

The Geology Department was then housed in Bacon Hall, a relatively old building of red brick that lay in the shadow of the Campanile—the tall bell tower—a landmark on the Berkeley campus. Bacon Hall had been the university's library at some earlier time; the Geology Department, as was so often the case, had inherited a second-hand building. I had no office or even a desk in the building, nor did any of the graduate students of my class. We had to study in the main library or in our rooms.

The faculty included A. C. Lawson (the "King"), the most senior member and certainly the most widely known; It was Lawson's last year of active teaching before his official retirement. Lawson had passed the chairmanship on to Louderback; both were full professors. I have mentioned Nicholas L. Taliaferro, who taught petrology and structural geology; he was an associate professor. There were also N. E. A. Hinds, geomorphologist, Perry Byerly, seismologist, Adolf Pabst, mineralogist—on leave in 1927—Carlton Hulin, ore deposits, and Howel Williams, volcanologist and newest member of the faculty. There were two others, Victor T. Allen and C. A. Anderson, both working for their degrees but also doing some teaching, particularly in the local field course. There were no paleontologists, for paleontology had split off some years before and become a separate department housed in the School of Mines building. All in all, it was a very young faculty. Except for Lawson and Louderback, all were in their late twenties or early thirties. Moreover, it was very much a California department. All had California degrees except Hinds (Harvard) and Williams(Liverpool) and, of course, Lawson himself (Hopkins). Two of the younger group, Williams and Anderson, attained distinction in their fields; both were elected to the National Academy of Sciences. Although it was a young department, it was still very much a Lawson department; he had set the program and direction years before.

The Paleontology Department had been established about 1912. I don't know the full story of how it came to be a separate operation. Rumor had it that Lawson had little use for paleontologists or their views, which is given some credence by Lawson's own writings. He once wrote: "for paleontologists and so-called historical geologists, geological history begins with the Cambrian. All that precedes the Cambrian is lumped together as the pre-Cambrian, a paleontologically uninteresting aggregate of rocks to be disposed of in a few paragraphs at the beginning of their fat textbooks on geology. It is difficult for them to grasp the notion that the Cambrian is a relatively late period in geological history" (1930, *Univ. Calif. Dept. Geol. Sci. Bull.* 19: 277). In another place he refers to their "lack of comprehension that would shame an imbecile." Of course the graduate students in paleontology came to Bacon Hall for some courses, but it was my impression that they were given a rather hard time.

I found my courses very interesting. Taliaferro—"Tucky" to the students—was a good lecturer. The textbook in the general petrology course was Tyrrell's *Principles of Petrology*, and the scope and content of Tucky's course were about at the level of that book. I took copious notes and every evening typed them up for future use; the second going over of the lecture material pretty well fixed the subject in my mind. The laboratory work in the course consisted of writing a description of hand specimens based on examination with a hand lens. The descriptions were very detailed—much more than I thought possible—often running to three or four closely written pages. We were expected to distinguish, using only a hand lens, between such fine-grained rocks as basalts, andesites, trachyte, and dacites. It became apparent to me then why California graduates in geology knew their rocks.

The thin-section course that followed, also taught by Taliaferro, was equally thorough. The text was Harker's *Petrology for Students.* The laboratory work in this course involved studying rocks in thin section. Each student had to make one or two thin sections without benefit of a diamond saw, motorized lap, or other modern equipment. A chip was ground down by hand on a glass plate with grinding powder. The results were not good. In fact, virtually all the slides we used in the course had been made by students in previous years. If one could master the subject using these wedge-shaped slides, commonly too thick, with feldspars and quartz showing bright colors, and clouded by bits of grinding powder and bubbles, one could surely identify and describe any rock in a properly made slide. But master the subject we did. The lectures in this course were mainly on the optical theory of mineral identification in polarized light under the microscope.

Tucky's structural geology was an equally well-organized lecture course. Tucky gave us a lot of fault problems, involving numerical data and requiring solutions mainly by calculation of the amount of fault movement, displacement of beds, location of fault segments or an ore shoot, and the like. The solutions were found by graphic construction using a "two-level contour projection" method—a species of descriptive geometry. Having studied descriptive geometry at Oberlin and having a great liking for it, I found these problems easy, though most of my classmates had trouble with them. Tucky did not say where the method or problems came from, but I afterward discovered that they had been worked out by W. S. T. Smith (a California Ph.D.) and published in *Economic Geology* (1914, 9:25–66).

Louderback's sedimentation seminar was indeed based on selected readings. The class was small, fewer than ten, all graduate students. Among them were three from Pomona College, a school where A. O. Woodford consistently turned out first-rate geology majors—Cliff Johnson, Bob Burger, and Dana Russell. Others in the seminar included Paul D. Krynine, son of a White Russian emigré, who afterward got his Ph.D at Yale and eventually became professor of petrology at Pennsylvania State College. Another was "Tubby" Winterer, who in midcareer abandoned soils to pursue geology. Tubby died several years later; his son became a geologist and is now at University of California at San Diego.

Louderback himself took little part in the seminar. He assigned the readings, some of which were in French (Androussov on the Black Sea) and some in German (Sauramo on varved clays in Finland), then called on one or another of the students to report on what he had read. Louderback sat quietly by, smoking his pipe, during the proceedings, asking a question or two at infrequent intervals. Krynine gave the most detailed reports. He had taken copious notes—seemingly just a paraphrase of the original paper. These he read in a monotonous manner that, owing to his slurred speech and Russian accent, was difficult to follow. The German and French articles gave the most trouble. Louderback made sure the graduate students learned to read and use German in particular. In fact, he taught a course on metamorphic rocks for which the text was Grubenmann's *Die Gesteinsmetamorphose* in the original German. I afterward found out that Louderback usually assigned the same articles each year, so there were translations floating around among the graduate students.

There was no text for the seminar, nor was there any systematic coverage of the subject matter. Instead the course was built around a reading list of the more important or "landmark" papers, which broke new ground and opened up new avenues of thought. Included also were some first-rate examples of thoroughness—models to be emulated. The first paper we read belonged to this genre, Harold Wanless's study of the White River sediments of the Badlands of South Dakota. I was not, of course, aware that I would soon be going to Chicago to teach sedimentation, but as it turned out Louderback's seminar had a great influence on my own approach to the subject. For example, the paper of J. A. Udden on the "mechanical composition"—grain size distribution—of clastic sediments led to a new way of thinking about sediments. Udden's approach was based on the premise that the grain-size distribution might be a clue to the agent or environment of deposition, a view that gained wide acceptance in the thirties. Even now the notion that the grading curve is a "fingerprint" of the environment is still entertained in some quarters, though doubts have haunted most of us.

C. K. Wentworth's earliest papers, on stream and beach pebbles, written about 1920, also were eye-openers. Here was a new way to look at old problems. Wentworth redefined terms like "roundness" and "shape," quantified them, and devised a way to measure them objectively so one could see how rounding progressed during stream and beach transport and study the rounding process experimentally.

The papers of Matti Sauramo on the varved clays of Finland opened a door for me. Studying the year-by-year records and constructing a varve chronology made a fascinating project. It sparked my interest in the subject, even led to my setting a student of mine at Chicago, Gordon Rittenhouse, to work on the varved clays of the Wabigoon area in northwestern Ontario. It led also to my error in interpreting the banded Archean slates and siltstones of the Minnitaki Lake area as varves. However, true varves did turn up in the Precambrian Cobalt argillites. Magnificent outcrops of varved argillites loaded with dropstones occur some miles north of Thessalon in the valley of the Mississaugi River of the North Shore district. These would convince even the most skeptical of the glacial nature of these deposits.

A few words about Louderback: Louderback ("Uncle George") was Lawson's right-hand man and handled all administrative matters. Next to Lawson he was senior. Louderback was then in his fifties and had the demeanor and look of a professor. He wore a goatee, smoked a pipe, and would, had it been permitted at the time, have had a stein of beer. He admired the German tradition of scholarship, which found expression in his insistence on thoroughness and familiarity with the German literature—in the original. His large office consisted of two connecting rooms, the walls covered by filled bookshelves and the tables piled high with correspondence and reprints. When a student came to see him he would

G. D. Louderback, professor of geology and head of the department at Berkeley in 1927. Reproduced by permission of the university archivist, Bancroft Library, University of California at Berkeley.

often recommend a paper, then after searching the piles for half an hour, give up the search and tell him to get it from the library.

Louderback was a Californian from the beginning. He was a student of Lawson's, got his degree at Berkeley, and except for a short interval at Reno spent his entire professional life at the University of California. It is said, however, that some years later he had a falling out with Lawson so that they never spoke to each other again.

Louderback liked organization and academic affairs—perhaps to the detriment of his science. He not only was chairman of the department but also was on various committees and boards both on and off campus. He established a chapter of Theta Tau, a national mining and engineering fraternity, on the Berkeley campus and not only was a patron of this group but was also active in the national organization, at one time being grand regent. Theta Tau was presumably a professional fraternity, but in 1927 it still had some of the trappings of a social fraternity, with its initiation rites and secret handclasp. I was invited to join and did so. The local chapter did not have a fraternity house, and its meetings must have been dull or seldom held, for I can recall little about it other than the initiation ceremonies.

Louderback contributed to the departmental excellence by his insistence on high-quality work by doctoral students; to ensure this he spent a week or more in the field with each at the conclusion of his studies.

I had no direct contact with either Byerly or the program in seismology. Nor did I study with Williams. "Willy," as he was known, was the newest member of the faculty, but he made an indelible impression because of his painstaking thoroughness and particularly his skill in illustrating his papers. His sketches were superb. He would spend a whole day making a single drawing of what he saw in a thin section. This talent no doubt reflects his background—he was a Welshman and a student of Greenly. The British petrographers illustrated their work with such pen-and-ink sketches, which are much more revealing than muddy photomicrographs. Williams's landscape sketches were likewise first rate. Today we have lost the art of sketching—an art highly developed by Holmes and others in the early days of the old Rocky Mountain Survey, before the establishment of the United States Geological Survey. Only when I met Robert Balk and Ernst Cloos, both from the European tradition, did I see similar use of pen-and-ink sketches. No doubt both Balk and Cloos learned the technique from Hans Cloos, who was the grand master of the art.

The course by N. E. A. Hinds was perhaps the weakest, though the field excursions were very worthwhile. Our first trip was to Yosemite, where we stayed in the floored tents of Camp Curry. At that time the California students combined geologic fieldwork with a fair amount of carousing. Every evening there were several card games under way accompanied by gin drinking—bootleg gin, of course, since Prohibition was in force. These activities went on long past midnight. You can imagine what shape many were in the next day, especially since Hinds's field trips involved strenuous hiking and climbing. I soon discovered my dislike of cigarette smoking and bootleg gin (and any hard liquor for that matter). The next day Hinds, who was young, thin, and wiry, would lead the class to the highest point around, scarcely pausing at all. I well remember the hike from the Merced River to the brink of Yosemite Falls, a three-thousand-foot climb on a steep zigzag foot trail. The gin drinkers of the night before took a lot of punishment.

The falls themselves were a disappointment. It was near the end of the dry season, so Yosemite Creek carried very little water, and what did spill over the rim was dissipated as mist and fine spray. But the view from the rim of the canyon was breathtaking. One had a full sweep, with the majestic Half Dome across the valley; the Merced River far below was only a thread. I really understood John Muir's rapture when he first saw these sights.

Upon attaining the summit, Hinds delivered a lecture on what was to be learned. We had a sort of Cook's tour—a marked contrast to J Harlan Bretz's manner of teaching, as I was to find out when I joined the Chicago faculty a couple of years later. Hinds, however, did a good job with the blue pencil. He went over our reports in great detail, correcting the English as well as the geologic thought.

The trip to Yosemite was only the first of many field trips during my year at California. Only at California (excepting perhaps at Oberlin and much later at Hopkins) did I find field excursions woven into the teaching program. Neither Minnesota nor Chicago did much outside the classroom. Most of the excursions, though not all, were an integral part of Hinds's course. We made a trip to the Calistoga area ("the Geysers"), where we saw the many roaring and hissing steam wells and hot-water pools. The steam is used to spin turbines and generate a good part of the electricity used in the San Francisco area. We also went to the Tiburon peninsula, then reached only by ferry. If I remember correctly, it was here we saw our first exposure of the Franciscan formation—a dark graywacke type of sandstone. It had an "igneous look" to it and the students were baffled, but it was familiar to me because it closely resembled the many Precambrian graywackes I had seen in the Lake Superior region. We also made trips to the Point Reyes and Mount Diablo areas; Tucky led the latter excursion. The most ambitious trip was to northern California. A monotonous drive up the Great Valley brought us to Redding, where we stayed the night. The next day we drove along the Pitt River (there was no Shasta Dam or lake at that time) to look at the Bully Hill rhyolite, the McCloud limestone, and other formations of this region. At one time we made a trip to see the Cretaceous resting on the granites of the Sierras—somewhere north and east of the Marysville Buttes.

The field course in the Berkeley Hills was one of the most valuable courses I had at California. The class was divided into small sections, one of which was supervised by Victor Allen. Allen had been an undergraduate student at Minnesota but had come to Berkeley for his doctor's degree. He worked on the Ione (Eocene) formation and was particularly interested in the clay minerals. We had a large-scale topographic map of the Berkeley Hills and were expected to plot the geology on it. The poorly consolidated Tertiary strata of the Hills are sharply folded; they included a banded chert formation, the Monterrey, a thick nonmarine sequence of gravels, the Orinda, and basalt flows, the Bald Peak basalts. When we reached an outcrop we were turned loose to "write it up"—to describe it in detail. Allen sat nearby saying nothing, but at the end of twenty or thirty minutes he looked over our field notes and quizzed us about what we had seen. On reaching a formational contact we would walk it out, using such outcrops as we could find, but more often relying on float. In the end each of us had made his own geologic map of a considerable part of the Berkeley Hills and had drawn his own geologic cross section. I came to understand why Berkeley graduates were good field geologists as well as petrologists. The strong emphasis on both was a legacy from A. C. Lawson.

I cannot recall any regular meetings of a departmental seminar, colloquium, or other forum at which either students or faculty talked about their research. There was one meeting of the Le Conte Club—a Bay-area organization—but my only recollection of that was of a tart exchange between Lawson and the bewhiskered Bailey Willis. There was also some kind of a departmental gathering at which Hans Cloos spoke. Hans Cloos, one of the leading German geologists of his day, the founder and chief proponent of "granite tectonics," lectured on some work he had done on the granite fabrics in the Sierra Nevada region, work his student (and younger brother) Ernst Cloos was to carry on. Karl Rode, also a student of Hans Cloos, was at Berkeley as a postdoctoral scholar. Hans Cloos was a dynamic man, full of enthusiasm for his work. I saw him once again when he was awarded the Penrose Medal of the Geological Society of America at its meeting in Chicago. We sat next to one another at the faculty club of the university and commiserated over our trials and tribulations as editors, he of the *Geologische Rundschau* and I of the *Journal of Geology*.

Because of the lack of a departmental forum, I had very little feeling for what was going on. I knew of Howell Williams's work on the

Maryville Buttes. I also knew something of what the students were doing, though for the most part my association was with the first-year graduate students, not with those well into their theses. I became aware only later, through publication, of Taliaferro's work on the Franciscan sandstone and cherts and of Lawson's interest in isostacy as applied to deltas, mountain ranges, and the like. But this was mostly after the fact. I don't think Louderback was involved in much beyond administration and related affairs, though he had done some work in the Basin and Range area. Byerly's work in seismology seemed remote and a thing apart. Paleontology was even more removed. I never met the Paleontology faculty.

In all, it was difficult to characterize the scientific milieu at Berkeley in 1927–28. As I noted, much of the student research was California-centered; much of it consisted of mapping quadrangles. I don't mean to imply that the mapping was routine—many areas were very complex indeed, and almost any field study would impinge on the problems of structure and petrology, But there was no overriding theme or motif to the research in the department at that time, unless it was California itself.

## ANDREW COWPER LAWSON

Lawson's seminar was an education in itself. Sooner or later all graduate students were obliged to take the "King's seminar," as it was called. There were, perhaps, a dozen students in the class at the time I was enrolled. We met in a large room, the departmental library and drafting room, but only the first row in front of the giant drafting table was occupied. Since it was Lawson's habit to call on one or another of the students at the ends of the row, one would if at all possible come early so as not to be "end man."

Lawson found out, at the first meeting, that none of us had read Gilbert. Grove Karl Gilbert was, in Lawson's view, one of the greatest geologists this country had ever produced, and until we had studied Gilbert we were not properly educated. So the first reading assignment was Gilbert's study of the Henry Mountains, a cluster of peaks in the desert of southern Utah. The study was a publication—a book in fact—of the old Geographic and Geologic Survey of the Rocky Mountain Region. Gilbert was indeed a major figure in the history of our science. In his Henry Mountain study he established the principles of both geomorphic development—the evolution of landforms produced by stream erosion—and of laccolithic intrusion. The Henrys were the type locality of laccoliths, those intrusive bodies with a flat floor and bowed top. We also read Gilbert's Lake Bonneville report, a formidable work of more than four hundred pages, published as monograph 1 of the newly established United States Geological Survey. In this work Gilbert clearly elucidated the principles of shoreline development. Gilbert's writing was flawless; his prose could scarcely be improved on. Perhaps this is why, some years later, I discovered that part of Chamberlin and Salisbury's three-volume *Geology* contained passages on the geology of shorelines taken from Gilbert with little or no modification (compare, for example, the middle of p. 35 in Gilbert with the second paragraph of Chamberlin and Salisbury, 1:321). Gilbert also clearly demonstrated depression of the earth's crust under the load imposed upon it by the waters of Lake Bonneville.

Lawson called on us to report on our reading. Anyone who began to give a resumé would be abruptly told to sit down, that we had all read the work and didn't need it summarized. Lawson did not want a *Reader's Digest* presentation—he wanted a critical analysis. What was the central question? How did the author go about answering it? What was the evidence? How did we evaluate the results? If a student erred by beginning with "I believe . . ." or "I think . . . ," Lawson promptly put him down with the remark that young men were not entitled to an opinion. Give us the facts—the evidence. We are not interested in what you believe or think.

It took us quite a while to adjust to this way of doing things. Lawson was a severe taskmaster. He acted the part of a prosecuting attorney—probing every statement, pointing out flaws and contradictions. He had no tolerance for shoddy thinking. One needed a thick hide to survive his piercing gaze and sharp tongue, which were enough to wilt all but the most durable. But the mental discipline he gave his students was invaluable.

Lawson did not browbeat only his students. He was no different in a public meeting. In a session of the Geological Society of America one could feel the tension mount as Lawson slowly rose snorting audibly, to fire a question or make a scathing comment on a presentation.

Lawson had a remarkable career. He was born in Scotland in 1861, but his family emigrated to Canada when he was a boy. His early education was in science, but necessity led him to a career writing for a newspaper. Quite by accident he took a course at McGill that turned him toward geology. He joined the Geological Survey of Canada and at age twenty-two was placed in charge of a field party to make a geological survey of Lake of the Woods, on the boundary between Minnesota and Canada. At that time the lake was beyond reach of the railroad and largely unsurveyed. Lawson had to survey the lake and map its many islands (sixteen thousand according to recent surveys) and very irregular shoreline. The work was done entirely from canoes. The resulting map and report, done in the brief period of two years, made history. Lawson showed that the Laurentian granite—previously thought to be the basement on which all else rested and perhaps the primitive crust of the earth—was in reality an intrusion into the country rock (1885, *Geol. Surv. Canada, Ann. Rept.*, vol. 1). To the latter Lawson gave the name "Keewatin," a designation that has become a standard part of Precambrian nomenclature.

Lawson was at once recognized as an authority on the Precambrian, though the Geological Survey was hesitant to publish his report because of its heretical views on the Laurentian.

Lawson went to John Hopkins University in Baltimore to study the theory and practice of thin-section analysis of rocks, a technique newly introduced from Germany by George Huntington Williams, then professor at Hopkins. In 1908 Lawson resigned his Survey post, and after a short period as mining geologist in British Columbia he joined the faculty at Berkeley. Lawson's work at Berkeley was equally impressive. He set the program of study and established the first systematic field *course* in America (as distinct from field excursions). Fieldwork was an integral part of the program. He and his students mapped the San Francisco Bay area, producing the San Francisco folio, covering five fifteen-minute quadrangles. This work established the stratigraphic and structural framework of the central Coast Ranges. Lawson's seminar instilled intellectual discipline and taught critical analysis. His work on the San Francisco Earthquake Commission, of which he was chairman, led to the elastic rebound theory of earthquakes, formulated by Harry Fielding Reid, also a member of the commission. Lawson initiated a long-term program of seismic studies at Berkeley promulgated by Perry Byerly. Howell Williams, and much later Jean Verhoogen and Francis Turner, joined the faculty. Lawson and all these others, members of the National Academy of Sciences, made Berkeley a leader in geology. Lawson founded and edited the *Bulletin of the Department of Geological Sciences.* The papers published there dealt largely with California problems; many were very long (E. F. Davis's paper on the bedded cherts was 197 pages), and many were accompanied by foldout colored geologic maps. The standard of publication of the *Bulletin* equaled or bettered that of any journal in America.

Even after retirement Lawson made news. As a guest in a field party studying the Precambrian of the Lake Huron region, led by Dr. W. H. Collins, then director of the Geological Survey of Canada, Lawson met Collins's daughter Isabel, then twenty-two. Rumor had it they eloped; in any case, Isabel and Lawson, then seventy and a widower, were married. Some years later, when he was eighty-eight, she bore him a son. Lawson was indeed a remarkable man.

Andrew Cowper Lawson, professor of geology, University of California. Reproduced by permission of the university archivist, Bancroft Library, University of California at Berkeley.

John Hazzard. Photo courtesy of the American Association of Petroleum Geologists and General Petroleum Corporation.

Even in 1927, then sixty-six and on the verge of retirement, Lawson had a commanding presence, standing tall and straight. His well-proportioned figure, his Scots complexion, wavy white hair, only a little thin on top, bushy eyebrows, piercing eyes, and drooping walrus mustache made him an imposing figure. He was the king and was treated as such—perhaps in part out of fear of a tongue lashing. Yet there was another side to his nature. Not many were aware that he wrote poems of great depth and sensitivity. Lawson was a fluent speaker; his lectures held listeners spellbound. He had a facile pen—acid at times—and his papers kept one awake. He was a genial host who invited all the graduate students to a breakfast at the faculty club each spring. Afterward he would place a cigarette in a long holder and light it, take a few puffs, and recount events from his colorful past.

Many of Lawson's students achieved prominence in the profession—they constituted a veritable *Who's Who* in the geologic world. Among them were such geologists as J. P. Buwalda, Chester Stock, A. O. Woodford, Adolph Knopf, G. D. Louderback, Charles Palache, and R. J. Russell—academicians all. But government and industry corralled their share, including E. F. Davis, C. L. Moody, Marcus Hanna, C. A. Anderson, Parker Trask, and Frank Calkins. Other well-known geologists who were former Lawson students were W. F. Foshag, Thomas L. Bailey, M. C. Israelsky, W. S. W. Kew, Mason L. Hill, E. B. Knopf, and E. N. Pennebaker. Lawson had a profound influence on the geological scene during the first quarter of this century.

## SOUTHERN CALIFORNIA

One of the graduate students at Berkeley whom I came to know well was John Hazzard. John had wavy black hair and such a dark beard that even after he shaved he still had five o'clock shadow. He was particularly susceptible to poison oak, of which California had plenty, and was always nursing a case of it. John was loquacious, his speech spiced with borderline epithets and expressions. He was an enthusiastic Californian and full of geology. John had come to Berkeley from the Univeristy of California at Los Angeles. In 1927 the newly established branch of the university at Los Angeles occupied the buildings and campus of a preexisting school—a military school I believe—and had not yet moved to its present location. Being a new institution, its program was limited; one could not work for the doctor's degree in geology, so Hazzard came to Berkeley to continue his studies.

When he registered he had the same initiation from Louderback as I did. Though he had had many courses at UCLA, he was obliged to repeat them at Berkeley. John was understandably irked to find he could not continue from where he left off. We were together in Tucky's courses, the Berkeley Hills field course, and Hinds's course.

At the Christmas break John invited me to spend a week at his home near Los Angeles, so I rode down with him. John was California-oriented and knew a great deal not only about the Los Angeles basin itself, but about the rest of the state. So I got a tour of the Los Angeles area, especially the Verdugo Hills where John had done some fieldwork. The Los Angeles basin itself was then a pleasant place, a region of small towns and cities widely scattered and separated by orange groves. The air was clean, and one could see the San Gabriel Range with its snow-capped peaks. My return many years later was a shock—one town next to another, no orange groves, and a sky filled with yellow smog. A most depressing place.

John was a great admirer of R. T. Hill. Hill was one of the old-time geologists who worked in various fields—stratigraphy, paleontology, structural geology, even ore deposits—an extinct generation. He spent much of his professional career in Texas, but he had retired when I met him, though he then had a one-year appointment to the geology faculty at the University of California at Los Angeles. At the time of my visit Hill was working on a report on the seismic hazards of the Los Angeles region. The story going around was that Professor Bailey Willis of Stanford University had been asked about the risks associated with the San Andreas Fault—responsible for the great San Francisco earthquake of 1906. Since the segment nearest Santa Barbara had been inactive for a long time, Willis suggested that the next quake might occur in the Santa Barbara region. As it happened, Willis was in Santa Barbara when there was a severe shock in that area. The story has it that he had predicted this earthquake and had gone there to see it happen. Now established as a seer of earthquakes, Willis was at once besieged by reporters asking where the next one would occur. Accordingly, he suggested that the next segment of the fault likely to move was that nearest Los Angeles. This statement precipitated a great ado—the Los Angeles Chamber of Commerce was in a panic. They needed a quick rebuttal of this dire prediction. Old R. T. Hill, now a prominent figure at UCLA, was tapped for the job.

When Hazzard and I arrived, Hill was reading proof on his response to Willis, a pamphlet to be published by the Chamber of Commerce. The job was being rushed and the task was confusing, so Hazzard volunteered our services as proofreaders. The problem was worse because the original manuscript had never had proper copyediting, so we tried to edit at the proofreading stage—an expensive and unsatisfactory procedure. But the writing was so bad—sentences without verbs, prepositions without antecedents—that it had to be done.

John and I frequently went to San Francisco on Friday or Saturday night, usually for dinner in one of the many Italian restaurants, where we had a bottle of wine (bootleg) with our spaghetti and meatballs. At that time there were no Bay Bridge and Golden Gate Bridge. One took the rapid transit—the Key System or the Southern Pacific—to the ferry dock in Oakland and rode the ferry thirty minutes or so to the dock at the foot of Market Street. I always thought ferries were the most pleasant way to commute: one could get a bite to eat, read a newspaper, have one's shoes shined, or just stand at the rail to watch the ships loom out of the mist and see the seagulls wheeling about. But with the coming of the bridges the ferries died, as did the rapid transit system, which had to be rebuilt many years later.

Except for an occasional encounter at the meetings of the American Association of Petroleum Geologists, I lost touch with John Hazzard. Apparently he wound up as a petroleum geologist working for the Union Oil Company. He did not take his doctor's degree at Berkeley but got it some years later at the University of Southern California.

FAREWELL TO EDEN

In retrospect, my time at California was perhaps the single most valuable year of my education. Certainly California taught me a lot. I was placed in seminars, exposed to the technical literature—primary sources instead of textbooks—and taught to read critically, to analyze a paper's premises and logic, and to be prepared to defend my analysis. Lawson in particular imparted a mental discipline that remained with me all my professional career. Also, California provided an opportunity to see much new geology—the Coast Ranges, the Sierras, and the Klamath Ranges of the north, and the Los Angeles basin in the south.

Yet I left California at the end of the school year, for several reasons. One was the offer of a half-time instructorship at Minnesota, at a stipend larger than my California fellowship. There I could live at home and save money, and I could take Grout's advanced courses, which I very much wanted. There were two other reasons, one being the opportunity to do a field thesis in the canoe country in northwestern Ontario; had I remained at Berkeley, I would have had to abandon this for a California thesis. Furthermore, Lawson had finished his last year of active teaching and was to retire the next year. Since I had come to California primarily to study with Lawson, my reason for being there had ended. Then there was the matter of German. I dislike German, and to stay at California would have imposed that language burden. A poor reason to leave, no doubt, but so it was. Louderback did not say much when I told him of my decision. He was, after all, taciturn. If he was disturbed he did not show it, but I had a feeling my decision was a surprise, since I had just been reappointed to my California fellowship. One does not leave the Garden of Eden by choice—an unpardonable sin indeed.

# 6

## Precambrian: A Lifelong Odyssey

My interest in the Precambrian began when I was an undergraduate student at Minnesota; my earliest firsthand look came when I was field assistant to Grout in the summer of 1924. Grout was then interested in what was called the "Coutchiching problem." Late in the nineteenth century A. C. Lawson, working for the Geological Survey of Canada in the Rainy Lake region on the Minnesota/Ontario boundary, described some mica schists of sedimentary origin that he called Coutchiching; these he placed below the Keewatin greenstones, until then thought to be the oldest in the world. Their *sedimentary* origin implied the existence of even older rocks, from which the sediments must have been derived by the ordinary processes of weathering and transportation. Lawson's interpretation of the Coutchiching schists as pre-Keewatin had been challenged by an international committee formed to reconcile Canadian and American views on the Precambrian. Thus the Coutchiching problem began. Lawson, in his restudy of the Rainy Lake area in 1911, reaffirmed his earlier conclusions. In 1924 the Minnesota Geological Survey was producing a new state map and needed a resolution of the problem. There were both greenstones and mica schists in the Burntside Lake area, so I went along as Grout's field assistant to check work done by John Gruner the summer before, as I recounted in chapter 2.

At the start of my 1927 canoe trip from Rainy Lake to the goldfields of Red Lake, I visited Grout's camp on Rainy Lake, the type locality of the Coutchiching, and in particular the exposures on Morton and Dude islands. I recall very well seeing the glaciated and wave-washed exposures on these islands and, with Grout, crawling over the surface on hands and knees looking for graded bedding—the upward coarse to fine gradation in grain size in the sandy beds. In this way we could tell the stratigraphic order in vertical beds and know whether the adjacent greenstones were above or below the Coutchiching metasedimentary schists.

On the 1927 trip to Red Lake I discovered a magnificent exposure of conglomerate of Archean age, filled with cobbles of pink granite, on an island in Abram Lake near Sioux Lookout, Ontario. This had been reported earlier by W. H. Collins but had never been mapped or studied in detail. The conglomerate became the subject of my doctor's thesis. Very little was known about the conglomerate and associated strata. I planned to map the conglomerate and try to determine its origin and the conditions prevalent during that time. Grout approved the subject, though I think he had some reservations. He wasn't sure what the "problem" was. Accidentally discovering a conglomerate in the course of a canoe voyage did not seem the way to choose a thesis topic. One must have a "problem," then look for a way to solve it—not just find an outcrop looking for a problem.

I well remember planning for the first field season—ordering an Old Town canoe through a friend in Oberlin, to be shipped to International Falls; riding north with Haymond Johnson, a former classmate at Minnesota; arriving at Rainy Lake, picking up the canoe at the freight depot, putting it on the top of the car, and driving across the International Bridge to Fort Frances, Ontario. I also remember buying provisions and driving to the lakeshore at Pithers Point, where I stripped the burlap from the canoe and burned the burlap and straw packing on the beach. I lovingly launched the canoe and loaded it, and, after storing the car, we set out for Sioux Lookout some 150 miles north. Our funds were too meager for us to travel by rail to Winnipeg, stay there overnight, then go by rail to Sioux Lookout. So we took the canoe route, a seven-day trip, retracing the route of my Red Lake trip the year before.

And I remember our arrival, setting up camp where no one had camped before, on the beautiful conglomerate outcrops on an island in Abram Lake. I could hardly sleep in anticipation of starting fieldwork. I was indeed now on my own—my first real independent effort with no one looking over my shoulder to correct or counsel. We were up at dawn, which is early indeed at this latitude in June, and after a hasty breakfast we crossed to the far shore and began work. As it turned out it was a troublesome spot—the rocks were of dubious character and revealed their secrets reluctantly. But we persisted despite initial discouragement. Mapping the shorelines was a pleasure. The mosquitoes and blackflies were few—a cooling breeze off the water saw to that. But at times the work was hard—leaving a sheltered cove to pull against the

(*top*) Lining the canoe down the Manitou River, northwestern Ontario. (Gene Hahnel and John Langwill, 1935). (*bottom*) R. M. Grogan and author on Sasakwei Creek, northwestern Ontario, about 1935.

Arthur C. Lundahl in burned area, northwestern Ontario, about 1938.

wind and waves, stowing the canoe ashore and traversing through the bush, often crossing muskeg swamps with their thicket of close-set scratchy black spruce, through windfalls and briar patches, up over rocky ledges, all the while pursued by a cloud of blackflies like smoke from a pipe. At times our efforts were poorly rewarded with uninformative lichen-covered outcroppings, but every now and then we would come upon a splendid exposure, often a critical one that resolved a troublesome problem that may have haunted us for days. Such an outcrop was like an opening in the woods that afforded an overview of the landscape; it gave us a glimpse of the ancient past. We forgot the discouragements and hardships of the day. Little by little the outlines of the geology began to take shape.

I returned to Minnesota at the end of the field season, spent a year completing my residence requirements, and took my oral exams in the spring of 1929. I spent yet another summer on my field studies, assisted by Carl Dutton, then an instructor at Minnesota, and later by Don Baker, one of my Oberlin students. I spent several summers mapping the conglomerates and their associated sediments, tracing them for about forty miles along their strike. I mapped not only the conglomerate beds—in places several thousand feet thick—but also the associated slates and graywackes and the several types of lava flows, now greenstone, and various intrusive plutons found in the Sioux Lookout region. Two seasons passed; we made the round trip from Rainy Lake to Sioux Lookout twice, collecting innumerable rock specimens to study under the microscope. At last I painstakingly drafted the final map, prepared the illustrations, and wrote the text, all of which grew out of the chance discovery of the conglomerate outcrops in 1927. My thesis was finished.

I came to know the Precambrian well, especially the oldest Precambrian, or Archean. I was much surprised that these most ancient rocks were so little altered. The slates and graywackes displayed the finest laminations; the greenstones showed pillow structures, undeformed vesicles, spherulites, and other volcanic features. The wave-washed lakeshore exposures revealed the most minute details. To be sure, in places the rocks were sheared, and near the large intrusives the metamorphic grade was such that the primary textures and structures were obscured. But elsewhere, though the strata were folded to verticality, the rocks were not schists in the usual sense, though they belonged to the "green schist facies." And, except for the enigmatic iron formation found here and there, the rocks were ordinary slates, graywackes, and conglomerates, or lava flows—mainly basaltic, in places andesitic—or, more rarely, rhyolitic. In other words, the world's oldest rocks were ordinary rocks much like the Paleozoic strata of the Harz Mountains or the

Mesozoic rocks in the Olympic Peninsula of Washington. To some this is perhaps disappointing—we might expect the rocks to be very different in ancient times. Yet in a sense it is even more astonishing to think that the earth has been much the same for about three billion years. After all, water ran downhill then as now, carrying sands and gravels derived from still older rocks; volcanic eruptions produced the same types of lava. That water existed at all is astonishing, for it shows that the surface of the earth was neither warmer nor colder than now. The conclusion seems inescapable also that the atmosphere and oceans were not greatly different from now. Some would not have it so; the atmosphere should be devoid of oxygen; these are the geochemists and cosmologists whose theories of planetary evolution demand an anaerobic atmosphere. But the rocks carry no such record. Some dispute this, and, true, the evidence is not all in, but the burden of proof rests on those who envision a different world in Archean times. In the end we will have to go to the geologic record for the answer. To this date evidence of an anoxic atmosphere is meager or ambiguous—certainly not conclusive.

When my thesis was completed I sent a copy to W. H. Collins, then director of the Geological Survey of Canada. I did so in part because Dr. Collins had mentioned the conglomerate in a reconnaissance report he wrote about 1910, before the construction of the Grand Trunk Pacific railroad, but also because I hoped the Canadian Survey might publish my study. Collins knew of my interest in the area but had not supported it in any way, nor had he hinted at possible publication. As it turned out, Collins was very interested in the results and offered to publish the work. I was delighted because Survey publication would ensure inclusion of the geologic map in color, whereas it would otherwise have been impossible to publish the map at all. American journals were chary of any map larger than a single page—not even foldouts were welcome, and color was unthinkable. In due time I received galley proofs of the text and color proof of the map. The results couldn't have been better—I was elated. But then the whole matter collapsed. It turned out that *after* I had finished my thesis, unknown to me and apparently also unknown to Collins, the Ontario Bureau of Mines had placed one of its geologists, M. E. Hurst, in the Sioux Lookout area. Hurst had completed his work, and his map and report were in press. For political reasons it would have been unwise for the Canadian Survey to issue a report on the same area at the same time. So Collins, much to his embarrassment, had to stop publication. But he did agree to provide me with three thousand copies of the map, which was already far along; only the Canadian Survey name would be deleted. It finally worked out—the manuscript was revised and shortened and appeared in 1934 as an article in the *Bulletin* of the

Geological Society of America, accompanied by the large colored map supplied by Collins. I had many inquiries about the map, since the Society at that time did not have the funds for colored maps. How did I manage it?

## THE OLDEST ROCKS: ARCHEAN

My initial Precambrian work was largely mapping. It was a program modeled after that of W. H. Collins, who when I first met him was mapping the area just north of Lake Huron. As he observed (1925, *Geol. Surv. Canada, Mem.* 143: 1), most of what we know about the geology of the Canadian Shield has been obtained from studies of mining camps. "[These] are apt to be far apart . . . the geological data obtained from them . . . are difficult to correlate and reduce to common terms. Particularly is this true of data relating to stratigraphy and its allied subjects, classification and nomenclature. . . . It becomes necessary, therefore, for the geologist to supplement from time to time the detailed study in mining districts with a certain amount of connective, or correlational work, in order that all can be woven together into larger contributions to earth history." Hence Collins selected "a series of small key areas" that would afford as complete a stratigraphical succession as possible, closely enough spaced so that the geological succession in one area could be identified with that in the next.

After completing my thesis, I mapped other selected Archean areas in northwestern Ontario—proceeding stepwise as Collins had done in the Huronian—to gradually extend our knowledge of Archean stratigraphy in the hope that a regional synthesis would emerge. This work was financed mainly by small grants—usually a couple of hundred dollars—from the Geological Society. Two hundred dollars would pay my expenses and those of an assistant for a three-month field season in the Canadian lake country, since we camped out in a tent. No salary, no fringe benefits, no overhead, no per diem—just out-of-pocket expenses. Graduate students at Chicago were glad to serve as field assistants for only their expenses; one of them, Gordon Rittenhouse, himself did a doctoral thesis on the Precambrian rocks of the Savant Lake area in northwestern Ontario.

The hoped-for regional synthesis did not fully materialize, but the new knowledge I gained from field studies led me to shift the focus of the investigations. Two things in particular grew out of this Precambrian work. One was an interest in graywackes and the graded bedding they displayed; the other was the contrast between the Archean assemblage and that of the Huronian of the North Shore of Lake Huron and similar strata of northern Michigan.

Graded bedding in Archean graywackes, East Bay, Minnitaki Lake, northwestern Ontario.

I was struck with the prevalence of graywacke. All the Archean "sandstones" were graywackes—dark rocks filled with angular quartz, feldspar, and rock particles. Why were the Archean sandstones so different in aspect from the clean, white (and cross-bedded) Precambrian quartzites of the Huronian of the North Shore of Lake Huron and the quartzites of the Michigan iron ranges? Moreover, the Archean assemblage was distinctive—greenstones and graywackes, with no limestones or quartz arenites (orthoquartzites of Krynine). I therefore read with great interest Tyrrell's paper "Greenstones and Greywackes," published in 1933 (*Réunion Int. l'Etude Précambrien, C. R.*, p. 24). Tyrrell's paper contained a clue. The greenstone-graywacke suite was characteristic of a certain tectonic environment, a particular type of mobile belt, the eugeosyncline of Stille or, in more modern parlance, the "island arc." I am not sure about the island arc analogy, but I am sure there are many younger examples of the Archean type of sequence. I was struck, for example, by the way the Franciscan formation of California, with its graywackes and greenstones, resembled the Archean.

I also read and reread Pentti Eskola's "Conditions during the Earliest

Geological Times" (1932, *Ann. Acad. Sci. Fennicae*, ser. A, 36:5–74). I was greatly impressed by this paper. By the early forties my thoughts about the Archean—what I had seen during a decade of fieldwork and what I had read—began to jell. I put them together in a paper "Archean Sedimentation," published in 1943 in the *Bulletin* of the Geological Society of America. In it I tabulated the peculiar features of the Archean assemblage and in parallel fashion tabulated the characteristics of the later Precambrian (Proterozoic). Later Marshall Kay published his classification of geosynclines. The Archean was a eugeosynclinal assemblage; the Proterozoic was a miogeosynclinal suite.

In the meantime, Paul D. Krynine began using the term "graywacke" for some of the Appalachian sandstones. I had not seen this term applied much outside of the Lake Superior region except, of course, in the Harz Mountains of Germany, where the term was first used. Krynine related it to a stage in his tectonic cycle—a concept that presumes that the mineralogical characters of the sands reflect the tectonic stability or instability of the depositional site. Active tectonism and consequent high relief and rapid deposition produce graywacke sands; stable areas yield the mature sands—the pure quartz sands that Krynine called orthoquartzites. Krynine's ideas provoked a good deal of discussion and debate. They were, perhaps, too simplistic, but they focused attention on sandstones and their classification and nomenclature and on the role of tectonics as well as other factors responsible for the several contrasting types. Krynine forced us to look at sandstones much more closely; to consider the role of tectonics in their production. We also focused on the nature of the bedding: graded bedding versus cross-bedding, a subject early commented on by E. B. Bailey (1930, *Geol. Mag.* 67:77), who ascribed the first to deepwater deposition and the other to a shallow-water environment—a remarkable insight, since nothing was then known about turbidity currents.

In 1960 I had a chance to visit the Harz Mountains, where I saw the rhythmically bedded graywackes and associated pillow lavas or greenstones—a late Paleozoic greenstone-graywacke assemblage. But most of all I wanted to see the rocks J. J. Sederholm and Eskola had studied. The opportunity came when the Twenty-first International Geological Congress held its 1960 meeting in Copenhagen. I elected to go on the excursion to southern Finland led by Ahti Simonen and Arvo Matisto. The excursion party, numbering about twenty-five, included a group from Cal Tech: Barklay Kamb, physicist turned geologist, Jerry Wasserburg, whom I had known at Chicago—not famous for his reticence—and Al Engel, whose uninhibited probing enlivened the expedition. Other participants included Erich Bederke of Göttingen, Adolf Watznauer, Ehrhard Voight of Hamburg, Janet Watson and her husband John

(*top*) Archean pillow lava, Yellowknife area, Northwest Territories, Canada. (*bottom left*) Pentti Eskola, 1960. (*bottom right*) Finnish excursion, International Geological Congress, 1960. Pentti Eskola (foreground) talking to Barclay Kamb (left) and A. E. J. Engel (right).

Sutton, both of Imperial College, and most especially Pentti Eskola. Eskola was going along for the first time as a participant rather than as excursion leader, yet he was very much a part of it all. He was then getting old and used a cane to get about, but get about he did. He wore a suit and tie despite the unseasonably warm weather. Eskola was a little smaller than I had expected, bespectacled and balding, but he hopped about using his cane to keep his balance. His English was impeccable, his inquiring mind as keen as ever. He had a philosophical overview that is rare indeed—all tempered by a delightful sense of humor.

In Finland everything but the place names was the same as in the Canadian Shield—the forests, the lakes, and especially the rocks. I had a preconceived image of Finns as taciturn, almost sullen. Not so. They were delightful—most friendly and hospitable. At one place the excursion stopped to look at an outcrop on a farm, a flat exposed surface between the house and the barn. After a time the farmer invited us all in for "tea." His wife had no doubt anticipated our visit, for we had not only tea but a table full of delicacies. We were met by newspaper reporters at our hotel and on one occasion interviewed on the radio.

We traversed southern Finland looking at rapakivi and orbicular granites, the Jotnian sandstone, and an assortment of Archean schists including conglomerates. Among the places we visited was the Tampere region, a place where Archean slates, interbedded siltstones, and graywackes are well exposed. The sequence consists of rhythmically graded beds, long ago described by Sederholm and Eskola, who thought they were annual layers, or varves. To see more of these rocks, Al Engel and I, guided by Simonen, spent a half day on our hands and knees looking at the outcrops on the shores of Lake Näsijärvi and studying the graded beds; the rest of the party spent the afternoon in the sauna. All in all, the excursion to southern Finland was a memorable event. It was a great privilege, having once met Sederholm, to see firsthand this classic locality he had described earlier and to be accompanied by Pentti Eskola. One cannot but express admiration for their monumental achievements.

My interest in the geology of Finland was not confined to the Precambrian. As a graduate student in Louderback's seminar at Berkeley, I had read two papers by Matti Sauramo on the history of the glacial retreat in Finland—a history pieced together from a study of the Pleistocene varved clay deposits. These papers, like most of the geological literature of Finland, were written in English (or German) and appeared in a Finnish publication with a French title!

I would have liked to return to Finland for a second visit, but I never did. I was, however, elected a corresponding member of the Geological Society of Finland—an honor I very much appreciated.

Sederholm and Eskola were interested in how far back in the earth's history one can carry the actualistic principle. How early can we presume that the processes operating were the same ones we see today? Were conditions then much the same as now? The question has been revived more recently by an upsurge of interest in the Precambrian—especially the earliest Precambrian. This revival of interest came from the rebirth of geochemistry and, more important, from the moon landings and the probes and fly-bys of the planets, especially Mars and Venus. The data gathered during these exploits led to speculations on planetary evolution—especially evolution of planetary atmospheres—and very naturally on the related evolution of the earth and its atmosphere as well as the problem of origin and evolution of life. It is presumed that other planets are in a state not unlike that which once prevailed on the earth or that they record a condition that may eventually prevail. More often than not models of planetary evolution and scenarios of atmospheric development have been proposed by chemists or geochemists, and they are often at variance with the geologic record. Still less has there been a concerted effort to examine that record to check the concepts proposed. Some of the evolutionary stages, of course, took place before the formation of the oldest accessible rock. The free oxygen in the atmosphere was the foremost problem. When did it appear and become abundant? Such geologic evidence as exists is meager and, as Dimroth and Kimberley (1976, *Can. J. Earth Sci.* 13:1161) have shown, is far from conclusive.

With the outbreak of World War II my fieldwork on the Archean ceased, and I began work on the late Precambrian in the Upper Peninsula of Michigan. By happenstance, however, I did further work on the Archean some years later, after I had left Chicago and moved to Baltimore. A Hopkins student, John B. Henderson, a Canadian employed by the Geological Survey of Canada, was investigating the Archean sedimentary sequence in the Yellowknife area of Great Slave Lake. In 1968, at the conclusion of his fieldwork, I went to see what he had done toward his doctoral thesis at Hopkins. Roger Walker, who had been a commonwealth fellow at Hopkins and was now at McMaster, went along.

The trip from Baltimore to Yellowknife was a long one. I flew to Montreal and stayed overnight, then went by Air Canada to Edmonton. Here I caught a plane to Yellowknife—the capital of the District of Mackenzie and a frontier gold-mining town on Yellowknife Bay of Great Slave Lake. The flight from Edmonton passed over a vast wasteland of watery swamp and sparse forest, then across Great Slave Lake, one of the great lakes of the world—some three hundred miles long—which straddles the boundary between the rocky Canadian Shield and the Great Plains, between the Precambrian and the Paleozoic. The East Arm with its myriad islands and rocky shores stands in great contrast to the expanded island-free western half of the lake.

The rock exposures around Yellowknife are superb. Being only a short distance south of the Barren Ground, the rocky surfaces have only a scattering of trees; hundreds of acres of naked rock, scoured and swept clean by the Pleistocene ice sheet, are laid bare. It is an ideal place for a geologist. We canoed around the Yellowknife Bay area to look at Henderson's Archean rocks, in which virtually all the features ascribed to turbidites could be seen.

My interest in the early Precambrian was rekindled. Our return flight from Edmonton took us across northwestern Ontario, where I had begun fieldwork forty years before. It was my first view from the air of Abram and Minnitaki lakes. I resolved then and there to revisit this area. Since my early work in the thirties we had learned a great deal—especially about graded bedding. From its use as a guide to stratigraphic order, we had turned to the question of origin. The rhythmic nature of graded bedding led to a search for a cyclic mechanism. Seasonal control seemed plausible, a concept given credibility by the annual layers, or varves, in the Pleistocene glacial sediments. So like Sederholm, Eskola, and Simonen I interpreted grading as seasonal. But the lack of ice-rafted cobbles—dropstones—and the absence of ice-laid morainal deposits—till—cast doubt on their glacial origin. Kuenen and Migliorini's classic paper in 1950 (*J. Geol.*, 1950, 58:91) unlocked the secret—the graded beds were turbidites, deposits of turbidity currents, bottom currents of dense, mud-laden water that transport sand down submarine slopes to great depths. I was now reasonably sure that the graded graywackes I had seen as a student were turbidites and were akin to the graded beds I had observed elsewhere—in the Carpathians, the Harz, and the Appalachians, in Finland, and most recently on the shores of Yellowknife Bay. But to resolve any doubt I wanted to revisit the area that we had just flown over and that I had studied long ago. But I had misgivings. Was my recollection of what I had seen right? Were the outcrops as I remembered them? How would I now judge the work I did as a graduate student?

Roger Walker agreed to go along to restudy these outcrops in the light of the new knowledge and our Great Slave Lake experience. We selected a critical area in the east part of Minnitaki, one showing the best exposures. We secured the newest air photographs and the following summer, 1969, embarked for the North. Instead of traveling by canoe, we could now drive our cars to the shores of Abram and Pelican lakes, near Sioux Lookout, where we found accommodations at a fisherman's resort. We also obtained a boat and motor for commuting to the work area on Minnitaki Lake. Were these Archean sediments truly turbidites? Our restudy of the sedimentary beds confirmed in every way their turbidite origin. Even the conglomerates in the Minnitaki Lake exposures proved to be graded and interbedded with the graywackes and siltstones, all deposited in deep water—at least in water below wave base. The turbidites were like those of many younger sequences and displayed the same graded graywackes rhythmically interbedded with siltstones and slates—a classic flysch assemblage.

In the course of our study we invited Dick Ojakangas of the University of Minnesota at Duluth to spend a few days with us. Dick had made a restudy of the Archean strata in northern Minnesota and concluded that essentially all the sediments there were water-laid volcanic tuffs and ash. The graywackes were the coarser volcanic debris—an interpretation not unlike that of Ayers for the sedimentary strata in the area east of Lake Superior. Dick immediately spotted volcanic quartz in the graywackes, recognizable by its bipyramidal form. I was skeptical, however, primarily because some of the sediments in the sequence contained too much quartz—40 percent or more—to be derived from volcanic sources. A plutonic source was required, and such a source was further indicated by the granitelike cobbles so abundant in some of the associated conglomerates, which implied a granitic crust of vast extent. This conclusion was incompatible with a volcanic source, which would be principally basaltic lava, at best andesitic, with only a limited volume of acid volcanics. True, the conglomerates also included cobbles of quartz porphyry, but these contained only 1 or 2 percent sand-sized quartz—not enough to form a quartz-rich sand.

So we had a dilemma—a granitic terrane was inferred to yield both quartz sand and granite pebbles and cobbles, yet the granites (which on a close inspection were found to be tonalities) in the region seemed to be intrusive into the sedimentary and associated volcanic strata and therefore younger. Where indeed was the basement on which the Archean strata rested and from which the sediments had been derived?

THE LATER PRECAMBRIAN: PROTEROZOIC

After I went to Chicago in 1929, I made many trips to the Upper Peninsula of Michigan, where I saw firsthand the strata of later Precambrian age. This proved an education, for I now saw the thick mature quartzites—rippled and cross-bedded—the dolomites with their oolites and algal structures, the thick sedimentary iron-bearing formations, and also an assortment of slates with interbedded graywackes.

Most of the earlier work on the later Precambrian (Proterozoic) of the

Lake Superior region had been exploratory, of a reconnaissance nature, or related to mining. Most was directed toward establishing the stratigraphy and attempting to correlate one mining district with another, from Minnesota to Michigan, and from the Michigan ranges to the original Huronian on the North Shore of Lake Huron. Except perhaps for the iron formations, nobody had really looked at the rocks as sedimentary deposits. Hence first at Chicago and later at Hopkins I set students to work on the sedimentological aspects of the later Precambrian. In all our work we made a major effort to map the directional structures in the sands, especially the cross-bedding, and to make a paleocurrent analysis, for I was then much interested in that subject. George Brett at Chicago was one of the first; he mapped the cross-bedding in the Baraboo quartzite of Wisconsin. A few scattered measurements of my own showed surprising uniformity of direction of current flow in the quartzites of the Huronian on the North Shore—all indicating a north-to-south current pattern.

Moreover, the thick quartzites—very nearly pure quartz—were a problem in themselves. How, in a time before land plants, could weathering have been so thorough and so complete as to leave a residue of pure quartz? One might presume that in the absence of a plant cover to stabilize the soil immature, partially weathered debris would be swept off the land to form highly arkosic sands. And under what conditions would one get such thick accumulations—thousands of feet of pure quartz sand? There seem to be few, if any, sandstones of comparable thickness and purity deposited in later times.

To look into these problems, in 1946 I set Jim Trow to work on the Sturgeon quartzite in Michigan. Much later, after I went to Hopkins, John McDowell went to work on the Mississagi quartzite and Don Hadley tackled the Lorrain quartzite—two prominent quartzites in the sequence on the North Shore of Lake Huron. My earlier observations, based on only a few random measurements, proved correct. The cross-bedding in the Mississagi and Lorrain in particular showed a generally southerly flow of the depositing currents. It is indeed amazing that the current directions in the Lorrain, for example, remained fixed throughout the deposition of more than five thousand feet of sand!

The old Menominee monograph, published by the United States Geological Survey, mentioned some conglomerates at the contact between the older basement gneisses and the Sturgeon. In 1941 I put Fred Hildebrand to work on them for a master's thesis. The conglomerate beds were thin and discontinuous and didn't seem to yield much. Hildebrand was discouraged, so I came up and joined him. We drove to the Fern Creek exposures near Norway, Michigan, on the only road then available—a single lane, just a pair of ruts in the sand. As we approached we saw rocks well exposed on high bluffs. As I came up to the outcrop, I was astonished to see tillites. No doubt about it, not only the typical diamictites but also interbedded siltstones and slates with beautiful dropstones! None of the other exposures of the Fern Creek beds, as we called them, showed these features. We had discovered an unrecorded glaciation.

My interest in tillites began with the discovery of the Fern Creek glacial beds, but I soon discovered that a good many formations reported as tillites proved to be of nonglacial origin. A few years later, in 1952, I was in Boston for a meeting of the Geological Society of America, where I presented a paper on the Fern Creek tillite. At this meeting I went on a field trip to the classic tillites at Squantum Head. R. R. Shrock, then of MIT, was the guide. Among others on this trip were John Crowell, of UCLA, and Hal James of the Geological Survey. Imagine our astonishment and dismay at seeing the Squantum for the first time—a classical deposit long cited as evidence of Permian glaciation in America. Crowell was the most outspoken; he had seen many deposits of this kind in California and had never considered any of them tillites. Indeed they were pebbly mudstones, probably products of submarine slump or other forms of subaqueous mass transport. Near Squantum Head were exposures of graded graywackes interbedded with slates, interpreted as deposits in glacial lakes. Shades of the Archean! So Crowell, James, and I agreed that the case for glacial origin of the Squantum was suspect if not downright wrong.

Crowell became interested in other reported cases of tillite and found many to be nonglacial. Some years later, when I was at Johns Hopkins, each of us, unknown to the other, put students to work on the Huronian Gowganda formation—long considered glacial. It turned out to be truly glacial, for not only were the tillites superb examples of the genre, but there were many meters of beautifully varved argillites peppered with dropstones.

Unlike the Archean, the later Precambrian has not only the pure quartzites but also limestones. These are of special interest because limestones, for the most part, are products of organic activity: they are accumulations of coral, shells, or other lime-secreting forms, most especially algae. Under what conditions and in what manner did the Precambrian limestones form?

Several of my students worked on this problem. Norman Greenman studied the Randville dolomite in Michigan. The Randville, as I later found out, was the Precambrian counterpart of the Conococheague, a late Cambrian formation in the central Appalachians. It had many of the same features—interbedded sand layers, mud-cracked beds, oolites, and stromatolites—probably formed in a tidal and subtidal environment.

The Denault in the Labrador Trough was described by Al Donaldson. It has an amazing display of stromatolites. But the most spectacular of all is the Taltheilei formation in the East Arm of Great Slave Lake, which was described by Paul Hoffman. Hoffman's masterly analysis of this formation and the associated strata has not been surpassed.

But the most baffling formations are unquestionably the iron formations. Their origin has defied all comers. Our contribution to the problem was to look more closely at the associated strata and so to circumscribe speculations on the environment of iron deposition. Walther's law is presumed to be valid even in the Precambrian, so that formations that overlie one another conformably are presumed to have been deposited side by side. It soon became apparent that there were two major types of iron formation—those associated with sandy deposits and those associated with muddy sediments. The first, the arenitic iron formations, accumulated in shallow aerated waters, associated with sands and displaying evidence of current action. The lutitic iron formations are associated with slates and carbonaceous muds bearing evidence of deposition in an anaerobic, relatively deeper, currentless environment.

IRON AND THE GEOLOGICAL SURVEY

I did not become involved firsthand in study of the iron formations and associated strata until World War II. As the war progressed and the teaching program at the university deteriorated, with lack of geology students on the one hand and an endless repetition of the Army Specialized Training Program classes on the other, I became convinced I should get out and into something more suitable—more geological. Carl Dutton, a fellow student during my last year at Minnesota, had been working summers for the Michigan Geological Survey, as had Carl Lamey of Ohio State University. Carl Lamey was a former student of U. S. Grant at Northwestern University. Obviously the Michigan Survey employed part-time staff, and I thought I might find a similar job. I had worked as a student for the Minnesota Geological Survey, and had for nearly ten years done independent work on the early Precambrian in northwestern Ontario. So I wrote to R. A. Smith, the state geologist, at Lansing, Michigan, and applied for a job. Smith's reply was evasive, but it was clearly a brushoff.

However, in 1943 the United States Geological Survey reentered the Lake Superior region, this time in a cooperative venture with the Michigan Geological Survey. The federal Survey had been very active in the 1890s during the development of the iron deposits of this region. Under the supervision of C. R. Van Hise, the Survey published a series of great monographs, one on each range, and in 1911 it issued one summarizing all the Survey work in the Lake Superior district (monograph 52). But the war stimulated the search for iron ore, so the Survey felt a return to the region was justified. The job fell to Charles Park, Jr., a Minnesota Ph.D., then geologist with the United States Geological Survey. He picked Iron County—the Iron River/Crystal Falls area—for a start. This range was the most poorly known, primarily because of the widespread glacial cover. It was here, perhaps, that geology could make its biggest contribution. He won the complete cooperation of the mining companies, who granted access to the exploration records and to their mines. Carl Dutton and Carl Lamey were transferred to full-time work on this project: Dutton was to work in Iron County, and Lamey was assigned to the Felch district in Dickinson County.

I found out about the program from Jerry Fisher, who had received an inquiry from E. T. McKnight, then chief of the metals section of the Survey. McKnight was looking for additional manpower for the project. Some correspondence followed between McKnight, Charles Park, and G. F. Loughlin, chief geologist, and in due time I received form 57—an application for civil service appointment. This happened in late June and early July. After what seemed like an inordinate delay, my appointment as geologist at $3,500 a year went through, and I finally received my travel authorization and vouchers the day before Labor Day.

Since it was now the end of the summer and school was about to begin, I left my family behind and took the night train, the Milwaukee Road, arriving in Iron River along with the first blast of fall weather—a cold snap that turned on the furnaces. The rail trip to Iron River involved a Pullman on the night train that ran from Chicago to Ishpeming, Michigan. At an early hour the Pullman was separated from the rest of the train at Channing and shunted onto the branch line to Iron River, with an intermediate stop at Crystal Falls.

So I began my work for the United States Geological Survey—work that was to continue for nearly ten years. Initially I took a leave of absence from the university and worked full time, but later I returned to Chicago and continued part time with the Survey.

I spent the first day on my new job with Park and Dutton, and Dutton gave me a tour of the Iron River area where, at this time, most of the mining was done. The ore was mined by underground methods, much of it from the Mineral Hills area north of Iron River proper. Park was spending most of his time mapping the underground workings; the area had few outcrops. I was to work in the Crystal Falls area, where there were more abundant rock exposures. So the next day Dutton drove me over to Crystal Falls along U.S. 41—about sixteen miles. In the course of this drive we saw one rather poorly exposed rock outcrop—everything else was morainal material, covered with second-growth timber, mainly

United States Geological Survey field party, Dickinson County, Michigan. Clockwise, starting at left: H. L. James, Carl Dutton, the author, Lorin D. Clark (concealed), and Carl Lamey. About 1945.

poplar, birch, some spruce and balsam, and muskeg swamp. I was dismayed and wondered how one could make a geologic map with so few exposures.

I checked in at the Crystal Inn, the only acceptable hotel in Crystal Falls, the county seat of Iron County. Crystal Falls is situated on a good-sized hill, with the courthouse at the top. The main street, lined with stores, runs due east, at a fairly steep grade, down to the crossing of the Paint River a mile or so from the courthouse. There was no Survey vehicle available at this time, so I was to begin on foot, mapping the outcrops in and about town, especially along the Paint River. Outcrops were numerous enough along the river so that it seemed worthwhile to map them by plane table. Jim Balsley, added to the project as a geophysicist, was to come over and run the plane table as soon as he returned from Washington.

In the meantime I started to work. I called at the city engineer's office and got blueprints of the plans of the city, showing streets and alleys. So I began my work by walking the sidewalks of town. The exposed rock was largely slate with some interbedded graywackes. Outcrops were generally small, not uncommonly occurring in the front lawns or backyards of private houses. I felt a little uncomfortable walking about in boots and field clothes checking small outcroppings—in some places greeted by the family dog, in others by furtive glances from behind curtained windows. But my compass and notebook must have allayed the fears of the housewives, for no one called the police. In the northeast part of town, in the lower ground near the dam and power plant, were some outcrops of the iron-bearing formation along abandoned railway grades, in test pits—now partly filled with discarded tires and other trash—and in some old mine pits and at the dam itself.

After a month of such activity—it was now early October, Jim Balsley appeared with plane table, rod, tape, and other paraphernalia. Jim had been back and forth between Iron River and Washington, D.C. In Washington he got wind of the aerial magnetometer—then a top-secret device for locating submarines. By some means Jim had secured the use of it and the aircraft and funds to try it out over land and apply it to the Iron County area. But he took time out to assist me in mapping the Paint River section between the dam and the lower bridge, a distance of about a mile. There being no adequate large-scale topographic map, we had to make one, on a scale of one inch to two hundred feet. I had no plane-table experience other than with an open sight alidade, so Jim took over as instrument man and I became the rod man. The Paint River ran in a gorge with rocky bluffs along the present river and former channel ways—relics, no doubt, of an earlier augmented flow during glacial retreat. The plane table, of course, was placed at strategic sites, high on the bluffs, with a good view. I skipped about setting the rod on various stations to give adequate control for contouring. But it was now late October and the weather was brisk—in fact downright cold—and on some dark days there were a few flakes of snow. I still remember seeing Jim standing by the instrument, flailing his arms, stamping his feet, and blowing on his hands to keep warm. This was especially true on the adjoining windswept golf course, on which there were a few small, poorly concealed outcrops.

When the topography was finished, Jim returned to his flying machine, and I took a print made from the plane-table sheet and plotted the geology. The venture proved highly successful. The sequence of strata exposed was critical. It extended from the iron-bearing formation at the dam upward into what was generally referred to as the "hanging wall"—the sequence of beds that overlay the iron formation. Not only did we establish the sequence, we got a feel for the tightly folded structures in which these beds were involved. The sequences included a chert breccia, which lay directly on the iron formation and was filled with debris from that formation, and also a highly magnetic slatelike member that in turn was overlain by a thicker series of ordinary non-magnetic slates. The chert breccia turned out to be of sedimentary origin and not the riebungsbreccia as some had thought—it was interbedded with and graded into graywackes with scattered bits and pieces of chert. The magnetic "slate" turned out to be a marker bed, traceable underneath glacial and other cover because of its magnetic character. We did not at first realize its importance, but later work established its uniqueness and continuity. It was this that enabled us to map large areas with few or no outcrops and to accomplish what otherwise seemed, on the first day, an impossible task.

By the time the Paint River outcrops had been mapped winter had set in in earnest, so in November, after some three months in the region, I returned to Chicago.

My work for the United States Geological Survey in the Upper Peninsula of Michigan was a most valuable experience for two reasons. It gave me a chance to study younger Precambrian strata, in contrast to my earlier work on the Archean. I had, to be sure, seen quite a bit of the younger Precambrian in the course of many departmental field excursions, but working in the field day after day and mapping is the only way to really understand the problems of these strata. Mapping is indeed the essence of geology, and those who think otherwise are grossly in error. An occasional field excursion will not do. Understanding comes only from prolonged daily field contact.

The other important aspect of my Survey work was my firsthand contact with geophysics, in this case with the earth's magnetic field and the magnetic anomalies related to the geology. I had no formal training in geophysics. Cursory examination of texts in the subject proved discouraging. The subject matter was presented in mathematical language I did not understand. The subject was for me too technical, too esoteric.

But as the Michigan work progressed the time came when I would have to look into the subject. On some of the Lake Superior ranges the iron formations can be traced beneath cover—swamp, lake, or glacial drift—because they are magnetic. And since the bedrock of the Iron River/Crystal Falls area was poorly exposed—being concealed by drift, in places continuous and commonly very thick—the problem of mapping seemed insoluble unless geophysical methods could be used. But the iron formation in this area consisted of chert and iron carbonate (siderite), both of which are nonmagnetic. In many places oxidation produced goethite and hematite, both iron oxides, but also nonmagnetic, so there seemed no possible way to trace the iron formation by magnetic methods. Moreover, earlier dip-needle surveys had had disappointing results. A few stray "magnetic lines" had been picked up, generally rather weak, and it was not clear what they were related to—perhaps a few discontinuous magnetic beds in the associated slates. To be sure, at Stambaugh, near the high school, there was an outcrop of highly magnetic rock of slatelike nature. A similar rock cropped out on a country road a mile or so west of the Tobin Mine near Crystal Falls, but no one knew whether these were the same, where they were in the stratigraphy, or whether they had any continuity. So to date the dip needle had not been very helpful.

But we had a dip needle, and with some help from Carl Dutton, who had used this instrument on the Menominee Range near Iron Mountain, I started to work. The dip needle is simply a magnetized needle that swings freely in a vertical plane, in contrast to a compass, whose needle swings in a horizontal plane. It can be used to measure the inclination of the magnetic lines of force—not their azimuth, as does the compass. But more often it is used to measure the relative strength of the magnetic field; it is the deviation from normal that is of interest—the so-called magnetic anomaly. By taking many readings at regular intervals along parallel traverses, one can map any such anomalies. The whole procedure is very simple and requires no mathematical ability other than averaging several readings of the oscillating needle (more convenient and quicker than waiting for the needle to come to rest). The traverses were run by pace and compass; readings were made every hundred feet on lines two hundred feet apart. In regions of very large and strong anomalies, the traverse lines would have to be run using a sun compass, since the ordinary magnetic compass would be unreliable. Fortunately this was not the case in the Crystal Falls area. The anomalies were usually so narrow that we could take a compass sight in an area of no magnetic disturbance that was adequate to carry us across the magnetic anomaly.

It soon became evident that the dip needle lacked the sensitivity required, so we switched to a Superdip—a dip needle modified by W. O. Hotchkiss. This was used in much the same manner as a dip needle, but it was tripod-mounted and properly oriented with a magnetic compass.

It soon became evident to me that the crux of the whole matter of a geophysical survey was in the interpretation of the results. One could readily teach a bright high-school lad the techniques of making the survey, but what does it mean? No sophisticated mathematical analysis can answer that question. The answer is basic geology. To what is the

(*top*) Tobin iron mine, near Crystal Falls, Michigan, about 1950. Stockpile of ore on right. (*bottom*) Lorin D. Clark and the Hotchkiss Superdip, about 1946.

anomaly due? Magnetite is a component of many rock types, and each of these has its own geometry; bed, dike, stock, and so forth. How does one relate the anomaly to geology? What criteria are used? As fieldwork and magnetic surveying progressed it turned out that, with very few exceptions, the anomaly was related to a relatively thin, fifty- to one-hundred-foot bed of slatelike aspect that lay a short distance *above* the iron formation. This proved to be a marker bed, and it made it possible to trace the structure under considerable cover, for the anomaly was centered over the concealed outcrop of this bed. Since the bed was steeply tilted and folded, the anomaly depicted faithfully each zig and zag of the concealed outcrop. In other words, the anomaly pattern could be interpreted just like a geologic map. The correlation of the geology and the anomaly pattern was excellent, so we had confidence that mapping could be extended into areas of few or no outcrops. There were complications, to be sure, since the anomaly weakened or disappeared in areas where oxidation had destroyed the magnetite.

The experience was illuminating. I learned that the problem came down to the relation between magnetic contours and geology—a relation established by empirical observations, not by esoteric calculations.

I worked for the Survey for nearly ten years—years that I regard as the most productive and rewarding period of my life. Nothing I had done was quite as enjoyable and satisfying, though just why this is so is a little difficult to figure out. Perhaps it was the nature of the work, the challenge it presented, and perhaps it was the tangible, visible results. It was field geology from beginning to end, running many long traverses, searching for obscure and all-too scarce outcrops and old test pits, taking thousands of Superdip readings, searching the company records for old drill holes, and underground mapping. The work was strenuous at times—hot and sweaty, with hordes of mosquitoes, swamps, and blackberry thickets. Perhaps it was the success of the plane-table survey along the Paint River that unlocked the "hanging wall" sequence. In any case, it was great fun to see the map grow little by little, to see things fall into place and a coherent picture emerge. Perhaps field geology has some of the elements of puzzle solving and the satisfaction it gives. Perhaps also there is the knowledge that the accomplishments have long-lasting value. A *good*, geologic map endures while theories come and go.

The Survey experience was enlightening in many ways. It introduced me to aspects of geology with which I had little or no previous experience—mine mapping, magnetic surveying, core logging, and the like. But perhaps more important, it gave me an insight into the workings of government bureaucracy. I was a bureaucrat—a member of a much-maligned class often demeaned by editorial writers, cartoonists, and at least one presidential candidate who forgot that the first man to walk on

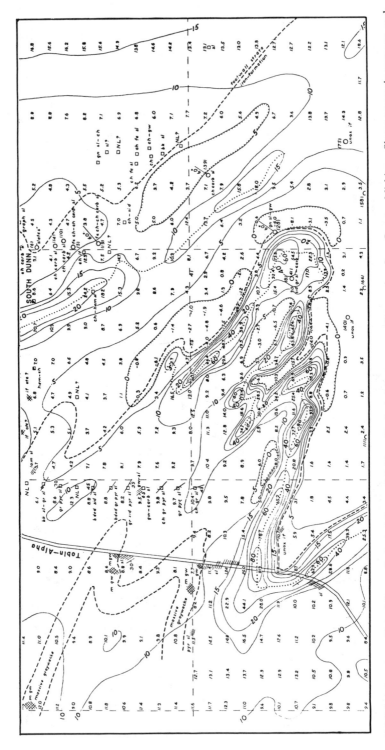

Published data sheet, United States Geological Survey/Michigan Geological Survey, near Dunn mine, Iron County, Michigan. Shows magnetic contours, rock outcrops, test pits, drill holes, and formation boundaries, 1972.

the moon was a government employee. The United States Geological Survey is a first-class scientific agency. Its senior scientists (bureaucrats if you will) are a distinguished group. A surprising number have been elected to the National Academy of Sciences—among them Tom Nolan, Bill Rubey, Jim Gilluly, Hal James, Bill Bradley, Tom Lovering, Luna Leopold, Preston Cloud, Bill Menard, and E-an Zen.

# 7

## Chicago: The Athens of the Midwest (1929-52)

My work on the Precambrian was indeed a lifelong odyssey—at Minnesota, Chicago, and Hopkins. But Chicago encompassed much more, for it was there I first became deeply involved in sedimentology. How did it begin? Chicago was looking for a "sedimentationist," and in response to a letter of inquiry addressed to Dr. Emmons, my name had been suggested.

Interest in sedimentation was then greatest in the Midwest. Courses in sedimentation, as the study of sedimentary deposits was called, had sprung up in the midwestern schools—Wisconsin, Iowa, Minnesota, and of course Chicago. The more conservative eastern schools were slower to follow. At Chicago such a course had been taught by J Harlen Bretz, but when Paul MacClintock left to join the Princeton faculty Chicago looked about for someone to fill the vacancy and take over the work on sedimentation.

I was trained as a petrologist and, though interested in all kinds of rocks, was not a "sedimentationist," or sedimentologist as we would say today. In fact this specialty did not exist. But Chicago was interested. Professor Edson S. Bastin, then chairman of the Department of Geology at Chicago, was going to Madison on other business and suggested I come there for an interview.

So in the spring of 1929 I went to Madison. My only qualification for the job was that I had taken a one-quarter course in "sedimentation" at Minnesota, taught by Ira Allison, and a two-semester seminar in the subject conducted by G. D. Louderback at the University of California at Berkeley. To be sure my doctoral thesis dealt with, among other things, ancient Archean sediments. Edson Bastin put me at ease. Professor Bastin, a large man, somewhat overweight and a cigar smoker, was phlegmatic and slow-spoken. There were long, somewhat awkward pauses in our conversation while he groped for words or busied himself with his cigar. I didn't feel I had acquitted myself particularly well, but nonetheless I received a letter offering me a job as instructor at a salary of $2,800 a year. I accepted and wrote Oberlin a letter of resignation. So I arrived at Chicago in the fall of 1929, along with the university's new thirty-year-old president, Robert M. Hutchins, the stock market crash, and the beginning of the Great Depression.

I had never liked the city of Chicago. It was too large, too dirty, and very dingy. I had of course seen the worst of it from the windows of the trains as I passed through on my way to and from Oberlin. And there was no escaping the confusion of a change of trains and depots in Chicago. Yet here I was committed to a job in the place. The university is on Chicago's South Side in Hyde Park, which in 1929 was a rather pleasant neighborhood between Jackson and Washington parks. Still, there were innumerable three-story walk-up apartments; I had had no experience with apartment living. Bastin, however, found me a room with a Mrs. Weller, widow of the late Stuart Weller, professor of paleontology, about a fifteen-minute walk from the university.

## THE CHAMBERLIN LEGACY

When the university was founded in 1891 by a gift from John D. Rockefeller, William Rainey Harper, its first president, had a vision of what a university ought to be—a community of distinguished scholars. He set out to create such an institution, and a great university was born. For his geology department he brought T. C. Chamberlin from Wisconsin, where Chamberlin was then president, and Chamberlin in turn brought together a distinguished group: R. A. F. Penrose, Jr., in economic geology, J. P. Iddings in petrology, R. D. Salisbury in physiography, and C. R. Van Hise, a leading authority on the Precambrian. Of the original faculty I met only T. C. Chamberlin. I heard him speak at the annual meeting of the Geological Society of America. But he was then rather old and had to be helped to the podium by his son Rollin, who was then on the faculty of the department. I knew little or nothing about Penrose, who later became the benefactor of the Geological Society of America which, together with the Philosophical Society, received several million dollars from his estate. I never met Iddings, though as a student I used his *Rock Minerals*. Salisbury I knew only as coauthor (with T. C. Chamberlin) of *College Geology*—my first book on the subject. Van Hise was well known to me by his monumental studies of the Lake

The original Chamberlin department. Left to right: Rollin D. Salisbury, C. R. Van Hise, Thomas C. Chamberlin, J. P. Iddings, and R. A. F. Penrose, Jr. Photo courtesy of the University of Chicago Department of Geology.

Superior Precambrian. By 1929 T. C. Chamberlin was dead, as was R. D. Salisbury.

When I arrived the original department had been wholly replaced, though in many cases by Chicago men. Thus the Chamberlin and Salisbury tradition and dogmas were preserved. The department was indeed very much a Chamberlin institution—his thought and philosophy still dominated, and it continued to bask in his fame long after that had faded into history. Chamberlin's son, Rollin T. Chamberlin, was then professor in the department and still taught the Chamberlin doctrines, which encompassed the permanence of continents and ocean basins (no such heresy as continental drift) and the planetesimal hypothesis of planetary evolution, all embodied in the three-volume Chamberlin and Salisbury *Geology* and its abridged younger cousin *College Geology.* Not surprisingly, the latter was *the* textbook in the beginning course at Chicago.

In 1929 the department was housed in two buildings: Walker Museum and Rosenwald Hall. Walker Museum, the older of the two, was a rather plain two-story structure and, as its name implies, a museum. The entire first floor was given over to exhibits of fossil materials, including a good many well-mounted and displayed vertebrate skeletons, particularly those of Permian amphibians—the special interest of Alfred S. Romer, vertebrate paleontologist. Contrary to the general rule for college museums, the museum was exceptionally well maintained, primarily owing to the two full-time curators—A. W. Slocum for invertebrates and Paul Miller for vertebrates. Paul Miller, in particular, was a skilled curator who accompanied Al Romer on his trips to Oklahoma and to South Africa to collect Permian amphibians. With their goatees, both he and Slocum looked more like professors than the professors themselves. The second floor of Walker contained work areas, a couple of offices, and a classroom or two. In keeping with buildings of that vintage, it had high ceilings. Rosenwald Hall was the newer building, constructed in 1915 specifically for geology. Like the other university buildings it was faced with Indiana limestone and had acquired a dark gray tone from the soot-laden atmosphere, for coal was then the universal fuel in Chicago. The building was pseudogothic—reinforced concrete with an overlay of stone, decorated with gargoyles and imitation gothic arches. Its gargoyles were carved to represent Permian reptiles; elsewhere on the building ammonites and other fossil forms appeared in bas-relief, as did various geologists of historical importance, including Lyell, Dana, Hall, and Logan. The building's tower was topped by an assemblage of meteorological instruments. The tower office was then occupied by the official weather observer for the Chicago area. Rosenwald Hall was shared with the Geography Department, as was the departmental library within; a very good library it was, with a full-time librarian, Margaret MacGregor.

The department was otherwise meagerly equipped. The petrographic laboratory had a good collection of Leitz microscopes; the mineralogy laboratory was very conventional; there were no X-ray facilities at all. All X-ray study of crystals was conducted by Zachariason in the Physics Department; the geologists had no access to his facilities, and as far as I knew none took his courses. There was a poorly equipped darkroom and a run-down shop for making thin sections, with no technician of any kind other than the two curators of paleontological materials. But five or six years after I came the department acquired Bill Schmidt, an out-of-work musician, who with meager funds gradually built up a shop and became a good thin-section maker and photographer.

Though in 1929 T. C. Chamberlin had been dead for two years, the department was a legacy from the Chamberlin era. Except perhaps for the timid move to add a course in sedimentation, the course offerings were largely those of the Chamberlin period. To my dismay—a dismay heightened by my California experience—the department did very little fieldwork; none was incorporated in the coursework at Chicago except the "local field course"—a course assigned to me. The department did,

Rosenwald Hall, housing Geology and Geography, University of Chicago, as it looked in the mid-thirties. Photo courtesy of the University of Chicago Archives.

however, offer two summer field courses—one in the Baraboo region of Wisconsin and the other in the Sainte Geneviève area of southeastern Missouri. The Baraboo course was taught by Bretz, and an excellent course it was—probably the best course taught in the department. It was run out of a tent camp in the state park at the south end of Devil's Lake. All geology majors took the course; it was a tradition, and Bretz was a superb teacher despite the masochistic tendencies shown in his insistence on a before-breakfast plunge into the chilly water of Devil's Lake in late September. The Sainte Geneviève course operated out of a permanent base camp, buildings and land belonging to the department. Fieldwork in the area had been initiated by Stuart Weller, late professor of paleontology. The funds for the purchase of the camp were donated by Bill Wrather, Chicago alumnus, oil man, and later director of the United States Geological Survey. It was called, appropriately, Camp Wrather. In 1929 and for a decade after, the Missouri course was taught by Carey Croneis. The field courses fell by the wayside with the onset of World War II, and with the drastic changes in the department in the postwar period they were never revived. A great pity! The department was the model for most of the geology departments in the midwestern universities, for the chairmen and faculties of these institutions were largely products of the Chicago department. Chicago itself was no exception.

Three of its four senior professors were Chicago products of the Chamberlin era: Bastin, Bretz, and Rollin Chamberlin; Jerry Fisher, a junior member, was also a Chicago man. Johannsen was a Hopkins product; Carey Croneis came from Harvard. All were geologists; in addition there were Al Romer and Adolph C. Noè. Romer was a vertebrate zoologist who taught vertebrate paleontology. Noè had an unorthodox career. For many years he had taught German and only belatedly pursued paleobotany. He had a split appointment, half in Botany and half in Geology. Romer and Noè went their separate ways and left geology to the rest of us.

The faculty was paid the prevailing salaries of the time—probably at the low end of the university's salary scale. Full professors got $4,500 to $5,500 a year. I advanced to associate professor at $3,800 during the later 1930s. Salaries increased somewhat in the postwar period; I received $8,500 as full professor at the time I resigned in 1952. Under Bastin's administration the departmental budget was woefully small. Aside from salaries, there was only $1,600 for everything else—most of which went for office supplies, postage, and the like. There was a good deal of unrest among the junior faculty over this niggardly budget. Funds for a graduate student's research in chemistry might be greater than the whole department's nonsalary budget. But complaints were to no avail.

Department of Geology, University of Chicago, about 1941. Lower row, left to right: W. C. Krumbein, E. C. Olson, Edson S. Bastin, Norman L. Bowen, Carey Croneis; top row, left to right: author, Paul Miller, Rollin T. Chamberlin, J Harlen Bretz, and D. Jerome Fisher. Photo courtesy of the University of Chicago Department of Geology.

Although Bastin was personally generous, he was miserly when it came to spending university money.

At my interview in Madison I was told that the lecture method of teaching was frowned on at Chicago—that this was "spoon feeding" and the Chicago courses were seminars. This, it turned out, was not true. Except for Bretz, all the faculty stood in front of their classes and lectured steadily until the closing bell. But Bretz was a very big exception. He was the personification of Socrates. The student read the text (Chamberlin and Salisbury, of course), but Bretz cross-examined him on what he had read and nailed him to the wall if he couldn't respond. It took a thick hide to hold up under this mode of teaching, but those who survived learned a great deal—to distinguish fact from fiction, to look for and evaluate evidence, to scorn unsupported opinions. Bretz's manner of teaching was said to have been modeled after that of Salisbury, under whom he had studied. A class taught by Bretz was not unlike the "King's seminar" conducted by A. C. Lawson at Berkeley. I can therefore speak firsthand of the effectiveness of the method and its disciplinary value.

Of all the department faculty when I arrived in 1929, Bretz was perhaps the most active and productive geologist. He was still engaged in his Scabland studies, was beginning his work on the Pleistocene of the Chicago area for the Illinois State Geological Survey, and soon embarked on his study of caves and related phenomena. Bretz was constantly going off to look at caves, and he inevitably took along from one to a dozen students. The trips were memorable affairs. Sleeping gear piled high, overnights in improvised quarters—often the gymnasium of a school or college. He taught the Baraboo field course with enthusiasm, and taking that course was an unforgettable experience, one of the best ways to learn what science was all about.

Bretz himself was something of a maverick. He came from a small town in Michigan and had gone to Albion College, then a somewhat fundamentalist church-oriented institution. Bretz soon found himself in hot water because of his heretical thoughts on theological matters. Nonetheless he graduated, taught high school near Puget Sound, and went to Chicago for his doctor's degree, submitting a thesis on the glacial history of the Puget Sound area. Bretz's sojourn in Washington led to his interest in the Scablands of that state. Bretz interpreted this maze of anastomosing deep, rock-cut channels, with their dry falls and plunge pools, as the product of a short-lived catastrophic flood generated by the bursting of an ice-dammed glacial lake, Lake Missoula. This reversion to catastrophism ran counter to the prevailing philosophy of geology— gradualism. Bretz's papers were sharply criticized, and his interpretation of the Scablands was rejected by the geological fraternity. At the height of the debate he received an invitation to present his views before the Geological Society of Washington (D.C.). This turned out to be a trap; all the big guns of the Geological Survey were trained on him. Bretz, though stung by the criticism, continued to work in the Scablands area, adding evidence bit by bit and piece by piece to bolster his case. Only many years later was he vindicated, and at age 97 he was belatedly awarded the Penrose Medal, the highest honor bestowed by the Geological Society of America.

Bretz left his mark on all the students he came in contact with. Relatively few studied under him for their doctoral degrees, but he was close to the students—his office door was always open. They accompanied him on innumerable field trips; they participated in a cooperative "luncheon club" that cooked and ate on the top floor of Rosenwald during the Depression years, producing odors of onion-flavored stew that permeated the stacks of Rosenwald Library, to the dismay of the librarian. Bretz put together and edited the departmental newsletter during the war years, a welcome item for the men in service here and overseas. His own research was interrupted by a trip to Greenland as

J Harlen Bretz, professor of geology, University of Chicago. Photo courtesy of the University of Chicago Archives.

geologist for the privately financed expedition of Louise Boyd—an epoch in itself. Bretz was an outspoken foe of Robert Maynard Hutchins, and especially of J. Mortimer Adler; he had little use for the Aristotelian approach to science. Despite his animosity, however, Bretz played no role in university affairs.

Rollin Chamberlin was perhaps the most widely known member of the department in 1929. He was born in Beloit, Wisconsin, where his father was professor of geology and later president of the University of Wisconsin. Rollin spent virtually all his professional life at Chicago. He received both his bachelor's and his doctor's degrees there and was a member of the faculty from 1912 until his retirement in 1947. No other person had as long an association with the department. This long, unbroken career was punctuated by his extensive travels—he visited every continent but Antarctica. He was editor of the *Journal of Geology*, founded by his father, from 1927 to 1947.

Rollin Chamberlin was a rather nervous man. He was a pipe smoker whose pipe continually went out, and a conversation in his office was always broken by intervals of silence for relighting it. His energy was in part expended in his active life outside the office. Of lean and wiry build, he engaged in strenuous sports. He was something of a baseball player in

Rollin T. Chamberlin, professor of structural geology, University of Chicago. Photo courtesy of the University of Chicago Archives.

his early days and a baseball fan all the rest of his life. He had an astonishing knowledge of teams, players, and plays. He was a good handball player, at one time champion of the university, a tennis player through his later years, and an active mountain climber all his life until a heart ailment put an end to his athletic activities. Rollin was justly proud of his mountaineering. In all he had sixty-three notable ascents to his credit, including the Matterhorn and other famous peaks in the Alps, various peaks in Alaska, the Pyrenees, the Tetons, the Sierras, the Cascades, and the Canadian and Colorado Rockies. He was a member of the American Alpine Club and a contributor to its journal.

Rollin had a good sense of humor and enjoyed a joke on himself as well as on others. He was basically conservative and a loyal alumnus of the University of Chicago, though very unhappy with the regime of Robert Hutchins.

It is not surprising that Rollin Thomas Chamberlin—named for his father, Thomas Crowder Chamberlin, and Rollin D. Salisbury, the two persons most closely identified with the early years at Chicago, and wholly educated in the department—should reflect, in his professional outlook and orientation, the tradition and philosophy of the Chamberlin and Salisbury era. It is all the more remarkable, therefore, that, though he was not an innovator or one to depart from tradition, he established a place for himself as an individual and a scientist of some stature. He had, indeed, severe handicaps to overcome—having so preeminent a father and remaining in the institution in which he was educated—yet to a considerable degree he overcame them. His early work on the degassing of rocks (his doctoral dissertation), his research on the field measurement and study of glacial motion, and some of his work on continental evolution were highly original and foreshadowed later developments. He shared the teaching of the course entitled Continental Evolution, in fact historical geology, a course geared to the last two volumes of *Geology*, by T. C. Chamberlin and R. D. Salisbury. This course, together with its prerequisite, Geologic Processes (taught first by Salisbury and later by Bretz), was the backbone of the Chicago curriculum for nearly four decades. These courses, taken by every Chicago student, were a memorable experience. Rollin sponsored more doctoral theses, perhaps, than any other member of the department.

Chamberlin was elected to the National Academy of Sciences—the only member of the department so honored during my stay at Chicago until the arrival of Norman L. Bowen. He was also elected to the American Philosophical Society.

Chamberlin was much interested in the structure of mountains. This interest led him to a period of experimentation with the pressure box or structure model. Fashioned along the lines pioneered by Bailey Willis and earlier workers, his experiments had the same failing—wrong materials and improper scaling. It is of interest that three of Chamberlin's best-known students worked on model studies. Francis P. Shepard was a coauthor with Chamberlin of a paper on some model experiments. T. A. Link, Ph.D 1927, wrote a thesis based solely on experimentation. Shepard later became known as America's first marine geologist, and Link became one of Canada's leading petroleum geologists. Best known for his concern for model studies was M. King Hubbert, who, though he performed no experiments, placed the whole subject on a firmer footing by carrying over the theories of model scaling from engineering to geology. Hubbert, though nominally a student of Chamberlin's, can hardly be said to have done his work under Chamberlin's direction or supervision. But undoubtedly his personal contact with the model studies of Chamberlin and his students, while himself a graduate student at Chicago, directed his attention to model studies. Hubbert provided the theoretical basis for model experimentation, though Hans Cloos and others had earlier achieved significant results by intuitive scaling.

An objective examination of Rollin Chamberlin's earlier publications shows that many were done to verify—or test—concepts earlier put forth by T. C. Chamberlin. His study of glacial motion was to test ideas developed by the elder Chamberlin as a result of his Greenland studies. Rollin's work on the depth of folding in the Appalachians and the Rockies applied a concept presented in the three-volume *Geology* (2:125) of Chamberlin and Salisbury. Even the study of occluded gasses was an outgrowth of the planetesimal concept of earth formation and generation of the atmosphere and hydrosphere as formulated by T. C. Chamberlin.

Chamberlin made many trips abroad at a time when foreign travel was not as easy or as commonplace as it is now. On one such trip, with his father, he went to China and on west through Siberia to Europe. Rollin made many contacts abroad, and as a result foreign visitors to the department were frequent. I was a guest at his house when J. J. Sederholm of Finland paid a visit and again when Hans Cloos of Bonn came to Chicago to receive the Penrose Medal from the Geological Society of America. Rollin apparently took a liking to me, since I was frequently invited to Sunday dinner at his home on Blackstone Avenue before I was married. When Rollin retired I became editor of the *Journal of Geology*. I am sure he had something to do with this.

Albert Johannsen taught petrology, including optical mineralogy. Johannsen, a shy and retiring person who found it difficult to speak in public, was a true scholar in the best Germanic tradition—exhaustive and painstaking. He had a command of the German language and, since he had gone to Johns Hopkins University to study with E. B. Mathews—who in turn had studied in Germany with F. Zirkel— Johannsen was a carrier of the German tradition of scholarship. George Huntington Williams, before Mathews, also had studied in Germany and had brought with him the thin-section method of studying rocks. Hopkins was the place to go to learn this new technique—the only place for a number of years. In reality, however, Johannsen did a disservice to petrology—his teaching gave little hint of the subject's possibilities, reducing it to classification and nomenclature. Johannsen took the view that a good description was immutable, whereas theories about how rocks form come and go with the changing fashions of thought. But in fact Johannsen's four-volume treatise on the igneous rocks marked the end of an era; though that era had really ended a decade or more earlier.

Johannsen's books were in the typical German *Handbuch* style—thorough to the point of exhaustion. His *Manual of Petrographic Methods* has not been surpassed. His citations are to original sources—none secondary—and were carefully checked before publication. Johannsen was always elated when he could trace a rock name back to the paper in which it was first defined and used. He was, in fact, a collector—a collector of rock names and of many other things. He built up an enormous rock collection—neatly trimmed and labeled rock specimens from the classical localities all over the world. Johannsen also collected postage stamps

Albert Johannsen, professor of petrology,
University of Chicago. Photo courtesy of
A. Johannsen.

and was said to have more than $2,000 invested in two-cent stamps
alone—stamps in blocks of four with the plate numbers. He collected the
engravings from which the illustrations of Charles Dickens's works were
printed, and most of all he collected original printings of dime novels—a
form of literature once very popular in America. After retirement
Johannsen wrote a major book, published by the University of Oklahoma Press, on the dime novel. He was also a gifted artist and painter. At
an early stage in his life he drew the fashion plates for the *Salt Lake
Tribune.*

I have mentioned Edson Bastin before. He was chairman of the
department from 1922 until his retirement in 1944 and was, of course,
chairman when I arrived. Bastin was a Chicago product, being the son of
a professor of botany at the old Chicago University—predecessor of the
present institution. After receiving his doctor's degree in 1904, Bastin
spent the next fifteen years in field studies of ore and other economic
deposits, done for the most part for the United States Geological Survey. He joined the Chicago faculty in 1919.

Dr. Bastin (as he was always called) began his career in Maine—he was
the author of several Maine folios for the United States Geological
Survey. At Chicago he was the economic geologist, teaching all aspects

Edson S. Bastin, professor of economic geology and head of the Geology Department, University of Chicago. Photo courtesy of the University of Chicago Archives.

of the subject except coal and petroleum geology, subjects he left to Fisher. His courses were well organized, systematic, and thorough. King Hubbert told me that it was in Bastin's course that he first became acquainted with curves of mineral production, and this acquaintance led to his analysis of growth curves in general. This interest in turn led to his forecasts of culmination and decline in both production and reserves of petroleum and natural gas, which turned out to be uncannily accurate. Bastin did an excellent teaching job; but though he assured me when we first met that Chicago did not teach by the lecture method, he did just that. He had, however, many suites of ore minerals from various mining districts that he had his students examine under the ore microscope to work out the mineral paragenesis—a subject in which Bastin was interested. His interest in this subject culminated in the publication of his *Interpretation of Ore Textures*, a memoir of the Geological Society of America.

Bastin was of a liberal persuasion both in politics and in religion. He was very active in the First Unitarian Church at Woodlawn Avenue and Fifty-seventh Street. He was concerned for the welfare of his students and his staff. His wife, Elinor Bastin, a New Englander, shared this concern but was perhaps a little too motherly at times.

Bastin's administration was a holding action. He was the conservator of the Chamberlin tradition, and no significant changes were made during his chairmanship. The department had stagnated. Time was not ripe, perhaps, for the dramatic changes that followed World War II, but lack of funds prevented even the modest advances the times called for. Funds were so meager that faculty members had to buy their own stamps, pencils, and scientific reprints, pay their own expenses to meetings, and so forth. The department had no X-ray facilities, no technicians other than paleontological curators—though this was later partially remedied—no drafting facilities, and very inadequate shop and darkroom equipment. It did have an excellent library and a capable librarian, but there was only one secretary and, at one time during the Depression, one telephone. These deficiencies were largely due to Bastin's inability to secure funds. Bastin had inherited the Salisbury tradition of never spending anything if it could be avoided. In the rough-and-tumble scramble for funds, Bastin came out last, and since this was before the days of grants and contracts and federal moneys the department fared badly indeed. Perhaps Bastin was too much of a gentleman. Even a small sum, such as Albert Johannsen's request for ten dollars for research, was hard to come by. The younger staff became very restless and persuaded Bastin to open up the budget-making process (salaries excepted), but the effort came to naught.

Dr. D. Jerome Fisher (Jerry to his students and colleagues) was a jack-of-all-trades. He was also a Chicago product, both undergraduate and graduate. Jerry had been a football player on the now-legendary Chicago team coached by Alonzo Stagg. This is now ancient history, since football disappeared with the coming of Robert Hutchins in 1929. Jerry had a good sense of humor, loved a prank or joke, and was always engaged in some horseplay—especially when Bretz was involved.

He early developed an interest in coal, mainly through his fieldwork in the Book Cliffs area of Utah for the United States Geological Survey and in Illinois for the Illinois State Geological Survey. In the course of this work he became adept with the plane table and hence taught plane-table surveying to the geologists before World War II and to others during the war. Quite by accident—actually by default—he was given the course in petroleum geology, which he had to organize from scratch and teach with only a few weeks practical experience. But his mainstay through the years was elementary mineralogy and crystallography. He was much handicapped in that, because of an earlier decision by Salisbury, then dean, X-ray crystallography went to Physics, not to Geology as in most schools. X-ray facilities did not become available to geologists until after World War II. Mineralogy was his main interest during most of my tenure at Chicago. He worked very hard on his courses, setting a high standard for himself and his students. Any book or reprint he owned was carefully read, and the margins were filled with his annotations or comments. He was a stickler for detail—for minutiae. His course was tough and to some extent was resented by many who had to take it.

Fisher had a penchant for gadgets, the most elaborate being the Emmons double variation apparatus, designed to measure accurately the refractive indexes of minerals by use of index liquids. The microscope was fitted with a thermal stage so temperature could be varied, and the wave length of the light used could also be varied—hence "double variation." But it was my impression that the equipment was little used.

Fisher himself did relatively little research in the field of mineralogy. He was of course greatly handicapped in that he had no X-ray facilities, since most mineralogical research involved X-ray analysis. As a result his publications were scattered short notes; his research had no major thrust or direction. It is my guess that this is why he remained an associate professor so long—promotions are not given for teaching. And since outside appraisals are needed for promotions, a handful of small notes is not likely to help.

He was however, made a professor a short time before his retirement. It was he, perhaps more than any other, who tried without success to loosen the departmental purse strings. And when with a change of administration funds became plentiful, he was pushed aside. With the advent of the Newhouse administration in the fifties, mineralogy and crystallography were given to others, petroleum geology and plane-table mapping were dropped, and Jerry was left out of the mainstream of instruction.

Jerry was a loyal member of the department in spite of the somewhat shabby treatment he received during the Newhouse administration. He wrote a very good history of the department through 1962.

Carey Croneis had been at Chicago only a year when I arrived in 1929; he had replaced the deceased Stuart Weller, professor of paleontology. He was a Harvard product (Ph.D 1928) and had taught at the University of Arkansas at Fayetteville before his Chicago appointment.

Although Carey was an undergraduate at Denison University in Granville, Ohio, he was very much a Harvard man. Although short and inclined to overweight, he was dapper and unflappable. Adept at bridge and a passable badminton player, he made every effort to know everybody who was anybody—the great and the near great. He knew and socialized with more members of the Chicago faculty than anyone else. As a result he was more knowledgeable about university politics than the rest of us. He also cultivated those in power in the geological fraternity at large—he knew most of the wheelers and dealers, especially in the oil industry—and so he came to play a major role in the inception and development of the American Geological Institute.

Robert Hutchins was a provocative person, and his educational policies split the faculty into two camps. In the department, Bretz and Chamberlin were strongly anti-Hutchins. Croneis never committed himself; he straddled the fence. Actually, he became much involved in the physical science survey course in Hutchins's experimental College. It was in connection with this course that he, with Bill Krumbein, wrote *Down to Earth*, a new-style textbook for nonscience students. The book tried to present geology in a light and entertaining manner. It was patterned somewhat after Harvey Lemon's *From Galileo to Cosmic Rays*, the first of the "new plan" texts and a model for the others that followed. Lemon's book, however, while written with a light touch, had a good deal of solid, albeit nonmathematical physics. The Croneis/Krumbein book had a considerable sale, but I believe it was relatively short-lived as such books go. I thought it was shallow. Another venture, associated with the physical science survey course, was a "stream table"—a flume-like structure to illustrate the work of running water and show meandering streams, deltas, and the like. But the results were rather a failure; the model was incorrectly scaled, and the landforms it was supposed to illustrate turned out to be only a braided stream—no more, no less.

Croneis had a penchant for becoming involved in activities, large and small, outside the department. The physical science survey course was only one such activity. He was also associated with Chicago's 1933 World's Fair—the so-called Century of Progress; he ultimately became director of its Hall of Science. In this capacity he was able to hire a great many graduate students in geology as guides—employment that proved a boon to students who could not then find other jobs, since we were in the middle of the Great Depression.

But Carey was ambitious. I don't know whether he thought he would become chairman of the department when Bastin retired in 1944. Indeed, there was some speculation on this; instead, N. L. Bowen became chairman, whereupon Carey promptly left to become president of Beloit College—a position for which he was eminently suited. A few years later he went to Rice University in Houston to head the newly formed Geology Department and ultimately became chancellor.

It is difficult to assess Croneis's role at Chicago. He did not come from the Chamberlin and Salisbury tradition as did most of the faculty. I do not think Carey had much influence on the general character of the department or of the direction it ultimately took. Little happened before Bowen's arrival; the major changes that were to take place were deferred by the war, and when they did occur Carey Croneis was gone.

Alfred Romer, who taught vertebrate paleontology, received his doctor's degree in zoology at Columbia. He was a comparative anatomist and looked on fossils as biological material that would shed light on evolution and other biological problems. More often than not in America, fossils were used as an aid to stratigraphy—a guide to correlation. In reality most paleontologists were biostratigraphers. Romer was not; he was a biologist, not a geologist—what some would now call a paleobiologist. In fact he boasted that he never had a course in geology. He objected to the constraints imposed on his students by the department and preferred to take zoology students with little or no geology and make them into vertebrate paleontologists. To solve the problem, Romer proposed a separate department of paleontology, a view supported by some of the biology faculty. Nothing came of the proposal because Bastin, who was not only chairman of the Department of Geology but also director of Walker Museum, which contained all the fossil collections, wouldn't budge. Later Romer's successor, E. C. Olson, solved the problem by setting up an interdepartmental Committee on Paleozoölogy that functioned like a department. Perhaps because of Romer's influence, the vertebrate paleontologists dissociated themselves from the geologists, formed their own society, and held separate meetings.

But Romer was able to pursue his research at Chicago, collecting vertebrate materials from the Permian of our Southwest and the Karoo region of South Africa. He had Paul Miller, a skilled curator, to assist him in collecting and to prepare the fossil materials. However, when in 1934 Harvard offered him an endowed professorship in zoology, he left Chicago. He was replaced by his student, E. C. Olson. Romer was a very productive worker, and his books made a significant impact on the field and led to his election to the National Academy of Sciences.

One member of the faculty during my tenure at Chicago who did not fit into any mold was E. C. Olson, known as Shorty to his friends. His career at Chicago began during the Bastin administration and extended beyond the Newhouse regime. Shorty was both an undergraduate and a graduate student at Chicago in the thirties. He became interested in vertebrate paleontology and got his Ph.D under Romer's supervision. When Romer resigned in 1934 Shorty was chosen as his replacement. Olson subscribed to Romer's point of view. Paleontology was an entity in its own right—not the handmaiden of stratigraphy. Fossils were studied for what they could tell us about the evolution of life, not to correlate strata or fix their position in the geologic time scale. To shake loose the departmental constraints placed on the students specializing in vertebrate paleontology, Olson put together a paleozoology program leading to the doctor's degree, a program organized in cooperation with the Zoology Department. Many of the requirements of the Geology

Department were waived and replaced by fundamentals of zoology. Degree candidates were examined by an interdepartmental committee. Olson also enlisted the support of the Field Museum of Natural History, moved all the vertebrate materials out of Walker Museum, and consolidated them with the even larger collections at the Field Museum. Olson also held most of his classes there.

Shorty proved to be a very good vertebrate paleontologist and, unlike many of that breed, knew a great deal of geology. He looked not only at the bones he collected but also at the matrix in which they were embedded. He felt it was necessary to know something of the environment in which the beasts had lived. He became enamored of statistics and, with Bob Miller, wrote *Morphological Integration*, a very original and significant book. He was belatedly elected to the National Academy of Sciences. It is of interest that upon election he joined the Section on Population Biology, Evolution, and Ecology—not the Section on Geology.

When Bowen was appointed chairman of the department, he took the job on condition that many routine matters would be handled by someone else. Shorty Olson agreed to be that someone else, and so he became the departmental secretary. He continued in this capacity when Newhouse replaced Bowen, and in 1957 he became chairman. He remained in the department after its merger with Meteorology when it became the Department of Geophysical Sciences—an anomalous position for a paleozoologist! In 1969 Olson left Chicago and joined the biology faculty of the University of California at Los Angeles, where he later became chairman of the Biology Department.

Adolph Noé was nominally a member of the department, but like Romer his work and interests were largely apart—he was a paleobotanist. Noé, or von Noé as his wife was wont to say, was a tall man with bushy, twitchy eyebrows and mustache, bad teeth, and an awkward gait—the last due, perhaps, to poor eyesight. He was an Austrian with a heavy accent and had an unusual career. He was educated at Graz, later at Göttingen, and last at the University of Chicago, where in 1905 he received his Ph.D. in German languages. He taught German at Stanford University and then, for twenty years, at Chicago. In 1923 he became an assistant professor of paleobotany, a subject in which he had had some experience at Graz.

Noé was a specialist in the study of the flora of the Carboniferous and, in particular, the plant fossil material in coal balls. In these concretions the cell structure of the plants is exquisitely preserved. His knowledge of geology was largely self-taught, gained mainly from his firsthand experience in collecting coal balls.

Noé was an unexcelled raconteur. He could entertain for hours, and his stories were enhanced by his gestures, heavy accent, and slight lisp. He belonged to the old school of European culture and tradition—a world long past. Noé was a student of library science, an expert in German language and literature, conversant with French, Spanish, and Russian, and familiar with both Latin and Greek. His linguistic ability and kind heart enabled many a graduate student to pass the reading examination in French and German required for the Ph.D. Noé liked people and was in turn well liked by rich and poor, humble and mighty. But his entry into science came late in life; he did not pursue science to the exclusion of other things; to a certain extent Noé was a dilettante. Hence as he approached retirement he had no major scientific work to his credit and, though the recipient of an honorary degree from Graz, was never promoted to a professorship at Chicago. Upon his death, just before his scheduled retirement, work in paleobotany at Chicago ceased. Noé's greatest contribution may have been his translation of Otto Stutzer's book on coal geology. When Noé died before it was finished, Gilbert Cady of the Illinois Geological Survey took over and finished the job for the University of Chicago Press.

With the arrival of N. L. Bowen in 1937, a new era began and the department was drastically altered. This change, however, was interrupted by the Second World War. For a few short years after the war Chicago was perhaps the leading department in the country. But first some remarks on students at Chicago.

## STUDENTS

One student had a profound effect on my thinking and on the course of events later in my life—M. King Hubbert. When I arrived in Chicago in the fall of 1929 King was one of the first graduate students I met. I was struck immediately by his personality. He turned out to be something of an iconoclast, a sharp critic with an excellent analytical mind and skill in mathematical and physical analysis. Nothing seemed to delight him more than finding a fatal flaw in someone else's analysis. Although he was a graduate student working for his Ph.D. under Rollin Chamberlin, I never could discover whether he took any courses, and I soon observed that, although Chamberlin was his adviser and supervisor, King neither needed nor accepted advice and supervision. He was a very independent individual—a student of nobody. Basically he was interested in geophysics, and at the time I arrived he had focused on isostacy.

King was not married at the time, nor was I, so both of us took our meals at the Gamma Alpha house on Dorchester Avenue. Gamma

M. King Hubbert. Photo courtesy of M. King Hubbert.

Alpha was a fraternity whose members were graduate students in the sciences. Although nominally a fraternity, it did not fit the usual stereotype of this genre—generally characterized by undergraduates more interested in social activities than scholarship and given to a great deal of beer drinking and noisy parties. Gamma Alpha was exceptional in the caliber of its membership—an unusual assemblage of very bright minds. Discussion at dinner was often very stimulating, especially with King Hubbert present. He nearly always provoked a heated debate.

King soon discovered my mathematical deficiencies. I had had college algebra and trigonometry at Minnesota, but no calculus. King was convinced I should remedy this defect at once, so at his prodding I got a book on analytical geometry and the elements of calculus and studied rather diligently for about a year. I went so far as to sign up for a course in mathematical analysis taught by Mayme I. Logsdon in the Mathematics Department. I mastered the basic concepts of integral calculus, then dropped the whole matter—it had little relevance to my geological studies. My mathematical skills rapidly vanished owing to lack of use—only trigonometry proved useful in later years.

King left Chicago without his degree to accept an appointment as instructor in geophysics at Columbia University. Still unmarried, he rented a loft somewhere in Manhattan and continued his research. He completed his paper on the theory of scale models—a study provoked, I surmise, by the model experiments of Ted Link, Fran Shepard, and other students of Chamberlin. These "pressure box" experiments with plaster of paris, wax, and diverse other materials were patterned on the well-known experiments of similar nature carried out earlier by Bailey Willis. King showed conclusively that all these experiments, designed to show how folds and faults develop, were incorrectly scaled—so badly so as to make them virtually worthless. King was persuaded to submit his study for his doctor's thesis, so Chicago finally granted him his degree even though his study had by this time appeared in print.

In New York City King met Howard Scott, who achieved considerable fame—or should I say notoriety—for his role in the technocracy movement. America was in the depths of the Great Depression, and Scott was the principal exponent of technocracy—in reality its founder. Scott contended that the price system under which we operate contained the seeds of its own destruction and that a new system—technocracy—would take its place. He published his views in a long article in the *Atlantic Monthly*. King became an ardent technocrat and wore a lapel pin bearing the emblem of technocracy.

After nearly ten years King became disenchanted with Columbia. He resigned his post and left an academic career to go with Shell Development Company, the research arm of Shell Oil in Texas. Shell had built a new research center in Bellaire, near Houston, and King was made a codirector of this laboratory. He was to remain there many years. While working in this capacity King wrote to me at Chicago and asked me to recommend an additional research scientist, since the laboratory was still building up its staff. Did I have any topnotch students—I recommended Robert Nanz, then a graduate student at Chicago. Bob had come to Chicago from undergraduate study at Miami University at Oxford, Ohio, and was something of a chemist, having worked as such for Schenley Distilleries at Lawrenceburg, Indiana. At Chicago he put together a rock analysis laboratory when Bowen took over the chairmanship. Nanz needed the facilities to run whole-rock analyses of Precambrian slates, a topic he was working on for his Ph.D. Nanz went to work for Shell and eventually became a Shell vice-president.

King remained at Shell for twenty-five years. He gave up his administrative duties early on and published a number of milestone papers. One of the best known was his "Theory of Ground Water Motion," sparked by a late-night bull session after an afternoon scientific meeting at which a speaker had set forth his ideas on how the proposed trans-Florida ship canal would affect the groundwater system. The debate was unresolved, but it set King to work and led to his monumental paper. King sent it to the *Journal of Geology*, but it was far too long for a journal article. Rollin

Chamberlin, then editor, arranged for it to appear as a supplement to a regular issue. It proved a popular item and went through a second printing. Among other papers King published were his work on hydrodynamic entrapment of petroleum and his study with Bill Rubey on the mechanism of overthrust faulting.

It is noteworthy that all King's papers were "pencil-and-paper" research. King did no fieldwork and virtually no experimental work. He developed his concepts from the first principles of physics, got his data from the literature, and used the information to test his general theories—of overthrusting, of entrapment, of groundwater motion. King's idol, if he had one, was J. Willard Gibbs, whose formulation of the laws of thermodynamics was a major achievement—an achievement purely intellectual, since Gibbs, like Hubbert, was not an experimentalist.

For his original work King was awarded the Day Medal of the Geological Society of America and later its Penrose Medal, the highest award. He was elected to the National Academy of Sciences. More recently he received the William Smith Medal of the Geological Society of London—ironically, named for the father of field geology but here awarded to a geologist who had done no fieldwork.

Perhaps King's most dramatic achievement was his prediction of oil depletion, which appeared in 1956 in a publication of the American Petroleum Institute. This paper dealt with the trend and future production of oil and gas in the United States; apparently it was generally overlooked or ignored, but King's presentation at the 1956 meeting of the Production Division, Southern District, of the American Petroleum Institute was not.

King clearly saw that at that time the discovery rate had peaked and production would soon culminate, and that it and our reserves would begin an irreversible decline. He predicted a peak production in 1970. His paper created a great deal of consternation in the oil world, and provoked heated controversy; he was roundly denounced. It was heresy indeed in a profession that is constitutionally optimistic and incapable of conceiving of its demise. It turned out, as we all now know, that King was right.

One task assigned to me was to teach the "local field course," involving weekend fieldwork in the Chicago area. This assignment worried me. The local area offered many Pleistocene deposits and landforms and a quarry or two in the Silurian Niagaran limestone. I felt uncomfortable with the Pleistocene, having had no firsthand experience with it, so I put the matter to my class—should we work on weekends as scheduled or put in an equivalent number of days in fewer but longer field trips? They opted for the latter, so we made four trips—a one-day trip to the

Thornton quarry in the Niagaran, one weekend trip to the LaSalle anticline and the Starved Rock area along the Illinois River, another to the Peoria coal-bearing region, and a week-long trip to the Marquette iron-bearing district on the south shore of Lake Superior. After the first year the Lake Superior trip became an annual event—to a different iron range each year. Very soon graduate students asked to be included, and eventually the faculty also participated as spectators. I was appalled to discover that many graduate students had never seen an igneous rock outside a laboratory. They could pass an examination on dikes and batholiths but had never seen them, and they didn't recognize either when confronted with them in the field. It was my policy, learned at California, to take students to an outcrop—of black diabase dikes cutting pink granite, for example—turn them loose for half an hour, then quiz them thoroughly on what they had seen. I soon discovered, and so did they, that they really hadn't seen very much. When asked what the rock was they gave a ready answer—perhaps right but more often wrong— but when asked to point out the minerals that were diagnostic or essential to the identification of the rock, they began to look for what they should have seen before naming the rock. And they soon learned the criteria for determining the relative ages of rocks and other fundamentals of field geology. It seemed to me that their education was woefully weak in many respects. This was not, however, unique to Chicago. California, by contrast, was rigorous and effective. You could be sure of several things about California graduates of that time—they knew their rocks and were excellent field men, and they knew how to use a petrographic microscope.

Upon arrival at Chicago I found out that in addition to the local field course and sedimentation, I was to teach elementary geology, both physical and historical, using of course Chamberlin and Salisbury's *College Geology* as a text. Students took these courses to satisfy a science requirement for the bachelor's degree. As might be expected, a large number of students passed through these classes over the years, but two in particular stand out: George Benton, who later became professor of meteorology and eventually a vice-president and colleague of mine at Johns Hopkins, and Charles Steen, who discovered the Mi Vida uranium mine and became a millionaire overnight, only to lose his fortune just as quickly. Of course there were other students— many of them. Some like Charlie Steen achieved notoriety; others like Arthur Lundahl achieved fame in fields other than geology. Art was a Chicago boy and, as his name implies, of Swedish extraction. He had a winning personality, was very outgoing, and made friends easily. Art was my field assistant for two summers in northwestern Ontario. When World War II broke out he was my assistant in the courses in photogrammetry I taught—we learned the subject together. But Art saw that the draft would soon catch up with him, so he enlisted in the navy. Because his record showed experience in teaching photogrammetry, he was assigned to further training in this field and eventually became a naval intelligence officer stationed on Adak in the Aleutians. At war's end he remained in the navy, but not long after he joined the Central Intelligence Agency and became director of their photointelligence laboratory. In this capacity he discovered the Soviet missile buildup in Cuba that precipitated the Cuban missile crisis. Art had to make a presentation on the missile installations to President Kennedy at the White House. I often say that I discovered the Cuban missiles—by proxy, that is. In connection with his CIA position, Art traveled extensively and served as consultant to many world leaders such as de Gaulle and Nehru. He became well known in his field, and in 1954 he was president of the American Society of Photogrammetry. I returned to geology; Art did not. Some years later, when I was at Hopkins, I received an invitation from Art to his investiture as honorary knight of the British Commonwealth at the British Embassy in Washington. Art was one of only four Americans to be so knighted; Dwight Eisenhower was another.

I also had John Scopes as a student at Chicago, though he did not remain long enough to get a degree. Scopes was made famous by the notorious "monkey trial" in Dayton, Tennessee, where he was a teacher in high school. He was brought to trial in 1925 for teaching evolution, contrary to state law. His transgression was deliberate, to test the constitutionality of the statute. The trial was highly publicized, since the chief lawyer for the defense was the well-known Chicago attorney Clarence Darrow. The other side was represented by the perennial candidate for president of the United States, William Jennings Bryan. Scopes was really the forgotten man in the proceedings. John was a most self-effacing person and must have felt very uncomfortable through the whole affair.

There were many other students also— too many to mention. Some including Hubbert, Krumbein, Wadell, Nanz, Potter, Hough, Ginsburg, Siever, and others, appear elsewhere in this story.

One thing that struck me when I arrived at Chicago was that every member of the faculty and many graduate students wore a laboratory coat. These, donned as soon as one arrived in the morning, were lightweight garments that snapped down the front. Even those who did no laboratory work wore laboratory coats—even Rollin Chamberlin, who spent most of his time behind his desk reading manuscripts. No place I ever went before or after followed this custom. At Caltech, when I visited in 1955, the garb was blue jeans—but not laboratory coats.

There was, in 1929, Kappa Epsilon Pi, a geological fraternity not affiliated with any national organization and, as far as I could tell, open to everyone. It had almost none of the attributes of a fraternity—no fraternity house, minimal initiation rites, and limited social functions. It was mainly a geology club that scheduled meetings and speakers. It did provide a forum for guest speakers—something Minnesota and California lacked. Each year it organized a mock Geological Society of America convention including full participation of all students, with programs, abstracts, and all the trimmings.

## JOURNAL OF GEOLOGY

When Rollin Chamberlin retired in 1947 he gave up the editorship of the *Journal of Geology*. I was asked to take on the job. The journal was one of many published by the University of Chicago Press. It had been established in 1893 by T. C. Chamberlin, its first editor, and I became its third editor. The *Journal* carried little advertising, and its revenues came principally from subscriptions plus some income from a $50,000 bequest of R. A. F. Penrose, Jr., onetime professor of economic geology at Chicago. Unfortunately, all the income from the bequest went to pay service charges levied by the University Press—bookkeeping and other expenses previously paid from general university funds. The *Journal* funded a part-time editorial assistant to handle correspondence and manuscript processing.

The *Journal* experience was an eye-opener. The variety and quality of manuscripts received was astonishing. Some manuscripts, submitted by organizations that did their own manuscript screening, such as the Geophysical Laboratory or the United States Geological Survey, were letter-perfect and could be sent to the typesetter at once. Others were bad—some very bad—with references in no coherent style and many missing, incomplete, or superfluous. The text might not be properly keyed to the illustrations, tables, or references. Illustrations commonly were poorly drawn or, even if well drawn, might be badly designed and hence ineffective. Worse still, the text was often poorly written, ambiguous, and with many grammatical errors. If such manuscripts were accepted, I became a ghost-writer. The authors' attitudes varied greatly—some appreciated editorial changes and were grateful for the help, but others were indifferent or even hostile and didn't want any editor "tampering with their manuscripts" or altering their deathless prose. The latter were for the most part Europeans, not accustomed to the American way of rigorous manuscript review and editing. One of the most difficult was Kalervo Rankama, who insisted on capitalizing earth, moon, and sun, contrary to University of Chicago Press practice.

On leaving Chicago in 1952 I gave up the editorship to C. Leland Horberg. I had managed, with the help of Jean Simmons (and later Mike Chappars), my editorial assistant, to get out six issues a year, some longer supplements, and a second printing of King Hubbert's "Theory of Ground Water Motion" and to upgrade the photographic illustrations by going to collotype, to the chagrin of the director of the Press. I spent all the surplus funds accumulated during the war years when the *Journal* had suffered a manuscript famine and accumulated unspent moneys.

We published several landmark articles, including Kuenen and Migliorini's "Turbidity Currents and Graded Bedding," a paper that really started the turbidite revolution, and Krynine's "Megascopic Classification of Sedimentary Rocks," which set forth Krynine's views on tectonic control of sedimentation and put the classification of sediments on a rational basis. The *Journal* also published a special issue on the feldspars growing out of the new studies of these minerals, in which the Chicago group played a major role. The issue met a mixed reception. It was hailed as a major event by those interested in the subject but not by those whose interests lay elsewhere.

### SEDIMENTATION AT CHICAGO

In 1929 sedimentation was a new subject, not a traditional component of geology curricula as were mineralogy and paleontology. It was becoming popular, and Chicago felt the need to offer a course. The interest grew out of the rise of the petroleum industry and the role geology played in oil exploration. The great demand for petroleum really began in the early twenties, after World War I, when the automobile, now mass-produced, became popular. The industry was destined to become a giant, and the insatiable demand for oil proved a boon for geologists. Since oil is formed in sediments and contained in sedimentary rocks, it soon became apparent that we needed to know more about sedimentary strata. Except as components of a stratigraphic section, their study had been generally sporadic and unorganized. The need was met in part by the creation in 1921 of a Committee on Sedimentation by the National Research Council, to stimulate interest in the subject. It was first led by R. C. Moore, a professor of paleontology at the University of Kansas, but W. H. Twenhofel, a professor at Wisconsin, soon took over as its chairman.

Twenhofel was also a paleontologist—or more properly a biostratigrapher. I first met him at one of the first Tristate Field Conferences, of which he, A. C. Trowbridge of Iowa, and M. M. Leighton of the Illinois Geological Survey were founders. Twenhofel reminded me in many ways of Calvin Coolidge—a soft-spoken, tall and lanky New Englander. He was, however, of German ancestry and a midwesterner from near Cincinnati—a region known for both its fossils and its paleontologists, including Foerste, Bassler, Ulrich, and Schuchert among others. Unlike

W. H. Twenhofel, professor of paleontology, University of Wisconsin. Photo
courtesy of Robert R. Shrock.

Sorby or Cayeux, he really knew very little about microscopic petrology. Nonetheless, he was a real scholar, an adept critic, and a productive
writer. Under his leadership the Committee on Sedimentation produced
its monumental *Treatise on Sedimentation*. an exhaustive summary of the
literature on the subject before its publication in 1926. Nothing so
ambitious had been published in America since Grabau's *Principles of
Stratigraphy* of 1913. Although nominally a Committee project, it seems
to have been written largely by Twenhofel himself. Twenhofel's *Principles of Sedimentation*, issued a few years later, was in many ways an
abridged version of the *Treatise*. It told the reader a good deal about
sedimentary processes but very little about the sedimentary rocks themselves. Twenhofel did much to establish sedimentology (a word he de-
tested) as a subdiscipline of geology and to make its pursuit respectable.
Twenhofel had studied the reefs of the Niagaran Silurian strata of the
Great Lakes area and had thus become an authority on reefs. When reefs
were found to be oil-bearing, the American Association of Petroleum
Geologists held a symposium on the subject at their annual meeting in
Saint Louis in 1949. Twenhofel gave the keynote address, summarizing
what was known about fossil reefs, to a standing-room-only audience in
the grand ballroom of the Jefferson Hotel.

In 1930 the Society of Economic Paleontologists and Mineralogists, a division of the American Association of Petroleum Geologists, launched the *Journal of Sedimentary Petrology*, with Ray Moore as its first editor. The SEPM, as it is known, was originally an organization of petroleum-oriented sample washers—those who constructed oil-well logs based on cuttings, microfossils, and, to a much lesser extent, heavy minerals. The organization, though at first industry-oriented, grew rapidly by addition of members with academic affiliation, who later came to dominate its leadership and determine its direction.

At the time the new journal was established, A. C. Trowbridge of the University of Iowa had suggested "sedimentology" as its title, but the suggestion was vetoed—mainly, I think, by Professor Twenhofel, who considered the term a bastard word owing to its derivation from both Latin and Greek. It was, as he put it in a printed discussion, poor terminology (also a hybrid word). Sedimentary petrology was the all-inclusive term dealing with the nature and origin of sedimentary rocks. Since I was trained in petrology at Minnesota, I chose to call my own course sedimentary petrology and made it just that—a course in petrology and all that implied.

The term "sedimentology" was then nowhere used in America, though Hakon Wadell, a graduate student at Chicago, published in *Science* (1932, n.s., 75:20), a note proposing it in place of "sedimentation." The suggestion fell on deaf ears in America, but "sedimentology" became widely used in Europe—first perhaps by the Dutch school, D. J. Doeglas in particular, who defined it to include both laboratory study and field study of sedimentary deposits, ancient and modern. Perhaps Doeglas felt the term "sedimentary petrology" had, by usage, become too restrictive; in the minds of some it had become the study of heavy minerals under the petrographic microscope. In time, owing to the energetic activities of the Dutch, the International Association of Sedimentologists was formed, and in 1962 this organization launched its own journal, *Sedimentology*. Subsequently the term "sedimentology" spread to the United States, where it had been first proposed and rejected. I later used it for advanced courses.

At Chicago Bastin told me I was to have a laboratory—it would be in the basement of Rosenwald Hall, in an area formerly used for storage. The basement seemed a fitting place, as Bastin put it, because no doubt I would want a "stream table," which would be a sloppy, wet operation. Then, too, I would be sieving sands with a Ro-Tap, a noisy mechanical shaker. Best to keep all this away from the rest of the building. Bastin was a bit taken aback when I said I would need petrographic microscopes to study thin sections of sedimentary rocks. All the microscopes were then in Johannsen's laboratory on the second floor, and because these were used only for Johannsen's petrography course he would have to discuss my request with him. Johannsen reluctantly gave up his two oldest models. He really didn't want to let them go, since no doubt my students would get sand in their stage bearings!

I give all these details to show the conceptions about the study of sedimentary rocks prevalent at this time and place. This was my first realization that sedimentation was conceived of as a "soft rock" subject, pursued in a different way from petrography. And so it had been in America. Nowhere was the chair in petrology held by a sedimentary petrologist. Petrology in America had become synonymous with igneous and metamorphic petrology ("hard rocks"). Not until 1937, when P. D. Krynine was appointed to the faculty at Pennsylvania State College, did this change. The reasons for this state of affairs were partly historical. Even though Henry Clifton Sorby, the "father of petrology" was primarily interested in sedimentary rocks, and despite the monographic studies of the great sedimentary petrographer Lucien Cayeux in France, the field of petrography was mainly exploited by students of igneous and metamorphic rocks, beginning with Rosenbusch, Zirkel, and others. The leading American students of sedimentary rocks were paleontologists or biostratigraphers—R. C. Moore and W. H. Twenhofel, for example. None except Marcus Goldman, of the United States Geological Survey, were petrologists; none had any significant training in petrologic methods. They made their observations mainly in the field in connection with stratigraphic studies; at most they used a low-power binocular microscope—the same one used to examine fossils. Hence it was generally presumed that the training for soft-rock geology, as it was called, was basically different. No need for crystallography, optical mineralogy, or petrography. Virgil R. D. Kirkham, a former member of the Idaho faculty and an oil geologist, was then getting his Ph.D. at Chicago. When I asked him why he took no courses in petrology, he simply said that when he wanted a rock classified he would hire someone to do it. This view epitomized the prevalent image of petrography at Chicago.

And not without reason, for Johannsen was indeed interested in little else than rock classification and nomenclature. It is small wonder that the few who took his courses had the notion that this was the aim and end of petrography. This came as a surprise to me, since Grout at Minnesota had a very different view of petrology—a view he instilled in his students. As he said in his textbook, *Petrography and Petrology* (1932, vi), "Reading the life history of a rock is a much higher achievement than a description and classification." So to me the study of thin sections was an approach to the interpretation of rock history. The whole of petrology— field and laboratory—was directed toward this end. Classification and rock names were but a step on the way, a way to simplify communication, not an end in themselves.

Clearly I was out of step with the concept Chicago had of the study of sedimentary rocks. They thought they were hiring a "sedimentationist"—not a second petrographer! Hence my request for petrographic microscopes was disconcerting and the response disappointing. So I taught a course in sedimentary petrography in spite of the handicaps.

One handicap was the lack of a rock collection. Johannsen had a superb collection of more than four thousand specimens from all the classic areas of the world—the Oslo region, the Scottish Highlands, the Auvergne region of France, the Eifel region of Germany, and many others—the type localities of virtually all igneous rocks—but no sedimentary rocks to speak of. So on every ensuing field trip I collected furiously and, with donations from many of my students and others as well, I acquired a suitable rock collection. I was destined, when I later moved to Hopkins, to do this job all over again. I persuaded Bastin to underwrite the cost of some thin sections, and later, when the department acquired Bill Schmidt as a technician, many were made in the departmental shop. I was in business.

Thin-section study demanded some skill in optical mineralogy, and my students soon learned that "soft rock" didn't mean soft courses. In my view the study of sedimentary rocks required precisely the same background in crystallography, optical mineralogy, and chemistry as the study of any other rocks. This approach was basic, and prerequisites in these subjects were required of all students in sedimentary petrography, to the dismay of those who came to Chicago for graduate study from backgrounds in paleontology. But it was a number of years before I finally had access to all the microscopes I needed and eventually had an adequate laboratory on the second floor of the building.

Two further circumstances had a significant effect on my work at Chicago. In the seminar on sedimentation conducted by G. D. Louderback at Berkeley, we had read the paper by J. A. Udden on the "mechanical composition" of sediments (1914, *Geol. Soc. Amer., Bull.* 25:655–744). Udden, who was professor at Augustana, a small Lutheran college in Rock Island, Illinois, had for many years made grain-size analyses of modern sediments in the hope of finding size-distribution patterns diagnostic of the several environments or agents of deposition. We read also two papers by C. K. Wentworth on his field and laboratory studies of cobble abrasion (1919, *J. Geol.* 27:507; 1922, *U.S. Geol. Surv., Prof. Paper* 131-C). I was much impressed with these papers. They seemed to open a whole new way of looking at sediments and sedimentary processes. Here was something to get one's teeth into. Gravels and sands had been described as well sorted, poorly rounded, and such, but such descriptions seemed subjective and ill defined. Here was a way to quantify these concepts—to measure them and study their modification during stream or beach transport. I incorporated this approach into my course; it was received in different ways. I had some students whose aim was to go into petroleum geology, strike oil, and become rich. This was particularly true of students from the oil fields of Oklahoma and Texas. They couldn't see what the roundness of a pebble had to do with finding oil. Nor could I, for that matter, and I didn't really care. Understanding was the motivation, not dollars. This approach, however, did fire the imagination of two of my students, Hakon Wadell and William C. Krumbein—two very different personalities. Wadell was a blond Swede with a noticeable accent, who was considerably older and more mature than most of his fellow students. He had been around—had even trekked across the ice cap of Iceland. He was a real scholar, a great admirer of the ultrathorough scholarship of the German tradition that produced the monumental *Handbuchs*—a scholarship epitomized by Johannsen, whom Wadell greatly admired. Wadell did much to clarify our thinking as he critically examined our concepts—especially about the shape and round-ness of detrital materials. He was, however, so dedicated to perfection that he had great difficulty completeing anything. He was fearful of overlooking some aspect or missing another reference. He became a perennial student, so much that his wife despaired of his ever completing his work for the Ph.D. and returned to Sweden.

Bill Krumbein, like Wadell, was older than the other students, but in other ways he was quite different. He was a graduate of the university's School of Business and was, in fact, a partner in a business—a collection agency that throve, no doubt, during the Depression years that followed. But he was not happy collecting overdue accounts and had greater ambitions. He returned to school part time to do graduate work in geology. He saw at once that grain-size analyses were susceptible to statistical treatment, a subject he had studied in business school. Udden and Wentworth had improvised statistical measures, but only Parker Trask, in his monumental study of source rocks of petroleum, made a rational approach to the problem by adopting several measures from conventional statistics, based on numerical values obtained from graphic plots of size analyses—the cumulative curves, to be specific. Bill Krum-bein saw at once what the problem was. The conventional measures based on equal class intervals were inappropriate for sediments, which are best analyzed and described by class intervals that are unequal—are geometric. Udden and his successors had intuitively seized on the geometric interval. Udden's grade scale based on the powers of two still prevails in America and has now more or less superseded the geometric scale based on the decimal system once very common in Europe. Krum-

William C. Krumbein, professor of geology, Northwestern University. Photo
courtesy of L. L. Sloss.

bein proposed his phi scale based on the logarithms to the base two. This
scale made calculations easy—the log intervals were equal. It eventually
became universal.

Bill's interest in sediments, particularly quantitative analytical
methods and statistics, expanded. Upon completing his thesis, a study of
the size composition of glacial tills, Bill received his Ph.D. and was
offered a post teaching physical science in Robert Hutchins's radical
College. He had the office next to mine, and in the course of the next five
or six years we were in close contact. I had acquired an associate
interested in sedimentation and sedimentary rocks. Bill read widely,
could handle German easily, and had a background in statistics and
mathematics that I did not have. It soon became apparent to both of us
that the laboratory analysis of sediments—especially unconsolidated
sediments—had progressed far enough so that a manual of laboratory
methods was badly needed. The methods of studying particulate materials were widely scattered, in the soils literature, in various industrial
journals, and elsewhere. Bill combed much of this literature and prepared a paper summarizing the history of particle-size analysis, which he
submitted to the *Journal of Sedimentary Petrology*. Twenhofel, who was
editor, accepted it somewhat reluctantly with the remark that all this was

just a passing fad. We soon collaborated to write a book. Carey Croneis put us in touch with Kirtley Mather of Harvard University, who was then adviser and editor of the Appleton-Century series in geology and related fields. Mather was interested, so we soon had a publisher and a contract. The book, *Manual of Sedimentary Petrography*, appeared in 1938. It had a long and ready sale, though never very large in any one year, and only in the seventies did it finally expire. Perhaps because of it, I was promoted to associate professor just after it was off the press.

The publication of our book ended an era, though we didn't know it at the time. In essence the approach Krumbein and I pursued was based on an unstated premise, one I found to be wrong but that some still have faith in today. This was the notion that the natural processes of sedimentation had left a textural imprint on the sediments—a fingerprint as it were—that would enable us to identify the environment (or agent) of deposition. This was the philosophy underlying Udden's work early in the century, and we presumed that by refining and sharpening our tools we could reach our goal. The clastic sedimentary deposit was looked on as a gross particulate system—a population of grains. If we could define the fundamental properties of these grains—size, shape, roundness, surface texture, and mineral composition—we could, by appropriate samples, estimate the makeup of the whole population. But the results were disappointing, and slowly disillusion set in. We could not, no matter how careful the sampling, the analytical techniques, or the statistical summarization, distinguish unambiguously between beach, dune, and river sands. After innumerable size analyses, calculations of statistical parameters, and scatter diagrams, we were still far from our goal.

In addition to applying statistics to grain-size analyses, Krumbein became interested in pebble abrasion—an interest sparked by the earlier studies of C. K. Wentworth. Krumbein built a "tumbling mill" patterned after that used by Wentworth. Using the refined concepts of roundness and sphericity developed by Wadell, Krumbein wrote equations that expressed the changes in roundness with distance of travel. He also extended his studies of cobble abrasion to present beaches and streams. He was thus the successor to C. K. Wentworth on the subject, though unlike Wentworth he did not apply his findings to the ancient rocks. As we found out later, the changes in rounding and shape of sand grains told us very little and the changes in pebbles were of minimal value. The size decline of the largest pebbles in the ancient fluvial conglomerates, however, was most informative. But Bill never made use of his findings. In addition to his other talents, he was a superb teacher of undergraduates; he was given an award for his excellence as a teacher.

As time progressed, Krumbein became more and more interested in statistical analysis of sedimentary data—particularly grain-size analyses. Statistical methods, not the geological questions, became the focus of his research. This line of work was temporarily halted by World War II, when Bill took a leave of absence from the university and went to work for the Beach Erosion Board, work that I presume had to do with studies of the beaches and coastlines of potential landing sites for invasion forces. After the war he joined the research group of the Gulf Oil Company at Pittsburgh and then, when apparently he failed to get a professorship at Chicago, he resigned to accept an appointment at Northwestern University in Evanston, Illinois. Our ways parted.

At Northwestern Krumbein became associated with Larry Sloss, a stratigrapher and also a Chicago Ph.D., and Ed Dapples, whose main interests were coal and sedimentary petrography. The three frequently collaborated; Krumbein and Sloss wrote *Sedimentation and Stratigraphy*, a well-received book published in 1951 by W. H. Freeman. His Northwestern appointment also brought him into contact with Bob Garrels. Bill was quick to see how Garrels's work on the stability of minerals under varying oxidation-reduction potential (Eh) and acidity/alkalinity (pH), could be applied to natural sediments. The two collaborated in a significant paper on this subject.

Bill became much interested in facies maps—maps depicting various stratigraphic measures such as net sand thickness, shale/sand ratio, and the like. Apparently he ran into this from a short period of association with the Gulf Oil Company, the data for the maps being derived mainly from well logs. This activity became very popular at Northwestern for a time. The results were mixed. The maps depicted the lithologic makeup and variations of a given stratigraphic interval in a very generalized fashion—a picture painted with a broad brush. They didn't greatly enhance our understanding of the sedimentary environments.

Bill turned more and more to statistical methods of greater sophistication, and when computers came into fashion he adopted the new technology. In short, Krumbein became a methodologist, more interested in the methods than in the geological problems.

Krumbein's greatest impact on sedimentology came from his earlier work—the basic principles of statistical summarization of the size frequency curve and the phi grade scale. And of course as the importance of size analyses declined so did his influence on the field. Bill was very ambitious, driven by a compulsion to succeed—a workaholic. He published a great deal, though some of his papers were only slightly modified versions of early ones. He made an effort to know the right people, to be at the right place at the right time, and, as he himself expressed it, "to put my thumbprint on as many things as possible." This side of his character irritated some of his fellow students—it smacked of "apple polishing."

Paul D. Krynine, professor of petrology, School of Mineral Industries, Pennsylvania State University. Photo courtesy of R. L. Folk.

Nonetheless, Bill had a very sharp mind and a great deal of ability. I learned all I know about statistics from him.

In the meantime Paul D. Krynine appeared on the scene. I had first met Krynine in Louderback's seminar on sedimentation at Berkeley in 1927 but had lost track of him until he turned up on the faculty of Pennsylvania State College (now university). He had left California and gone to Yale, where he took his Ph.D. under Adolph Knopf, submitting a thesis on the Triassic sediments of the Connecticut Valley. He had become a skilled petrographer in spite of his bad eyes. He had also become vociferous in his approach to the study of sedimentary rocks, his principal approach being thin-section petrography. Since thin-section petrology had been a mainstay of my teaching at Chicago, I had at last found a kindred spirit on the American scene. Paul achieved considerable fame from his American Association of Petroleum Geologists Distinguished Lecture tour in 1943, when he presented his classification of sandstones and discussed the role of tectonics in their composition. He prepared elaborate mimeographed lecture notes, which he distributed freely. His tour lectures were accompanied by a demonstration of his thesis with thin sections. I remember hearing Paul say that when he gave his lecture in Tulsa he had to borrow Ira Cram's personal microscope—

none were to be found in the offices or laboratories of the petroleum companies. This was then an unfamiliar tool to the oil-field geologists, and to most sedimentationists for that matter.

Paul had changed quite a bit since Berkeley days. He still had the same awkward gait, the same thick glasses and atrocious eyesight, but he had become much more assertive—perhaps aggressive is the word. He was much in evidence at the meetings, often very critical of a presentation, very positive in his views, almost bullying at times. His mannerisms were not such as to make friends. But Paul and I got along well enough. We argued a great deal, in particular about graywacke—its definition and significance. The term was used in the literature on the Lake Superior Precambrian but seldom if ever anywhere else in America. Krynine was using it freely for many sandstones that did not seem to be graywackes as I understood the term. Perhaps to convince me of his views, he invited me to come to Pennsylvania State College and spend a few days with him. I accepted and, loaded with specimens and thin sections, boarded the train at Englewood Station in Chicago. It was then wartime, and the trains were usually late, generally crowded with servicemen coming home on leave or just returning to duty. The coach was full—no empty seat anywhere—so like many others I was obliged to sit on my luggage in the aisle. I was bound for Altoona, Pennsylvania, an all-night ride. The Pennsylvania coaches then had a section at the end of the car with broad shelves for storing luggage. I shuffled the bags about when night came, made a space large enough to crawl into, and went to sleep. As promised, Paul was at Altoona; he had saved his gasoline ration coupons and driven more than forty miles to meet the train. I stayed at his home, but we spent most of the time in his laboratory looking at thin sections. Paul was very stubborn and insisted that arkose was feldspathic but graywackes were not. But in the end he conceded that my Archean graywackes were indeed graywackes, even if richly feldspathic. Then and there he set up two classes:"high-rank" and "low-rank" graywackes—the first with feldspar, the second without. But in general we were in agreement about sedimentary rocks—on how they should be studied, on the role of tectonics in controlling the sandstone composition, and on the classification of sandstones. We were both petrographers and spoke the same language.

One project of Krynine's that never came to fruition was his "sedimentological institute," an organization designed to do for sedimentary rocks what the Geophysical Laboratory in Washington had done for igneous and metamorphic rocks. Krynine proposed establishing such an institution to do the fundamental research on sedimentary rocks and processes. It was to be a nonprofit enterprise supported by the petroleum industry, each company pledging a certain annual sum. The proposal, made in 1944, was that the oil companies pool their resources to prose-cute basic research in the field. The institute would do only fundamental science, which would become public knowledge. The companies would work out the applied aspects. It seemed more sensible to mount a cooperative effort of this kind than for each company to set up its own research program, with duplication and overlap of effort. Krynine enlisted the support of Krumbein and myself, and we wrote out a prospectus for this institute. A. I. Levorsen, a prominent independent oil geologist, became much interested in the idea and arranged a meeting at the Baker Hotel in Dallas in connection with the 1944 meetings of the American Association of Petroleum Geologists. A dozen or so attended—mostly the chief geologists of the major oil companies—including G. C. Gester, Mose Knebel, Theron Wasson, Earl Noble, K. C. Heald, Rodger Denison, and A. I. Levorsen. Krynine also went to New York to discuss the proposal with Eugene Jablonski of Socony and R. F. Baker of the Texas Company. Later Ira Cram, then president of the American Association of Petroleum Geologists, and Lou Weeks of the Jersey Company became involved in the discussion. Despite the enthusiasm and tentative commitment of support by several companies, the others held back. Ira Cram, for one, didn't think thin sections were worth two and a half million dollars. Clearly Cram got the wrong impression of what had been proposed. Eventually, for whatever reason, the whole matter fell through. Shortly thereafter the companies organized their own separate research laboratories. This was rather a pity, I believe, for the available talent was thinly scattered, duplication of research was rampant, and the results were classified. In fact, Gulf Oil already had its own research laboratory. In the thirties, Ben Cox of Gulf tried, without success, to persuade Bill Krumbein and me to join their research group, though Bill did work there for a short time after World War II.

Paul freely distributed reams of mimeographed materials to one and all, but it was difficult to get him to put his thoughts into formal journal articles. I did eventually get his classification of sedimentary rocks for the *Journal of Geology*. My contacts with Krynine were very stimulating and helped shape my own thinking. Unhappily, Krynine died a few years later of leukemia. The Krynine tradition has been perpetuated to some extent by his students, the best known being Robert Folk. And Bob Folk has acquired, perhaps unknowingly, many of Paul's mannerisms, for he was indeed a great admirer of Krynine. A Krynine trademark, which Folk acquired, was cartoonlike illustrations.

World War II had by now broken out, and though the regular coursework was an early victim, I continued my work—now directed toward publication of *Sedimentary Rocks*—originally designed to be another joint venture with Bill Krumbein. Again Carey Croneis steered us to a publisher, this time Harper and Brothers, for Carey had become editor of their newly established Earth Science series. Bill and I signed a contract. But shortly after, Bill left Chicago for war work and I was diverted to teaching of photogrammetry and work for the United States Geological Survey. But at war's end I went to work again on the book. Bill, in the meantime, had resigned his Chicago post to accept a job at Northwestern University; he lost interest in the book and bowed out. Under a revised contract the job was done by 1948. The book embodied my philosophy of the study of sediments. To my surprise, and at first to my dismay, I discovered that I had done myself out of a course. What could I say? Everything I would have presented in class was now in the book. Surely I couldn't stand in front of the class and repeat it chapter by chapter. The students were presumed to know how to read. So I made a radical change in my teaching pattern. The classes were now to be two hours long—in the laboratory. Each student had a thin section and a hand specimen from the same rock. A half hour would be spent studying the rock and the thin section, with a view to writing a description and interpretation. At the end of the half hour I quizzed the class on what they had seen (or not seen). The information thus obtained, cross-checked by everyone, was the basis for a written report to be prepared later. Then began a discussion on the significance or meaning of our observations. The obvious conclusions emerged, as did problems partially or wholly unresolved. Each student then put together all he had learned into an extended report. After a half-dozen sessions of this kind on a particular class of rocks, sandstones for example, I would devote a period to lecture and discussion of topics common to all—such as cements—beginning the discussion with what the students had seen. In this fashion we covered the sedimentary rocks, beginning always with firsthand observations, followed by an orderly marshaling of the facts using the observations as evidence for the conclusions to follow. The students learned to formulate the criteria for reconstructing the history of the rocks in question.

This was also the procedure in the field, to teach students to observe, to assemble the evidence, to reason from that to a conclusion, to recognize and formulate the unresolved problems. All this proved stimulating and I think an effective mode of teaching. No more lecturing—the "Bible method" of teaching, as my friend King Hubbert called it. Though this philosophy of teaching, the Socratic method some would say, was employed by Bretz, it was not the pattern at Chicago. I did not come to it all at once, but it remained with me until the end of my teaching career.

An aspect of sedimentation or sedimentology that I mentioned earlier is the stream table. These were in vogue when I came to Chicago and, as

I mentioned, it was presumed that I would have one—hence one reason for placing my laboratory in the basement. Some years later a stream table actually was installed in the basement of Rosenwald for Carey Croneis, who used it as a demonstration for the general physical science course he helped teach. The demonstration confirmed my view that such stream tables had minimal value—certainly none as a scientific experiment. This view was not held by many. I think W. H. Twenhofel at Madison had one; Ed McKee certainly did, and for many years he gave papers on the subject at the meetings. But all these stream-table experiments were naive and directed to the wrong objectives—to make deltas, meandering streams, terraces, and the like.

The first flume experiments that impressed me were those of Lucien Brush, who in 1958 used the big flume of the United States Geological Survey in Denver. In 1914 G. K. Gilbert had done some experimental work with the flume as a result of his investigation of the transport of debris from the alluvial mining in California. Gilbert's work was very good, and the Survey maintained the facilities for further research on sediment transport. Brush gave a short paper at the Saint Louis meetings of the Geological Society and showed a time-lapse motion picture of the formation and migration of sand waves as seen through the glass side of the flume. Here you could see with your own eyes how cross bedding was formed and how cross-bedded layers were superposed on one another. It was very dramatic, and for the first time I had a clear picture of how this structure formed. It was not the product of advancing microdeltas as some had claimed. But Brush's experiments were closely controlled—the parameters of flow were carefully measured, discharge, velocities, grain size, and such, were measured and recorded. The relations between bed forms, sedimentary structures, and flow conditions could thus be studied under rigidly controlled conditions. Kuenen's flume experiments with graded bedding were equally impressive, especially his motion picture of turbidity currents—a presentation he made at the meetings in Chicago in 1950. Well-controlled flume studies like these have been pursued in more recent years by A. V. Jopling at Harvard, J. R. L. Allen at Reading, and John Southard at MIT. Their work has shed a good deal of light on sedimentary structures and their relation to bed forms and flow conditions. This is a far cry from the earlier work with stream tables. Flume studies of the more recent sort presume considerable understanding of fluid mechanics, an ingredient wholly lacking in the earlier stream-table approach. Few geologists have the knowledge and skill to pursue these studies.

Early in 1950 I had a letter from Ph. H. Kuenen of the University of Groningen in the Netherlands. Kuenen was planning to come to Chicago for the meetings of the American Association of Petroleum Geologists and Society of Economic Paleontologists and Mineralogists, to be held in April of that year, and especially to participate in an SEPM-sponsored symposium on density currents—most of which we now call turbidity currents. The symposium had been organized by M. L. Natland, a micropaleontologist who had noted that some California sandstones—presumably shallow-water in origin—contained unquestioned deepwater Foraminifera. The sands must have been deposited in waters three thousand feet or more in depth. They also contained some forams of shallow-water habitat. Natland concluded that the sands were resedimented—redeposited—having originally accumulated in shallow water and having then been transported to waters of great depth. The presumed mechanism of transport was a density current—a current of water denser than the ambient waters because it was mud-laden—a turbidity current in modern parlance. The whole subject of density currents was a new one. Only a few years before, Daly had suggested that density currents might have cut the great submarine canyons. These astonishing features had long been a puzzle, and Shepard, Kuenen, and others had speculated about their origin. Kuenen, an inveterate experimenter, had set up an outdoor flume—in reality a canal—and had produced turbidity currents. Moreover, he had noted that such currents formed graded beds. Meanwhile C. I. Migliorini, a geologist from the University of Florence, had been making a field study of thick sequences of graded beds in Italy and had reached the conclusion that such beds were deposited not by ordinary bottom currents but by some unknown kind of current. Chance brought Kuenen and Migliorini together, and they wrote a joint paper on turbidity currents and graded bedding.

The point of Kuenen's letter to me was to inquire if I, as editor of the *Journal of Geology*, could find a place for this paper. Kuenen pointed out the timeliness of the paper; could I publish it so that it would appear just before the SEPM symposium? On seeing the paper I agreed, and by juggling the publication schedule I got it into the *Journal*. It proved a winner—a classic paper that turned our thinking around.

I had never met Kuenen, though I knew of him through his published papers. He was one of the few remaining "generalists," an imaginative, highly original thinker. His career began with the *Snellius* expedition of 1929/30 to the Dutch East Indies, where he acquired an interest in marine geology, which led to his study of submarine canyons, atolls, the rate and mass of deep-sea sedimentation, and eventually to his book *Marine Geology*, one of the first of its kind. But he is probably best known for his experimental studies; he was the Daubrée of the twentieth century. His first experiments reflect his earlier interests, the mechanism of foldings and ptygmatic folds, but he is better known perhaps for

Ph. H. Kuenen, professor of geology, University of Groningen, the Netherlands. Photo courtesy of L. M. J. U. van Straaten.

his experiments with density (turbidity) currents, a line of investigation he began in 1937.

Kuenen, accompanied by his wife, came to Chicago and spent a day with us at the university. He was tall, with a commanding personality, and spoke perfect English, with a British accent he owed to his English mother. The next day he presented his paper at the symposium. He also showed a short motion picture, in slow motion, of turbidity currents in action—currents generated in a smaller glass aquarium. The effect was sensational, and the turbidity current revolution was launched.

Kuenen's Chicago paper marked a turning point in his own research. He now devoted most of his attention to sedimentary deposits and their structures. Not only did he continue his studies of the flysch with its graded beds, but he became interested in their sole marks—assorted markings on the undersides of the turbidite sandstones—features long ago described in the Devonian of New York State by James Hall but little understood. But Kuenen also returned to experimental studies, this time on the abrasion of sand both by wind and water. Instead of a "tumbling mill" he used a circular flume.

Kuenen continued his scientific studies unabated until the death of his wife. This traumatic event led to deep depression, and his scientific studies abruptly ceased. In his last letter to me he seemed overwhelmed by self-doubts notwithstanding the many honors bestowed on him, including the Penrose Medal of the Geological Society of America. His depression proved intractable—a great pity, because Kuenen had one of the most imaginative and original minds of any geologist of his generation.

What seems so obvious to us now was totally revolutionary in 1950. Sands had always been considered shallow-water deposits, products of rivers and beaches. Moreover, the sands along the coastlines were confined to a near-shore fringe and gave way to silts and muds farther from shore. Graded beds were "old hat" to the Lake Superior geologists, who had crawled on their hands and knees to study the grading and determine stratigraphic order—the "way up" in vertical beds. Curiously, graded beds were not widely known to geologists in general. There is no mention of them even in formations such as the Martinsburg, where they abound. And even as good an observer as Ernst Cloos seems not to have noted them in the Wissahickon formation of Maryland. Not until I came to Hopkins were these pointed out, for I was very familiar with graded beds from my studies of the older Precambrian of northwestern Ontario. I had speculated on their origin. The thinner beds, a few centimeters thick, resembled the varves of some Pleistocene deposits; the thicker ones up to a meter in thickness could be "drainage varves"—those deposits formed in a single year by the sudden drainage of an ice-dammed lake. Moreover, thick sandy varves are known in these deposits of some areas. So I interpreted the graded Archean graywackes, with their interbedded slates, in the Sioux Lookout area of northwestern Ontario as year layers. One major flaw in this view was the absence of any associated ice-deposited material—till—or of any ice-rafted pebbles or cobbles, features found in the Pleistocene glacial beds. Kuenen and Migliorini's paper made it all clear. I had chosen the wrong model. Turbidity currents were the mechanism, not seasonal glacial melting. The age-old concept of equating sands, even coarse sands, with shallow-water deposition had died.

Kuenen's papers stimulated research, and graded beds—turbidites—appeared everywhere. Many went overboard and reported turbidites where there were none. Curious markings on the undersides of many turbidites, the sole markings—noted long ago by Hall in the marine Devonian of New York State were rediscovered and given close scrutiny. It became evident that these were paleocurrent features etched on the mud bottoms by the flow of turbidity currents and preserved as "casts" on the underside of the overlying sand bed. When I moved to Hopkins I set two of my students, Earle McBride and Norman McIver, to work on some of the turbidite formations of the mid-Appalachians—

the Ordovician Martinsburg and the Devonian "Portage." Outcroppings of these formations were plentiful in the nearby areas of Pennsylvania. Several years later, when Kuenen was in this country again, I took him and Preston Cloud out to see them, but in the midst of our trip a blizzard completely covered the outcrops. I also took Stan Dzulinski and M. Ksiazkiewicz, two well-known Polish geologists who had studied the turbidites of the Carpathian flysch of Poland, together with their escort, Bob Neuman of the United States National Museum, out to see the same exposures. A. Seilacher, of Tübingen, was another visitor to these exposures.

With the growing interest in sedimentary deposits there was a concomitant revival of interest in marine geology—a field much neglected after the pioneer studies by Murray and Renard of the *Challenger* expeditions. Francis P. Shepard was about the first American to show interest in the subject. Shepard had been a graduate student at Chicago under Rollin Chamberlin. He submitted a thesis on the Rocky Mountain Trench and received his Ph.D. in 1923.

I first met Shepard on a field excursion in Illinois. At that time he was teaching structural geology at the University of Illinois at Urbana. I was struck with his accent, which seemed to place him in the Newport set, and indeed he came from a wealthy family that owned a seagoing yacht. Despite the handicaps of such a heritage, Fran Shepard established himself as a marine geologist, using the family yacht as a base of operation. His early work brought sneers from the macho field geologists. Imagine spending your summers yachting and pulling up a bottom sample between cocktails! Tough life, no? But Shepard persevered—at first largely without any clearly defined goals—a description of the bottom samples of Cape Cod Bay or an extended description of the sediments on the Atlantic Shelf. But the pendulum swung his way, and marine geology was due for a revival.

At first Shepard was pretty much alone; only H. Stetson of Harvard kept him company. But in later years he was joined by Kuenen, W. H. Menard, K. O. Emery, Robert Dietz, Bruce Heezen, and many other marine geologists as well as by geophysicists and oceanographers.

Shepard became interested in submarine canyons, now depicted much more accurately with the sonic depth finder. This interest led to a more structured research program and brought him to the forefront. Now attached to the Scripps Institution, Shepard had the ship time and equipment he needed. His work had become respected. The subject of marine geology has now far outrun its early beginnings.

Shepard's 1948 book *Submarine Geology* is a readable, largely descriptive account of the subject. Now the field has become more esoteric, encumbered with equations and other embellishments. The field of

Francis P. Shepard, professor of marine geology, Scripps Institution of Oceanography, La Jolla, California. Photo courtesy of Francis P. Shepard.

oceanography, including marine geology, underwent a renaissance after World War II. It became much more than a study of bottom sediments and encompassed marine geophysics—gravity, seismic, and magnetic surveys. The new sonic depth finder made study of bottom topography infinitely easier, and waves, currents, and chemistry also came under scrutiny. These developments laid the foundations for the concept of plate tectonics, which was to overturn many cherished and hoary dogmas.

But to me the study of bottom sediments, despite improved coring techniques, was unappealing. In fact the whole trend among sedimentologists toward the study of modern sediments was unattractive. I did not see where these studies led; they were often a mere cataloging of data—collect samples and analyze the hell out of them. Grain size, grain shape and roundness, carbon content, oxidation-reduction potential, and a multitude of other parameters were plotted on appropriate maps and contoured. And so what? What did these papers do for me when I stood in front of an outcrop? Not much. Not until I became a consultant for Shell in 1952 and grew familiar with the work of Hugh Bernard, R. J. LeBlanc, and Robert Nanz on the Holocene sediments of Texas was I convinced of the value of the study of modern sediments, despite the often-quoted dictum "the present is the key to the past." But the Shell story belongs in the Hopkins chapter.

For all the years I lived at the edge of Lake Michigan, I never set sail upon it, nor did I become involved in a study of its sediments except for a very cursory look at the minerals of the beach sands from the southern part of the lake. My back was turned on the lake, and I faced toward the "hard rocks" of the Precambrian—an orientation to be repeated when I moved to Baltimore on the shores of Chesapeake Bay. But there was one exception.

I had a student, Jack L. Hough, who was an incurable sailor, and he wanted to study the lake sediments for a master's thesis. I rather reluctantly gave my approval. Jack fashioned his own tools—a gravity coring tube and a clamshell sampler—the latter made by carving a wooden model, then having molds made and the parts cast in a local foundry. To try these out we went to the marina at Jackson Park, rented a rowboat, attached my very small outboard motor—a one and a half horsepower Johnson weighing twenty-seven pounds—maneuvered around the anchored yachts, and passed out of the harbor and into the lake. The weather was clear, so we went about a mile offshore and cast the equipment overboard. The core sampler collected nothing; the snapper did sometimes pick up gravel, some quite coarse, though more often than not it too came up empty. But we continued, going north past Grant Park and the Planetarium, past Navy Pier, almost as far as Evanston. In places we picked up a pebble or two; more often nothing. Our cruise ended a few hours later, with minimal results. We didn't know at the time but found out later that we were trying to sample a very coarse lag deposit—a gravel pavement produced by winnowing out of the fine materials from the local boulder clay or glacial till. But Jack wasn't discouraged. His wife was the daughter of Anton J. Carlson, distinguished professor of physiology at the university. Carlson was a Swede from way back, and though he had come to the States many years before he never lost his Swedish accent. His Viking ancestry led to a belated investment in a sailboat, a very sturdy, broad-beamed craft, decked over with the cabin equipped with bunks, galley, and such for open-water cruising. Jack was the one Carlson had relied on for advice in buying and operating the craft, so he let Jack use it for his lake studies. Hough made several traverses across the southern part of the lake, collected many bottom samples, and completed his master's study. So in a sense I got involved with marine geology—albeit freshwater and by proxy.

In summary, my interest in sedimentary rocks began quite by accident—the accident of my appointment as an instructor at Chicago to teach, among other things, a course in sedimentation.

THE WINDS OF CHANGE

In 1937 Albert Johannsen reached retirement. He quit with alacrity; he had been looking forward to retirement so he could devote full time to other pursuits—his research and writing on the dime novel or more correctly, on the house of Beadle, one of the publishers of this form of literature. His interest in petrography waned after his four-volume work on the igneous rocks was published by the University of Chicago Press. I don't remember very well the faculty deliberations that led up to Norman L. Bowen's appointment, but evidently word had gotten around that Bowen was ready to leave the Geophysical Laboratory, where he had spent most of his professional career. The reason he gave for leaving was to introduce experimental petrology, especially the body of knowledge generated by the subject, into the universities. Up to this point the teaching of petrology had gone along much as before with little incorporation of the rapidly expanding new ideas generated by the work at the Laboratory. And in no university was comparable work being prosecuted.

Bowen's appointment, as Charles L. Hutchinson Distinguished Service Professor of Petrology, marked a turning point in the history of the department—the first real thrust forward since T. C. Chamberlin's retirement. Petrology was now wholly reoriented, away from the classification and nomenclature under Johannsen to petrogenesis under Bowen. Bowen's appointment was an omen of change—revolutionary change not only at Chicago but elsewhere, though that change had to wait until the end of World War II.

Bowen was a Canadian, a graduate of Queen's University at Kingston, who did his graduate work at Massachusetts Institute of Technology. In 1906 the Geophysical Laboratory of the Carnegie Institution of Washington was established to study the problems of mineral composition and the origin of rocks. The Director, Arthur L. Day, brought together a group of chemists, physicists, and geologists, and in 1910 Norman L. Bowen joined the group. His doctoral thesis was based on his work at the Laboratory, and in 1912 he received his degree from MIT. He remained at the Laboratory, except for a short interim appointment at Queen's, until he came to Chicago in 1937. He became one of a dozen or so distinguished service professors who were paid significantly better salaries than ordinary professors—$10,000 a year, as I recall.

Bowen required a laboratory to continue his research and to induct students into the art, and that condition was attached to his accepting the appointment. The university administration accepted the condition without batting an eye. So a laboratory—costing perhaps $10,000—was set up. Bill Schmidt constructed the furnaces, ancillary facilities, and all.

Bowen's work was on phase equilibriums, on simple systems at first, just two components. Mixtures in varying proportions were prepared, then a very small sample or charge was placed in a tiny envelope of platinum foil and placed in an electric furnace. Here it was held at a known temperature until equilibrium was achieved, then dropped into a dish of mercury to quench the material. The results were examined under a polarizing microscope to see what minerals, if any, were present. This type of study involved running a great number of mixtures at a great many different temperatures so as to locate the curve showing the course of crystallization. It was a purely empirical approach to mineral equilibrium. By working out many two-component mixtures, and later three-component mixtures, much light was shed on the course of crystallization of magmas and the origin of the igneous rocks. Bowen's book, *Evolution of the Igneous Rocks*, published by Princeton University Press in 1928, was a landmark in petrology; the great diversity of igneous rocks was explained by fractional crystallization of a common parent magma. His book had a profound influence on the younger generation of geologists because it emphasized the importance of sound understanding of the principles of physical chemistry that underlie rock formation. The reaction principle—expressed in Bowen's reaction series—was, according to Pentti Eskola of Finland, one of the most important contributions to petrology in the present century. True, the systems studied in the laboratory were very simple—two, three, or perhaps four components and in the early days anhydrous—but the work pointed the way to go.

So with Bowen's appointment—a distinguished service professor, a member of the National Academy of Sciences, and later recipient of the Penrose Medal and numerous other honors—the department regained national stature. But the war shortly interrupted its normal activities. Bowen returned to Washington and became involved in classified war research. But his return to the university after the war, brief as it was to be, led to even more profound changes in petrology and set in motion a development that can be truly characterized as a revolution—the coming of age of geochemistry and the profound restructuring of the curriculum in geology at Chicago—a change that afterward spread to nearly every graduate department in the United States. It all began at Chicago with Bowen's appointment.

Bowen himself was a very modest person; he was not a large man, rather less than average height. He was quiet-spoken, with a dry sense of humor and usually a quizzical smile. Bowen was something of a hypochondriac, always sure he had some serious illness even when medical evidence proved otherwise. He enjoyed field trips and, though he did no fieldwork himself, had, like most Canadian students, a good deal of earlier field experience in the Precambrian "bush." He willingly joined the departmental field excursions, which were mostly to the Lake

Norman L. Bowen, professor of petrology, University of Chicago. Photo by Julian R. Goldsmith.

Superior region. I first met Bowen in the summer of 1937 just before he came to Chicago. Edson Bastin was going to visit a student of his, B. T. Sandefur, who was working on the ores of the Cuniptau mine near Timagami, Ontario. Bowen and I joined Bastin and not only visited the Cuniptau property but went on to Kirkland Lake and to the Rouyn area in Quebec.

Bowen's soft-spoken manner was deceptive. He held strong convictions and was capable of harsh judgments. His criticism of H. L. Alling's book *Interpretive Petrology of the Igneous Rocks*, for example, was severe (see *Amer. Mineral.*, 1936, 21:813). Because his stature as a scientist was of the highest, he had the complete confidence of the university administration. Later, when he became chairman, university funds were as easy to get as they had been difficult under Bastin's chairmanship.

### THE WAR YEARS

With the outbreak of World War II the situation at Chicago changed. After Pearl Harbor the old pattern disappeared. The draft decimated the ranks of graduate students; classes dwindled. The university went to part-time operation. It undertook a program of war research, most notably the so-called Metallurgy Project, which proved to be a part of the larger Manhattan Project—in reality the development of the atomic bomb. The Physics Building and other parts of the campus were restricted areas, buildings were closed to the public and guards were posted. The areas closed included the stands at Stagg Field, the football stadium. What had been indoor tennis courts beneath the stands became a closed laboratory. The whole matter was secret, but it required no special savvy to guess the goal. Not metallurgists but the nation's top atomic physicists were involved. It was already known that the atom contained enormous energy; it was only necessary to find out how to release it. Clearly this was what all the fuss was about. And they did succeed, for it was under the stands at the football field that the first self-sustaining nuclear reaction was achieved.

The Geology Department played no role in this drama. But like other parts of the university we did assume new responsibilities. The nation needed maps and mapmakers. The United States itself, though the richest nation in the Western world and one of the most advanced, was inadequately mapped. There even were no good maps of much of our own coastline, to say nothing of remote areas of the world—now all potential theaters of war. So the government instituted a crash program. Air photographs made mapping a great deal easier and more rapid. But the art of converting an air photograph (a perspective view) into a map (an orthographic or other projection) was not widely known. The science of photogrammetry had been developed in earlier years by the Swiss, who carried their cameras to mountaintops and compiled their maps at leisure in the drafting room. The Canadians had experimented along similar lines and had mapped part of the Canadian Rockies in the same way. But with the advent of the plane the problem became one of constructing a map from pictures taken from an unstable camera station at an unknown or very crudely known location and altitude. The Canadians were able to develop methods for rapid reconnaissance mapping of the vast, nearly flat terrain of the Canadian Shield. The United States was somewhat behind the others in mapping techniques and experience and now had to catch up fast.

The university was asked to set up a program to train mapping technicians. Three courses were involved: photogrammetry, plane-table surveying, and map drafting. Since Jerry Fisher had taught plane-table mapping to the geologists for years, he had the experience and equipment and took on this course. Henry Leppard of the Geography Department took on map drafting. It fell to me to teach photogrammetry. My experience was nil; I had, to be sure, looked at some of the Canadian air photographs in my search for rock outcroppings to reduce the blind search on foot in the woods. To my surprise the theory and techniques of photogrammetry proved interesting, and the problems could be solved by graphic methods. Here a course I had taken years ago, descriptive geometry—a course in projections and the graphic solution of problems relating to them—proved invaluable. The essense of photogrammetry was to take a perspective projection and make an orthographic projection from it; just the reverse of the problem facing an architect, who takes the blueprints (orthographic projection) of a building and makes a perspective view of it for his client. I was fortunate to have Art Lundahl as my assistant.

We secured the known manuals, those of the Canadians and of the United States Army, and went to work. I taught the nine-week course several times to civilians—those who saw the handwriting on the wall and for patriotic or other reasons wanted to get into war work. The course was organized to teach the basics of descriptive geometry, then the fundamentals of their application to mapping techniques, the latter leading to actual construction of a map, each member of the class contributing a part. For the Canadian method with oblique photographs—those taken from a plane but showing the horizon, much like a view from a mountaintop—we used perspective grids on large glass plates. Each student drew one or more grids on paper, which were photographed down and printed as glass positives. The student would select the proper grid, superimpose it on his picture, and transfer details from grid to an orthographic net on another sheet of paper. For the vertical air photos then used in the United States, we followed the Department of Agriculture slotted template method. Bill Schmidt built a template cutter, and with a suitable collection of photos we assembled a map that scaled true despite considerable relief in the terrain being mapped. As the war effort intensified, the civilian classes were replaced by the Army Specialized Training Program (ASTP). But the fun went out of it. The army recruits were there not because they wanted to be but because they had to be. They marched in to class and marched out again, but the interest and zest were gone. To keep them on their toes and to keep close records on performance I had to give them a ten-minute written test every day. These were the so-called objective tests where one checks a word or number in a list of possible answers to each question—"multiple choice." Since I had a number of classes in succession with ten-minute breaks between, I soon discovered the same test would not work for all sections. To ensure original work, I would prepare a series of different tests that looked alike, but a minus sign on one was a plus on another. This was the hardest and least rewarding teaching I ever did. I was glad when it came to an end.

I looked about for somethng better than teaching photogrammetry to unwilling army cadets. An opportunity to join the United States Geological Survey and participate in its program in the Lake Superior region came at just the right moment. The initial work was to be in Iron and Dickinson counties in Michigan, the former being the most poorly mapped and understood of the various iron ranges. I applied for the Survey job and, after considerable negotiation and formalities, received my appointment.

## THE POSTWAR ERA AND
## THE REMAKING OF THE DEPARTMENT

At the close of the war changes came rapidly. In 1944 Bastin retired as chairman and professor of economic geology and moved to Ithaca, New York, where Cornell University provided workspace and library facilities. When Croneis resigned to become president of Beloit College in Wisconsin he was replaced by J. Marvin Weller. Weller was a tall, handsome chap who had worked for twenty years for the Illinois Geological Survey since getting his Ph.D. at Chicago. He was a biostratigrapher and had made a name for himself through his work on cyclothems—the sedimentary cycles in the coal measures of the Midcontinent fields (1930, *J. Geol.* 38:97–135). Actually these cycles had been discovered and well described in 1912 by J. A. Udden in his study of the Peoria Quadrangle. Weller refined Udden's work and broke the cycle at the base of the sandstone instead of the coal. Weller taught both paleontology and stratigraphy. Marvin started his work at Chicago with high hopes but soon became disillusioned and rather bitter about what he viewed as a general deterioration of the department—the teaching of highly specialized courses in esoteric subjects and the total neglect of the fundamentals of geology.

In 1946 W. H. Newhouse was appointed to replace Bastin in the field of economic geology. Newhouse had been at Massachusetts Institute of Technology for some time, essentially as successor to Waldemar Lindgren, but I gather he was unhappy there and had a falling-out with W. J. Mead, the chairman, so he was willing to come to Chicago. Bowen in the meantime had a letter from Tom Barth of Oslo indicating that he wanted to leave Norway and hinting, if not asking, whether there might be a place for him at Chicago. Bowen approached the faculty and raised the question of making Barth an offer. The faculty concurred, and in 1946 Barth was offered an appointment, which he promptly accepted. Bowen knew Barth personally, for Barth had spent some time at the Geophysical Laboratory. Barth was a typical, rather gaunt Norwegian. He had gone through the German occupation of Norway and had been affiliated with the resistance movement. He was a good geologist, with quite a bit of field experience. Barth had shuttled back and forth between Norway and the States, never seeming to make up his mind where he wanted to be. But he had a clear notion of where he thought geology should be going—to him geochemistry was the way. And America offered a better chance than Norway to achieve this goal.

Barth wanted to bring along B. Bruun, his chemical analyst, Kalervo Rankama from Finland, who was a geochemist and spectroscopist of the Goldschmidt tradition, Hans Ramberg, a student of Barth's who was interested in the thermodynamics of petrologic processes, and also Franz Wickman, a Swede of diverse interests less clearly focused. This was a big order. Would the university administration approve and provide the funds? Bowen obtained approval—a major shock to those of us who had lived through the Bastin era of austerity. Clearly the administration had confidence in Bowen. Rankama, Ramberg, and Wickman came as research associates on term appointments. But with the Scandanavian influx—to our dismay—Bowen resigned for reasons not clear to me and returned to the Geophysical Laboratory in Washington.

The department, faced with Bowen's resignation, had to find a replacement in petrology and a new chairman. The first problem was readily solved by the appointment of Julian Goldsmith, who was at this time working for Corning Glass. Goldsmith was well qualified to continue the work in experimental petrology, for he had been a student of Bowen's. But the chairmanship was a thornier problem. Bowen's resignation was very unsettling, as the search for a chairman always is. Bowen sounded me out; Would I accept the chairmanship? I declined with alacrity. Nothing could be further from my liking than the chairman's job. (Little did I know then that I would inherit the chairmanship at Hopkins!) After an interval of confusion and uncertainty, Newhouse was appointed.

It soon became apparent that Newhouse considered geology as currently taught and practiced at Chicago and elsewhere a decadent discipline. He had a low opinion of the *Bulletin* of the Geological Society of America, regarding it as largely worthless. If it contained a paper he approved, he tore out the relevant pages and put the rest in the wastebasket. He had an even lower opinion of *Geotimes*—"high school stuff." He was ready to sweep out all of "classical geology" and those who practiced it. He was much impressed by the avant garde in geology, though I don't think he understood much of it. Newhouse proved to be a disaster. He did not have the knack of working with a faculty of diverse interests, points of view, and philosophies. Newhouse was small and, as commonly happens with small men, he overreacted—he seemed almost paranoid at times. He was not able to accept disagreement or criticism and appeared very insecure. Within a short time the department became sharply polarized, a state of affairs from which it recovered only after

Robert Balk, professor of structural geology, University of Chicago. Photo courtesy of Christina Lochman-Balk.

half the faculty resigned or retired and Newhouse gave up the chairmanship.

Even before Bowen resigned the search had begun for someone to replace Rollin Chamberlin, now at retirement age. Negotiations were entered into with Robert Balk, then at Mount Holyoke College in Massachusetts. Balk was an Estonian, educated at Breslau (now in Poland), where he had been a classmate of Ernst Cloos and student of Hans Cloos. He was also a classmate of Karl Rode, whom I had known at Berkeley and with whom I explored the Henry Mountains of Utah in 1928. Balk was the Peter of the Peter and Paul team described in Hans Cloos's *Conversation with the Earth* (p. 351). Paul was Ernst Cloos.

Balk was a very friendly, outgoing person who loved geology more than anything else. He had come to the United States on a ticket provided by an uncle in New York. Arriving from war-torn Europe he was half-starved and penniless and without a job. He lived in a garret in New York City subsisting primarily on oatmeal. But he inaugurated a study of Duchess County, New York, and applied his considerable skills to the study of the rock fabrics—cleavage, schistosity, and lineations. He was the author of a Geological Society Memoir on structural petrology—the first book on the subject in English. He later obtained an appointment at Mount Holyoke, a women'scollege, where he continued his field studies on weekends and vacations. He worked for the United States Geological Survey in Massachusetts but eventually embarked on a field program in the Adirondacks, where he apparently worked alone in that wild and rugged terrain. He had prodigious energy. He married Christina Lochman, a Hopkins Ph.D. in paleontology, then teaching geology at Mount Holyoke.

Perhaps owing to a change in the chairmanship at a critical time, there was a breakdown in communications. Balk thought he had a firm offer and had resigned his Mount Holyoke post, as had his wife, but final action had apparently not yet been taken on his Chicago appointment. All this put Newhouse in a hole, and only after a lot of difficulty was the Balk appointment approved. Balk arrived in the fall of 1947. In my estimation he was a good choice, for he was a field geologist and provided good balance to the laboratory- and theory-oriented group at Chicago. Moreover, he was a disciple of Hans Cloos, who had introduced a new approach to structural field studies.

Balk's stay at Chicago did not work out. No doubt he felt out of place, out of step with the trend to geochemistry, but I think the problem ran deeper than that. I clearly recall one doctoral oral examination. The candidate was Morris Leighton, son of M. M. Leighton, himself a Chicago Ph.D. and then chief of the Illinois State Geological Survey. Young Leighton, mainly at my suggestion, had undertaken a study of the Mellon gabbro, a Precambrian intrusive in the Penokee region of northern Wisconsin and Michigan. Associated with the gabbro was a "red rock" differentiate of granitic or syenitic composition. Neither had been studied in any detail. Leighton spent a season or more mapping these rocks and followed his fieldwork by thin-section study of collected materials. Hal James of the United States Geological Survey and I spent a day in the field going over the area with Leighton. Hal's comment at the end of the day was that Leighton's work was first-class—a very good piece of work indeed. Balk was Leighton's adviser and hence a member of the examining committee, as was I. Newhouse was also present. Leighton presented his thesis and defended it well. At the end, while the candidate was out of the room, the committee reached its verdict—to pass Leighton even though Newhouse remarked that his study was "the kind of thing we are trying to get away from." I could tell by the look on Balk's face that then and there he concluded it was time to move. I felt the same way. In any event, Balk resigned and went to the New Mexico School of Mines at Socorro, only to meet a tragic death shortly after when his plane crashed into Sandia Mountain.

Bretz also retired about the same time, and in 1947 C. Leland Horberg was appointed his successor. Lee had come to Chicago a few years before from Augustana College to take his Ph.D. He was a physiographer, or geomorphologist as we say today, and a student of Bretz's. Lee was an excellent field man, skilled in landscape analysis, a very original and productive scholar. I had known him well as a student and later as a colleague. His career was tragically cut short by cancer.

When Newhouse became chairman, Rankama and Ramberg received faculty appointments; Franz Wickman returned to Sweden, To accommodate the new personnel and program, Rosenwald was extensively remodeled. A classroom had been converted by Bob Nanz to a laboratory for rock analysis while Bowen was still chairman. Johannsen's laboratory was cut in two; half went for a spectrographic laboratory for Rankama. I moved out of the basement into a second-floor laboratory made from a classroom.

Rankama was a tall, rather humorless Finn—very stiff-necked and with positive and rigid views. I was then editor of the *Journal of Geology* and had to deal with him. In keeping with the new spirit of the Chicago department, he thought the *Journal* should become a journal of theoretical geology—we should accept no more papers based on field studies. He also did not want any editor tampering with his manuscripts. Rankama was a tremendous compiler. He and T. G. Sahama had written a treatise on geochemistry (Goldschmidt variety), and while at Chicago they brought out a revised edition in English that was published by the University of Chicago Press.

Ramberg was a Norwegian but had been a student of Barth's at Oslo. He made a tremendous impression on Barth. Ramberg wanted to reduce petrology to thermodynamics. At the moment he was interested in diffusion, particularly diffusion and metamorphic differentiation, whereby rocks in the solid state seem to yield several unlike end products during metamorphism. Even granite might be such a product. Barth, who liked the concept, went so far as to explain large granite plutons as the product of a "cloud of ions." Newhouse was equally impressed with the new approach and regarded "classical geology" as passé. Ramberg was also rather humorless. The students sensed this and attempted to make up for the lack. At a talk Ramberg gave before the faculty and students, illustrated by lantern slides, the students inserted a few slides of nudes, *Playboy* style, into the series being projected. Ramberg was embarrassed and didn't know what to say; the students were greatly amused. Ramberg wrote *Metasomatic and Magmatic Rocks*. As the departmental representative of the faculty advisory committee to the University of Chicago Press, I was able to facilitate the publication of Ramberg's book as I had earlier done for the Rankama book.

The situation at Chicago had deteriorated badly. George DeVore and A. J. (Mike) Frueh were added to the faculty, DeVore to replace Balk.

Jerry Fisher was pushed aside, and his mineralogy courses were given to Mike Frueh and Ramberg. Frueh was a crystallographer, a recent Ph.D. from MIT whom Newhouse had known; DeVore was from the University of Wyoming and had worked with Newhouse in the field.

Faculty meetings were grim affairs. On one side sat Balk, Horberg, Fisher, Weller, and myself. On the other were Newhouse, Barth, Ramberg, Rankama, and eventually Frueh and DeVore. The polarization of the department put Shorty Olson in a difficult position. He tried with some success to maintain a neutral stance and with less success, to play the role of peacemaker. Perhaps because of his junior rank and newness of appointment, Goldsmith also maintained a discreet neutrality. It was apparent that Newhouse and Barth had decided on the next course of action; Newhouse announced the decision. We were presented more often than not with a fait accompli rather than a proposal for discussion. If we dissented Newhouse turned to his followers for backing; he always got it. The decisions further eroded support for field studies or field requirements and led to closing of the Missouri field camp, disposal of the Sainte Geneviève property, and dropping the Baraboo field course. They also decided to rename all the courses, to remove the stigma Newhouse fancied attached to the old names and to identify with the new avant-garde science. Petrology became thermodynamics of rock-making minerals, structural geology became tectonophysics, paleontology became paleozoölogy, and so forth. On one occasion some of us objected vigorously to one of Newhouse's decisions; the result was that Newhouse lost control of himself, stormed out of the meeting, and said, as he slammed the door, that he was resigning. But he did not give up the chairmanship while I was still there.

For me the final straw came shortly afterward. I had for many years conducted extended field trips to one or another of the iron ranges of Michigan, for reasons given earlier. The last trip was to be a joint effort with Heinz Lowenstam, who had now joined the faculty of the department. The group signed up was rather large; there didn't seem to be enough private cars, so we chartered a bus. But this added quite a bit to the cost, so I thought the department should contribute to the expenses—they would be shared by both the department and the students participating. I went to Newhouse to get the several hundred dollars required. Newhouse refused to approve the expenditure, pleading poverty; a week later he gave Ramberg $5,000 to build a calorimeter. That settled it. It showed all too clearly what the priorities were. At the first opportunity I would resign. Balk had already left; I did so shortly; and, not long after, Lee Horberg died. Lowenstam also left to join the Caltech group. Barth had already returned to Norway, and Rankama to Finland.

The Chicago department was depleted. The alumni were alarmed; What had happened? I never learned the full repercussions.

GEOCHEMISTRY

What brought about the "geochemical revolution"? A revolution it was. Before World War II very few, perhaps none, of the universities had geochemists on their faculties or offered courses in the subject. Perusing the programs of the annual meetings of the Geological Society reveals few or no papers on geochemistry. Today, however, there is a super-abundance of activity in the field—a journal, *Geochimica et Cosmochimica Acta*, a Geochemical Society with a plethora of sessions and symposia at the annual meetings, and at least one geochemist on every graduate departmental faculty. How and why did it come about? And where did it begin?

It began at Chicago, mainly in the immediate postwar years. But even before the war N. L. Bowen, with his great prestige, loosened the purse strings at Chicago; he brought the field of experimental petrology to the university. From a niggardly $1,600 for nonsalary items, the Chicago department's expenditures went up by an order of magnitude. Bowen's laboratory was established and equipped, as was a laboratory for rock analyses. Yet it might all have stopped there but for two further circumstances. One was the arrival shortly after the war of Tom Barth, who had visions of a geochemical institute and who brought along Kalervo Rankama, a spectroscopist and geochemist of the Goldschmidt type, B. Bruun, a chemical analyst, and Hans Ramberg, whose forte was thermodynamics and rock-forming processes.

But there was an additional and most important circumstance. During World War II, research related to the war brought together the nation's top nuclear physicists and chemists. After the war Robert Hutchins boldly offered them faculty status and positions in the several new institutes created at that time: the Nuclear Institute, the Institute of Metals, and the Institute of Radiobiology. Hutchins made this move without having in hand the funds to underwrite this commitment. So regardless of his pronouncements about science and his love for Thomas Aquinas, Hutchins turned out to be one of the best friends science could have at Chicago. Among those who accepted Hutchins's offer were Harold Urey, Claire Patterson, Harrison Brown, Willard Libby, Clarence Zener, and Cyril Smith. Only Smith and Zener were bona fide metallurgists, and they were theoretical rather than applied in orientation.

Of all these, Harold Urey was most significant. More than the others

Harold Urey, professor of chemistry, University of Chicago, and students. Lower left, Cesari Emiliani; lower right, Gerald Wasserburg. The young woman, Sybil Kochen, was a lab technician. Photo courtesy of the University of Chicago Archives.

he had a real, wide-ranging curiosity about geology. Urey was the only one who came over to Rosenwald—came into your office to inquire, to learn, to try out a new idea. There was a never-ending freshness about his approach to problems. The real creative mind is, I believe, one that can link seemingly unrelated things in a new way. Urey had this ability, coupled to a fertile imagination that provided the stimulus. He attracted students from geology, students like Jerry Wasserburg and Harmon Craig.

Isotopes had been discovered just a few years before—both radioactive and stable isotopes—and, as has often happened in science, new developments in one field or discipline spilled over into another. So it happened at Chicago. Urey was then studying the distribution of the stable isotopes of oxygen and their possible use as a geothermometer. Libby had studied the carbon isotopes and saw possible geochronological applications—carbon 14 age dating, an achievement for which he was awarded the Day Medal by the Geological Society of America. Harrison Brown was interested in the age and composition of meteorites and the mantle of the earth. Interest developed in geochronology and the use of the various isotopes, K/A, Sr/Rb, and Pb/Pb for determining mineral ages. Claire Patterson worked on lead and the age of the earth. Urey was also interested in the chemistry of the planets and their satellites—especially the earth/moon system.

All these activities involved geological materials, so it was natural that interaction and communication developed between these chemists and the geologists—especially Tom Barth and his colleagues. Joint seminars and colloquiums were common; students, mainly geologists, crossed over and learned the techniques of mass spectrometry. Jerry Wasserburg became a student in Urey's laboratory and worked on the K/A method of dating. Urey and associates turned to the geologists for samples and geological data. Heinz Lowenstam left the Illinois Geological Survey to become a geological associate assisting in Urey's paleotemperature research.

In short the situation at Chicago, fortuitous though it was, provided the climate for a major expansion in teaching and research in geochemistry unrivaled anywhere else at that time. Chance had brought together a group of exceptionally brilliant minds. The atmosphere was electric, mutually stimulating, and creative. Urey, Libby, Samuel Epstein, Wasserburg, Brown, Craig, and Lowenstam were all elected to the National Academy of Sciences. But the integrity of the group was short-lived, for the geochemical revolution at Chicago was soon exported to Caltech. In 1950 Chester Stock, then chairman at Caltech, died and Bob Sharp assumed the chairmanship. Under his leadership the department reassessed where it was and where it wanted to go. Vertebrate paleontology, Chester Stock's field, was dropped. According to Sharp, Al Engel and Ian Campbell urged the addition of a geochemist. They consulted with Linus Pauling, distinguished chemist and Nobel Laureate then at Caltech, who suggested going after Harrison Brown. So Brown left Chicago and joined the Caltech faculty, to be followed in short order by Sam Epstein, C. R. McKinney, and Claire Patterson. A few years later Heinz Lowenstam and Jerry Wasserburg followed. The raid placed Caltech in the forefront of the field.

The whole development of the program at Chicago was greatly helped along by—probably could not have happened without—the Office of Naval Research and later the National Science Foundation, which underwrote the purchase of the equipment needed and funded the research programs themselves. Departments were obliged to find laboratory space, to alter buildings designed for other purposes, to purchase X-ray diffraction equipment, mass spectrometers, and ancillary apparatus, and to hire "chambermaids" to keep the whole thing going. A revolution had indeed taken place.

There were, of course, other developments elsewhere. Bob Garrels at

Northwestern, and later at Harvard, developed "cold water" geochemistry—the study of geochemical processes in aqueous solutions at low temperatures. One of my students at Chicago, Ray Siever, went to Harvard to study with Garrels. Ray felt that the next step in the study of sedimentary rocks was best achieved by understanding the chemistry of the processes that led to the formation of the "chemical" sediments and the diagenesis of sedimentary deposits in general. At the conclusion of his work under Garrels, Ray was appointed to the Harvard faculty. K. Krauskopf at Stanford was in the game early on, but the roster in this early period was small and most of it concentrated at Chicago, spreading later to Caltech and eventually everywhere. The development of "cold water" or sedimentary geochemistry was also linked to the resurgence of oceanography and modern sediment work. Among those active in this field were Gustaf Arrhenius and E. D. Goldberg. But the real pioneer in the subject, was Carl "Papa" Correns, who did more than anyone else in the thirties. He was, however, very much alone; the real push came in the postwar era. Geochemists were in great demand. Isotope geology was the rage, and mass spectrometers became commonplace. Papers on geochronology, geothermometry, and mineral equilibria flooded the journals and the programs of the annual meetings.

| | 95 | 1900 | 05 | 10 | 15 | 20 | 25 | 30 | 35 | 40 | 45 | 50 |
|---|---|---|---|---|---|---|---|---|---|---|---|---|
| **PALEONTOLOGY** | | | | | | | | | | | | |
| Vertebrate | | | | Williston | | | | Romer | | Olson | | |
| Invertebrate | | | Stuart Weller | | | | | Croneis | | | J.M. Weller | |
| Paleobotany | | | | | | | | Noe | | | | |
| **SEDIMENTATION** | | | | | | | Bretz | | | | | |
| **SEDIMENTOLOGY** | | | | | | | | | | Pettijohn | | |
| **GEOMORPHOLOGY** | | Salisbury | | | | | | Bretz | | | | |
| **GLACIAL GEOLOGY** | | | | Atwood | | | | MacClintock | | Horberg | | |
| **STRUCTURAL GEOLOGY** | Van Hise | | | Leith | | | | R.T. Chamberlin | | | Balk | |
| **ECONOMIC GEOLOGY** | | Penrose | | | Emmons | | | Bastin | | | | |
| **PETROGRAPHY PETROLOGY** | | Iddings | | | | Brokaw | | Johannsen | | Newhouse / Bowen | | |
| **CRYSTALLOGRAPHY MINERALOGY** | Iddings | | | | | Brokaw | | Fisher | | Ramberg | | |
| **GEOCHEMISTRY** | | | | | | | | | | Frueh / Goldsmith / Rankama | | |
| **GENERAL AND HISTORICAL** | | Salisbury | | | | Bretz & R.T. Chamberlin | | | | Barth | | |
| **GEOPHYSICS** | | | | | | | | | | | DeVore | |
| **GENERAL AND COSMOLOGY** | T. C. Chamberlin | | | | | | | | | Cook, Riley | | |
| **FIELD GEOLOGY** | | Salisbury / Atwood | | Trowbridge | | S. Weller | | Bretz / Croneis | | | Horberg | |

Geology faculty, University of Chicago, 1893–1952.

Where does this leave us? At Chicago the explosion of geochemistry dazzled Newhouse, who, though not a part of it, was overawed by the field and those who pursued it. I have noted the results—a downgrading of what was termed "classical geology," a renaming of the courses in the department, Rankama's feeling that the *Journal of Geology* should be a journal of theoretical papers only and that those based on field studies should be rejected, Newhouse's decision not to fund, even in a very small way, field excursions but to buy a calorimeter costing ten times as much, and a general "putdown" of field studies as "something we are trying to get away from." The rush to be fashionable led many other schools down the same path to a greater or lesser degree. Stratigraphers, paleontologists, and mineralogists were replaced by isotope chemists, specroscopists, geochemists, and the like. They dropped field courses and many other "traditional subjects" such as map reading and plane-table surveying. They became, as Ernst Cloos described it, like a dough-nut—a lot of exotic fields around the periphery and nothing in the middle. Hopkins, contrary to the trend of the times, kept its equilibrium and was able to blend the newer realms of geochemistry with the core subjects of geology and train students who were at home in both. It was one of the few schools to do so.

# 8

## Hopkins: A New Beginning
## (1952–Present)

I had resolved to leave Chicago, but the problem was when and where. Where could one go without seeming to move downward? For the first time in my life I was at a loss: I had never had to look for a job and was uncertain how to go about it. Fortunately a solution again presented itself. I received a telephone call from Ernst Cloos of Johns Hopkins University in Baltimore. He was going to be in Chicago and would like to drop in to see me at my office—nothing was said about a job. I had become acquainted with Cloos when we were both members of the Council of the Geological Society of America in the late forties. In fact we had been forced to share hotel room on Times Square when the Hotel Pennsylvania (later the Statler) was overbooked.

In a day or two Ernst Cloos turned up, along with Aaron Waters, whom I had not met though of course I knew him by reputation. Ernst was not coy. He simply informed me that I had been appointed a professor at Hopkins! Ernst had learned something of the Chicago situation from Robert Balk, for Cloos and Balk had been classmates at Breslau years before and were close friends. J. T. Singewald, Jr. had just retired at Hopkins, and the president, Detlov Bronk, had given Cloos the chairmanship and also a mandate to upgrade and rebuild the department. Hopkins had a long and distinguished tradition in geology, but, as sometimes happens, it had become rundown and somewhat second rate. It was indeed in need of rebuilding. Cloos had persuaded Aaron Waters, who was disenchanted with Stanford, to join him in this effort. Together they made their plans—to secure Jim Gilluly and me. To cut red tape, Cloos persuaded the Academic Council at Hopkins to act on the appointments even before he made contact with the prospects.

After my initial surprise I agreed to consider the Hopkins offer seriously and set a date to visit Baltimore. I admitted a deep dissatisfaction with the Chicago situation, but even so one does not lightly resign a tenured professorship at Chicago.

I flew to Baltimore early in March 1952. Ernst met me at Friendship Airport, and I saw Baltimore and Johns Hopkins University for the first time. It was raining and mild and must have been so for some time, since the grass was the greenest of green and the earliest spring flowers were out. It was a welcome contrast to the drab and chilly landscape of Chicago.

Hopkins is housed in a group of Georgian buildings on a city campus, but one marked by large open spaces and wooded patches of giant beech and tulip trees. The grounds are well manicured and very attractive. The buildings were designed to harmonize with the Homewood House, a one-story Georgian-style dwelling built in 1803 by Charles Carroll, one of the signers of the Declaration of Independence. The university itself, founded in 1876 by Johns Hopkins, a Baltimore merchant, moved to the Homewood campus in 1916. Geology occupied Latrobe Hall, originally constructed as a civil engineering building, along with the Maryland Geological Survey and the Civil Engineering Department.

My visit to the department was a letdown. Latrobe was a dimly lit, depressing place with creaky wooden floors. The classrooms were shabby; the laboratories ill equipped. Collections were stored in a motley array of wooden cases; the laboratory tables and chairs were equally shabby and mismatched. There was, however, a good departmental library with a librarian, and there were Ernst Cloos and Aaron Waters and also J. D. H. Donnay, crystallographer and mineralogist. Donnay, however, held a joint appointment with chemistry and had his office and laboratory in Remsen Hall, the chemistry building. But the contrast between Latrobe at Hopkins and Rosenwald at Chicago, the latter with its new laboratories and equipment, was striking. Latrobe had a rundown late nineteenth century look about it—rolltop desks and all.

The next day was clear and sunny and very springlike. Cloos and Waters drove me to Annapolis, where we boarded the *Maurey*, the research vessel of the Chesapeake Bay Institute—a Hopkins institution focused on a study of the Bay. They presumed I would be interested in doing some work on the sediments of the Bay, so we spent a delightful day on the water and saw the operation of sample collecting with a free-fall coring tube and the like. The cook on board served a generous lunch.

On the last day of my Hopkins visit Cloos took me to President Bronk to talk about the future of geology at Hopkins. I was struck with Bronk's small stature, but what he lacked in size he made up in energy; he clearly saw that to build a department, or a university, you needed to lay hands on the best scholars in the country—or abroad, for that matter. Nothing definite came out of the meeting except the promise to meet my needs for a laboratory, since Hopkins had no laboratory or equipment for a sedimentologist and no sedimentary rock collection. But such a laboratory would be forthcoming and equipped according to my specifications, ready for classes in the fall. In the end I did no more than promise to consider the offer and to make a decision within ten days after my return to Chicago.

I did not go to Newhouse or the dean but agonized over the problem by myself. My wife was quite ready to pull up stakes and cut our ties of more than twenty years. A week later I accepted the job and wrote a letter of resignation. The move clearly was not a promotion—it was a move sideways at the same salary, then $8,500 for an academic year, and a move from a well-equipped laboratory with a rock collection built up over twenty years to the promise of a laboratory and no rock collection. Shorty Olson, then secretary of the department at Chicago, who handled all the routine business, graciously let me take my teaching materials, both thin sections and rock specimens, with me to Hopkins. This was a big help in getting started.

In May my wife and I drove to Baltimore, spent a week house hunting, and ended up buying a house still under construction. At that time of year Maryland was at its best. The pink dogwood and the azaleas were out everywhere. It was breathtaking. The area is one of rolling wooded hills, occasional rock outcroppings, and beautiful homes—a far cry from the endless row houses and walk-up apartments of Chicago that I had endured for twenty years. The prospects of a suburban house and garden in a tranquil area some fifteen minutes' drive from the university was a pleasant prospect. The problem now was to sell our Chicago row house—a difficult task. Since it was in a "changing neighborhood," even though adjacent to the Chicago campus, there were few interested parties and no bank or other financial institution would underwrite a mortgage. Time came for Hopkins to start, so I had to go to Baltimore and leave my family behind. My wife persisted and through her own efforts finally found a buyer who was able to swing the deal. Our move was completed, though we were delayed a little longer until our Maryland house was finished. By Thanksgiving we were in our new home.

The shift to Hopkins turned out to be one of the best moves I ever made. True the facilities and equipment were at the start antiquated and inadequate, but—as I soon learned—it was the spirit of the place that counted. The whole milieu at Hopkins was a great contrast to that at Chicago. Cloos and Waters were field-oriented; Cloos took his classes into the field every weekend. And what a field area we had! The crystalline rocks of the Piedmont were exposed on the campus—along the Piedmont streams, the Gunpowder, the Potomac, the Susquehanna. Then there was the Blue Ridge and beyond that the Great Valley with its limestones and dolomites and the folded Appalachians—the Ridge and Valley province—at most an hour's drive away. Moreover, the department had a field camp—a converted Appalachian mountain farm, log cabin and all—hidden in the Bear Pond Mountains. It provided overnight accommodations and served as a summer field camp.

Clearly fieldwork at Hopkins was an integral part of geology, not "something we are trying to get away from." I never regretted my move. The change of scenery, the friendly atmosphere of the place, and the warmth and enthusiasm of Ernst Cloos made all the difference. Gone were the hostility, the put-downs and the tensions of the last years at Chicago. I had a chance to start a new career—to see the magnificent Paleozoic sequence, Cambrian to Permian, well exposed in the Appalachian Mountains.

In 1952 Hopkins had a small geology department with a faculty of six: Ernst Cloos, J. T. Singewald, Jr., J. D. H. Donnay, and Harold Vokes, professors, and G. A. Anderson and Tom Amsden, associate and assistant professors respectively. By the time I arrived things had changed: Singewald had retired; Anderson, denied a professorship, had resigned; and Aaron Waters was on board. With the arrival of Hans Eugster several years later the department grew to seven, but there it remained.

THE HOPKINS TRADITION

Geology at Hopkins had a long and honorable tradition. Shortly after Hopkins opened its doors it became one of the leading schools for the study of geology—especially petrography. What was this tradition and how did it come about? When Hopkins was founded in 1876, the stir caused by Gilman's coming to Baltimore and launching a real university was great. Daniel Coit Gilman built his university on the German model—a true university, a community of scholars in pursuit of knowledge—not an academy or college. At first there were no undergraduate students as we now know them, and even after undergraduates were admitted graduate studies dominated the Hopkins scene. In 1952 there were still as many graduate students as undergraduates.

Geology at Hopkins began when George Huntington Williams was appointed to give instruction in mineralogy in 1883. He soon advanced to professor of inorganic geology, and he was joined four years later by William Bullock Clark. Clark taught stratigraphic geology and paleontology. Clark, like Williams, was a product of the German universities and understood the meaning of scholarship.

George Huntington Williams was unquestionably the outstanding member of the department during its formative years. Despite his very short time at Hopkins, 1883 to 1895, cut short by his death at thirty-eight, Williams made Hopkins *the* place to study petrology, for he brought to America the new technique of thin-section study of rocks under the polarizing microscope. Williams had studied at Heidelberg, where he received his doctor's degree, summa cum laude, under the famous German petrographers H. Rosenbusch and F. Zirkel. Owing to Williams, Hopkins quickly became the leading school, and for a time the only school, giving instruction in microscopic petrography. In a very short time Williams had gathered a group of students who in turn became leaders in the field. Even after Williams's death, others still came to Hopkins to study petrography, so great was its reputation in the field. Williams accomplished much in a short time. He was an indefatigable collector; his collections are still an important asset at Hopkins. He was a true scholar in the best Germanic tradition and was able to impart this tradition to his students. His own publications, including monographs, were numerous. Williams did much to establish the igneous origin of the dark schists in the Appalachians and the Lake Superior region and thereby to eradicate the last vestiges of Wernerism.

Upon Williams's death, Clark became head of the department. At the same time E. B. Mathews was appointed instructor to take over the work in petrography. Mathews not only had been a student of Williams but, like Williams, had also studied under the German masters. Harry Fielding Reid also joined the faculty to give instruction in geological physics, and a few years later E. W. Berry joined the group. So, despite the loss of Williams and the youthfulness of its faculty, Hopkins remained a strong department. Three members, Clark, Berry, and Reid, were eventually elected to the National Academy of Sciences. But it was mainly H. F. Reid and E. W. Berry who gave Hopkins its stature.

Reid had taken his bachelor's degree at Hopkins in 1885 and his Ph.D. in 1890. After ten years of teaching mathematics and physics, first at Case in Cleveland and then the University of Chicago, he returned to Hopkins and remained until his retirement in 1930. His early years were spent in the study of glaciers, a pursuit that took him to Switzerland and Alaska; in Alaska he explored the Muir glacier and discovered and named several others, including the Gilman and Hopkins glaciers. Later his interests shifted to seismology and the study of earthquakes. He was a member of the commission formed to study the San Francisco earthquake of 1906, and as a result of this work he formulated his elastic rebound theory of earthquakes—perhaps his most famous work.

E. W. Berry was the most colorful member of the early faculty. He lacked any formal education beyond high school, and after a checkered career he ended up in newspaper work. Berry was self-educated in both botany and paleobotany. As a result of a chance meeting with W. B. Clark, then head of the department, Berry was appointed assistant in paleontology in 1906 at a salary of $500 a year. Berry proved a prodigious worker and was soon firmly established at Hopkins, where he later became professor, then dean, and ultimately provost. He was known as the "degreeless dean," for indeed he had no degree of any kind. Berry's seminars were famous and well remembered by all participants. He was a disciplinarian, and nobody was spared, not even the high and mighty. Jim Gilluly has remarked that no other person had a greater impact on his education and subsequent career. I saw Berry only once, at the Pick and Hammer show in Washington. This show, an annual event, pokes fun at the Survey brass and any others deemed worthy targets. This particular show had a skit, a song and dance act, about the Berrys of Baltimore—the elderberry and the gooseberry, father and son. The impersonation was very good—glasses with black ribbons and all.

There was one other member of the early department who was, perhaps, the best known in the Baltimore community itself—C. K. Swartz. He entered the university in 1884 and received his bachelor's degree in 1888, then dropped out of school because of his health. He later entered Oberlin Theological Seminary and received the bachelor of divinity degree in 1892. whereupon he became a parish minister. Some years later, in 1904, he returned to Johns Hopkins, where he received his Ph.D. He then joined the faculty of the college as instructor in geology. He was then forty-four, and he continued his career as collegiate professor until his death in 1949. I mention Swartz's career because even when I came to Baltimore in 1952 his reputation as an eloquent lecturer was still fresh in the minds of many who had attended his exceedingly popular classes. He was not well known as a scientist, but undoubtedly he was the outstanding teacher of his time—perhaps unexcelled before or since. His career spanned nearly the whole history of the university, from its founding almost until my arrival in 1952.

As might be expected, the department attracted many students, some of whom became well known themselves. Among these were Albert Johannsen; A. C. Lawson, whose Rainy Lake study was in part his Ph.D. thesis at Hopkins; George Otis Smith, later director of the United States Geological Survey; U. S. Grant, head of geology at Northwestern University; W. S. Bayley, petrographer; Wendell Woodring, paleontologist; Florence Bascom, one of the first women to receive a Ph.D. in geology; and also Charles Keyes, who used his wealth to finance his *Panamerican Geologist* and his personal vendettas. Others who studied at Hopkins but went elsewhere for their degrees included Frank Dawson Adams, H. Foster Bain, and Jim Gilluly.

After its initial period of preeminence, the department had slowly slipped into mediocrity. By the start of the Second World War Clark and Williams were long gone; E. W. Berry was retired, as was Mathews, Williams's successor. Swartz, former minister, had also retired, as had H. F. Reid, eminent seismologist. Latrobe had become shabby; the department was ill equipped to pursue geology in the forties.

The situation was much like that at Chicago during the thirties. As with Chicago there was a brilliant beginning when the university opened, followed by a replacement of the original department by its own graduates and a gradual decline in stature. In 1943 Joseph Theophilus Singewald, Jr., had become the chairman. He was a Hopkins product, having received his Ph.D. in 1909. Like some of his predecessors, he had traveled and studied in Germany. Joe was outspoken, frank, and utterly honest, but he was also frugal, a trait that saved the university money but proved detrimental to the welfare and advancement of the department. Singewald was like Bastin at Chicago, generous to a fault but parsimonious with university funds. To secure approval for even small expenditures one had, as Ernst Cloos expressed it, to present a lawyer's brief. He had, as Ernst Cloos also pointed out, the wrong approach to spending money. It is not the chairman's job to save university funds; it is his job to spend them wisely. But under Singewald's leadership the department had not only ill-equipped classrooms and laboratories but also a less than first-class faculty. But there were two notable exceptions—both immigrants to America—J. D. H. Donnay from Belgium and Ernst Cloos from Germany.

Donnay started his career in mining engineering at the French-speaking university at Liège, then came to Stanford, where he became a geologist. After getting his degree in 1929 he worked in French Morocco as a petroleum geologist. In 1931 Donnay joined the Hopkins faculty as an associate in mineralogy, but he left Hopkins in 1939 to accept a professorship at Laval University in Quebec. Apparently the move to Laval did not work out, and Donnay wanted to return to Hopkins. To make this possible he had to accept a split appointment as professor of mineralogy and crystallography, supported equally by Chemistry and Geology. He did so in 1945. Donnay was small, endowed with a good sense of humor, and a demanding teacher—the most methodical, most logical, and most exacting. He demanded rigorous thinking and was indeed a good disciplinarian. All geology graduate students went through his courses in crystallography and mineralogy, which screened out those of marginal capabilities. Donnay was a true scholar, with the highest standards, and demanded the same of the students. He was respected by his peers and served as president of the Mineralogical Society, which later awarded him its highest honor, the Roebling Medal. He was also president of the Crystallographic Society.

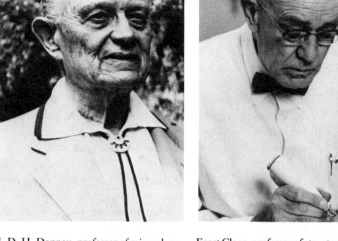

J. D. H. Donnay, professor of mineralogy, Johns Hopkins University, 1981. Photo courtesy of J. D. H. Donnay.

Ernst Cloos, professor of structural geology and chairman of the Department of Geology, Johns Hopkins University, 1952. Photograph by R. W. Linfield.

Donnay had been married a second time to Gabrielle Hamburger—also a crystallographer with a Ph.D. from MIT, where she had been a student of Martin Buerger. She had established a reputation as a scientist and secured a post at the Geophysical Laboratory in Washington. She was later elected to the Hopkins Society of Scholars. I think she had a somewhat low opinion of geology and geologists, which she expressed as "Astrology is to astronomy what geology is to geonomy." Her opinion of the science was, I might add, shared by others. This was just another way of expressing the belief that only by becoming quantitative and mathematical would geology become a science—a naive and simplistic view of the matter.

Ernst Cloos was beyond all doubt the outstanding scholar in the Hopkins department. Cloos came to Hopkins in 1931 from Germany, where he was educated. He took his Ph.D. at Breslau, where he was a pupil of Hans Cloos, his older brother. Ernst had come to America to study the fabric of the granites of the High Sierras in California, and on his way home he stopped in Baltimore and was offered a lectureship. He remained for the rest of his life. At first he had no space of his own but sat at a desk in the office of E. B. Mathews and had to endure Eddie Mathews's cigars.

Ernst had tremendous enthusiasm and energy, He soon fell to work on the crystalline rocks of the Piedmont and eventually those of the Blue Ridge Mountains and the Appalachians. He loved fieldwork and believed the field was the only proper place for a geologist. He even taught his class in structural geology in the field—all day every Saturday. The last outcrops were seen by the headlights of the cars.

Cloos soon became well known in American geological circles. He was the authority on mid-Appalachian geology and became active in the National Research Council, being chairman of the Section on Geology and Geography, and also in the affairs of the Geological Society of America, of which he eventually became president.

In 1952 Detlov Bronk, then president of Johns Hopkins, asked Ernst to become chairman of the department after the retirement of J. T. Singewald. Geology at Hopkins underwent a renaissance and became a distinguished department. Five members of its faculty, including Cloos himself, were elected to the National Academy of Sciences, though only three were at Hopkins at the time of election. This is a record unequaled in any geology department anywhere or in any other Hopkins science department. For about ten years the department attracted a larger number of National Science Foundation fellows than any other geology department and achieved a high status in national surveys, yet it was not half as large as the smallest of the more distinguished departments. It was housed in an old building, somewhat improved from the Latrobe Hall of 1952, and did not have the popular gadgets of the times—no mass spectrometer, no electron microprobe or electron microscope, and a minimum of technicians. It had only a single handyman and, for many years, only one secretary.

GEOLOGY AT HOPKINS

With the appointment of Aaron Waters and myself the department was not enlarged, since we were in a sense replacements for Singewald who had retired and Anderson who had resigned. Nor were the program or facilities greatly altered. Waters was one of the top petrologists of the time, albeit a "classical" petrologist. He taught an excellent course, and attracted many first-rate students; he brought two with him when he came to Hopkins: Jim Moore and Cliff Hopson. Among his other students were George Fisher, Hans Schmincke, Don Swanson, Carter Hearn, Don Lindsley, and two French Canadians, Pierre Sauve and Gilles Allard. Waters himself had been at Stanford for many years, then with the United States Geological Survey during the war, after which he returned to Stanford. But Stanford enrollment in geology had mushroomed, and the outlook was for assembly-line teaching, with

Aaron C. Waters, professor of petrology, Johns Hopkins University, 1952. Photo by Gayla Myers.

which Waters felt very uncomfortable. He was therefore delighted to come to Hopkins where he could work more closely with his students. He did a superb job of teaching petrology. He continued his work on the Columbia River basalts, and many of his students worked on these or related problems. Waters regularly attended the meetings of the Geological Society of Washington, often accompanied by a carload of students. In part because of his Washington contacts, we had many guest speakers from both the Geological Survey and the Geophysical Laboratory: Bill Bradley, Bill Rubey. Bill Pecora, and Phil Abelson among many. Very commonly after Journal Club meetings the faculty and speaker were dinner guests of Joe Singewald at his home on Tunbridge Road in Homeland—they invariably had filet mignon. Joe was a genial and very generous host. After dinner the students were invited, and when the faculty retreated to another room they had free access to the speaker, along with beer and pretzels.

Upon my arrival I became very busy putting together my program in sedimentology—getting the laboratory into shape, building a sedimentary rock collection, and having thin sections cut to supplement the meager collection I brought from Chicago. I also went out every week with Ernst Cloos and his class to learn what I could about the Piedmont, the Blue Ridge, and the folded Appalachians—a region vastly different and infinitely more exciting than the flat, drift-covered plains of Illinois.

In reality the facilities changed very little. Laboratory space was obtained by subdividing large drafting rooms once used by the civil engineers. Engineering was undergoing a change at Hopkins—it was now "engineering science," and the usual things such as surveying and drafting were discontinued. My laboratory and that of Aaron Waters were carved out of a room previously occupied by the departmental library, which had been moved to a still larger drafting room. The old incandescent lights were replaced by fluorescent fixtures, the creaky wooden floors were covered by asphalt tiles, and in due time the building was changed from direct to alternating current. Cloos bought a good many steel cases to store the new collections and to house the old Williams mineral and rock collections previously stored in the heating tunnel beneath the building.

But basically the department remained the same, both in size and in program. The faculty, six in all (Cloos, Waters, Donnay, Vokes, Amsden, and myself), met regularly for lunch at the faculty club. It was here that we discussed and settled departmental matters. Of course problems were also discussed at other times by two or three of us, but, unlike the situation at Chicago, the faculty did not just meet to hear what had already been decided. Our course of action usually was taken by consensus.

But the science of geology was rapidly changing; geochemistry had come of age, and a veritable revolution was in progress. The "geochemical revolution" finally caught up with Hopkins as it had elsewhere—first at Chicago in the forties, then at Caltech, and finally nearly everywhere. In 1956, when Ernst Cloos was on leave in Europe on a Guggenheim Fellowship, Aaron Waters was acting chairman. Waters invited Hans Eugster to come over from the Geophysical Laboratory in Washington once or twice a week to teach a course in geochemistry, based mainly on the experimental petrology that had been pursued at the Laboratory since the days of N. L. Bowen. A couple of years later Hans was persuaded to join the department at Hopkins full time. The university administration concurred, and Eugster was soon established in a laboratory on the third, or "attic," floor of Latrobe. Thus geochemistry began at Hopkins. But, unlike the case at Chicago, geochemistry did not expand by elbowing out field geology.

Hans Eugster, like N. L. Bowen, had been brought up on field geology. Hans had mapped the rocks of the Alps in his native Switzerland and done fieldwork in the Labrador Trough in Canada. Even though he was now an experimental petrologist, he never lost sight of the rocks and was an enthusiastic supporter of the field program at Hopkins,

Hans P. Eugster, professor of experimental petrology, Johns Hopkins University, and student, Ron Spencer. Photo by William Denison. Hopkins field party. Left to right: J. J. Reed (from New Zealand), C. A. Hopson, and George W. Fisher. Excursion to Bear Island in the Potomac River.

leading some trips himself. Hopkins had succeeded where Chicago had failed, in creating a successful blend of field, laboratory, and theory. With very few exceptions, Hopkins students were equally at home with thermodynamics or on an outcrop. Geochemistry had become an important part of Hopkins research and teaching without detriment to field geology.

But the changes did not end with the arrival of Eugster or the extensive remodeling of the top floor—once the workplace of many graduate students—with all its rewiring, heavy-duty air conditioning, new laboratory benches, electric furnaces, and ancillary equipment. Phil Abelson, then director of the Geophysical Laboratory, proposed a lecture series to be jointly sponsored by the Laboratory and the Department of Geology, to be held in Latrobe. I believe the Laboratory provided funds to secure speakers once a week. The lectures were then collected and published in 1959 by John Wiley as *Researches in Geochemistry*.

One of the papers included in the volume was by Charles Milton, on the minerals of the Eocene Green River formation of Wyoming. Bill Bradley had done a great deal of work on the geology of these beds, but it was Milton who looked into their interesting mineralogy. Abelson asked Eugster to review the paper before publication. Hans saw at once that one could go beyond cataloging and describing the minerals; one could look at the mineral assemblages in terms of phase equilibriums, just as one would look at a mineral assemblage from a metamorphic or igneous rock. After some discussion Hans Eugster and Charlie Milton revised the paper as a joint publication. Thus began Eugster's interest in the nonmarine evaporites. As it happened, however, the concept expressed in this paper, and by many earlier workers, was based on the presumption that the Green River evaporites were the products of a perennial salt lake. Later examination in the field clearly showed that the lake had been intermittent, more akin to a playa than a perennial lake. Eugster was soon convinced, and with R. C. Surdam he wrote a revised interpretation. Clearly sedimentology comes first, geochemistry second. Eugster's interest in the nonmarine evaporites expanded and consumed much of his time thereafter. He and his students worked further on the Green River and on Saline Valley and Searles Lake in California. Eugster himself went to the Rift Valley of Africa to study Lake Magadi, another trona-depositing lake. Here he became involved in the chert problem, which in turn led to a renewed interest in iron formations. He later studied Lake Chad in the Sahara and some high-altitude salt lakes in Bolivia. Together he and L. A. Hardie reexamined the Miocene salt deposits of Sicily; they too turned out to be deposits of an ephemeral lagoon and strandline environment. All these studies led into the question of the origin of the brines as well as their crystallization.

It soon became apparent that the program needed someone in the field of "cold water" geochemistry. So Owen Bricker, a student of Garrel's, joined the faculty in 1964 and remained until 1975. G. M. Lafon and Abe Lerman were also involved for shorter periods.

Another consequence of the program in geochemistry was the need for greatly expanded financial support—for travel to remote places as well as larger and more expensive laboratory facilities: an X-ray diffractometer and other laboratory hardware. National Science Foundation grants were the principal source of funds, though some support was provided by the Petroleum Research Fund and NASA. The era of grants and grant proposals had arrived. Before 1957, when Eugster first came, the department received no grants other than the small sums, usually under $1,000, available from the Geological Society of America or Sigma Xi. Grants suddenly became much larger; the departmental total was at least two orders of magnitude greater.

The program in geochemistry and the funding it generated attracted many students, both post- and predoctoral. Among those were Al Turnock, W. Gary Ernst, George Skippen, L. A. Hardie, K. B. Halferdahl, Bevin French, Blair Jones, J. Stephen Huebner, and Frank Kujawa.

Unlike geochemistry, geophysics had a long history at Hopkins. Instruction in the subject began with the appointment of Harry Fielding Reid, who joined the Hopkins faculty as professor of geological physics in 1895 and taught that subject until his retirement thirty-five years later. His course, first listed as "geological physics" but later changed to "dynamic and tectonic geology," dealt mainly with what we now call geophysics, with some structural geology thrown in. He is best known, perhaps, for his elastic rebound theory of earthquakes. When the university moved from downtown to the Homewood campus in 1916, its first building, Latrobe Hall, was constructed to include a free-standing pier that extended down to bedrock, on which was to be placed a seismograph, though I am not sure whether such an instrument was ever installed.

When Reid retired in 1930 instruction in geophysics lapsed, to be revived a few years later by Ernst Cloos, who taught the subject until about 1949. Cloos often taught two courses, one on the principles of geophysics and one on applied geophysics. He was especially well qualified to teach the latter, since he was on the first field party to succeed in using seismic refraction techniques to locate salt domes in the coastal plains of Texas and Louisiana. This work was done by Seismos G. m.d.

H. of Hannover, a geophysical company founded by Lutger Mintrop, for the Gulf Oil Company. Geophysical exploration for oil was launched.

Instruction in the subject lapsed again, except for a brief period in 1954 when it was given by Edward Byerly, son of the California seismologist Perry Byerly. It was resumed with the arrival of Bruce Marsh in 1973.

William Bullock Clark was the first to give instruction in paleontology at Hopkins. He was, in fact, professor of organic geology—just as George Huntington Williams was then professor of inorganic geology, the two of them constituting the whole department. Clark was more than a paleontologist; he also taught what he called "applied geology" a subject akin to what we now call "engineering geology," as well as the first course in "economic geology," the geology of both the metallic ores and the nonmetals. Perhaps his interests in those subjects stemmed in part from his being the first state geologist. He was appointed to this job at the inception of the Maryland Geological Survey, established by an act of the State Legislature in 1896 and housed on the Hopkins campus. The work of the Survey was by necessity of an applied or practical nature. When E. W. Berry was appointed Clark turned most of the work in paleontology over to him but reserved for himself the course in historical geology. Historical geology was the essence of geology, since geology was conceived of as the "history of the earth and its inhabitants." All else was contributory to the unraveling of that history. Geology was then much more history-oriented, not so process-oriented as now. In the first part of this century paleontology was largely concerned with taxonomy and classification—systematic paleontology and research centered on the description of the faunas (or floras) of a specific group of strata or an extended review of the structure and makeup of a given order or family or even genus. Under Berry's leadership this is what paleontology at Hopkins was all about. Berry himself was interested in plant fossils, a field that set Hopkins somewhat apart from other schools of that time. Berry was a most prolific scholar—he has more than five hundred titles to his credit.

The first real change in the direction and scope of paleontology came with the appointment of Dave Raup in 1957. Raup was, for that time, a most unusual paleontologist. He tackled new fields, investigating the crystallography of echinoids—the optical orientation of the plates of the calyx—using the universal stage and the polarizing microscope. He explored the laws of growth exhibited by the shelled invertebrates. He even went so far as to generate shell forms by computer by varying the parameters of the growth spirals, a considerable advance over D'Arcy Thompson's pioneer work on shell growth and form. Raup's approach to the subject is best expressed in the book, *Principles of Paleontology*, he and Steve Stanley wrote in 1971, which went far to change the course of paleontology and give it new life. Both were at Rochester at the time, Raup having left Hopkins shortly before. But this new or revitalized paleontology returned to Hopkins when Stanley was appointed in 1969. Those who now pursue the subject prefer to call it paleobiology so as to disassociate themselves from the systematists and biostratigraphers.

A. Seilacher joined the faculty as lecturer for only one year, 1963. He was a most stimulating fellow, interested in the relations between organisms and sediment and in tracks and trails, or "trace fossils," including their life positions and habitats and their burial. We tried to keep Seilacher, but this proved difficult because of his visa problems. In the meantime he was offered the professorship at Tübingen, the top position in paleontology in all of Germany. After a protracted interval of indecision he declined the Hopkins offer and accepted the Tübingen job. This was a blow to Raup, who then resigned and went to Rochester. After a short interval Steve Stanley joined the faculty; recently Bob Bakker, the dinosaur man, was added.

Hopkins had a long tradition in economic geology. As I noted, W. B. Clark taught a course in the subject. Upon the appointment of J. T. Singewald, Jr., in 1908, courses in ore deposits were listed in the catalog. Joe continued to teach the subject until his retirement in 1952, forty-four years later. Singewald himself was active in the field, participating in the Hopkins expedition to the Andes and serving as consultant to various mining companies.

The Andean expedition of 1919 was underwritten by the family of Professor Williams and was known as the "George Huntington Williams Memorial Expedition." Singewald investigated the copper, silver, and mercury deposits of Peru and Bolivia; Berry studied the floras of the associated strata. The first three issues of the newly established *Johns Hopkins Studies in Geology* were devoted to the results of the Andean studies. Singewald's Peruvian ore collection is still stored in the heating tunnel.

Singewald was a member of the Society of Economic Geologists and for many years was its treasurer. Much of the work on ore deposits was then descriptive—a review of the principal deposits of the various metals, history of discovery and production, classification of the deposits, and a lesser attention to the processes of ore deposition. The content and scope of economic geology was essentially that embodied in the texts of the day, those of Emmons and Lindgren. With Singewald's retirement, instruction in the subject ceased and was revived only briefly when George Brimhall was at Hopkins in the 1970s.

Petroleum geology, which became a field in its own right when the petroleum industry was stimulated by the mass production of automobiles, was given little attention at Hopkins. A course in the subject was taught by Anderson from 1941 to 1951, but it ceased altogether with Anderson's resignation.

When Hopkins went over to the central library system and the new Eisenhower building opened, we lost our departmental library and librarian. We did, however, keep some books to be placed in a "reading room," which ultimately became a bootleg library. Dr. Leslie Gay, personal physician and close friend of Singewald, donated funds to equip a room in Latrobe to house these collections. It was called the Singewald Reading Room. Singewald's own bound journals, especially *Economic Geology* and the *Bulletin* of the American Association of Petroleum Geologists, formed the nucleus of the collection. To these were added others donated by Quentin Singewald, John Brown, and various members of the faculty.

When I arrived in 1952, training in field methods and geologic mapping was given during the summer at an established field camp, Camp Singewald, in Washington County in western Maryland. This camp had only recently been acquired. Since about 1945 Ernst Cloos had given formal summer instruction in field geology, operating out of a log cabin in the Bear Pond Mountains. He was then working on the geology of Washington County for the Maryland Geological Survey. During the course of this work he found a ten-acre bottomland Appalachian farm, with a log house and a few small outbuildings, and was able to secure funds for its purchase from alumni and friends of Joe Singewald. This became Camp Singewald. The hand-split shingles were covered with corrugated metal roofing, electricity was brought in, and water was electrically pumped from a well and piped into the lean-to kitchen added to the old log house. Thus a permanent field station was established. Additional funds from both the alumni and Joe Singewald made possible the construction of two additional buildings—a dormitory and a classroom building with student drafting tables, acquired when the drafting program at Homewood was dismantled. These buildings were cinder block with steel casement windows and corrugated metal roofing. But the camp never became plush; the privies of the mountain farm remained. Cleaning them out periodically was a chore shared by all, including the camp instructor.

Before the summer field program established by Cloos, instruction in field geology had been handled in an irregular manner. Mark Secrist taught courses in the subject at Homewood during most of his tenure at Hopkins. Before that Reid had offered courses in "exploratory surveying" that perhaps grew out of his own explorations in Alaska. Even Mathews at one time taught a course in field methods. But all of these

Hopkins students at "Siebert's pasture," Washington County, Maryland. Hopkins field camp (Camp Singewald).

were given in the classroom, not the field. Weekly field excursions were part of the Hopkins program from its inception; these were often followed by a week-long excursion at the end of the academic year, a transect of Maryland from the plateau in the west to the coastal plain in the east led by Professor Swartz. Joe Singewald also took his students on a week-long visit to one mining district or another.

Field study has thus been an integral part of the Hopkins program, though Hopkins did not have a field camp until late in its history. George Huntington Williams had a clear understanding of the relation between laboratory studies and fieldwork. Though a prime mover in establishing microscopic research on rocks in America, he wrote, "The writer is not aware that the most ardent advocate of the study of petrography (microscopical or otherwise) considers this branch as more than an aid to geological research. Divorced from field observations it becomes unreliable and trivial." And he concluded, it is "the acknowledged duty of every petrologist to be at the same time a field-geologist, and to study his material in the laboratory in the light of his own observations in the field." Very good advice, and as relevant today as it was one hundred years ago.

Another aspect of Hopkins that sets it apart from other schools and has been an important factor in its program in geology has been its proximity to Washington and the Geological Survey. This has made possible a close liaison with the Survey and also the Geophysical Laboratory of the Carnegie Institution and the Smithsonian. From time to time Hopkins has had guest lecturers from these institutions, and in some cases Survey personnel have filled in and taught courses at Hopkins. In 1895, for example, G. K. Gilbert gave two lectures a week for three months on physiographic geology; in the same year Bailey Willis lectured twice a week on stratigraphic and structural geology. Even in more recent years courses were taught by Washington guests, as, for example, when Thomas Gibson of the United States Geological Survey gave the lectures in paleontology and stratigraphy. Raup had resigned and his replacement, Steve Stanley, was not yet on board.

In some cases doctoral dissertations were done under Survey auspices; in other cases the facilities of the Washington institutions were made available for graduate student research. John Graham's landmark study of magnetism in sedimentary rocks was done at the Department of Terrestrial Magnetism.

The Hopkins program in geochemistry was helped immeasurably by the cooperation of the Geophysical Laboratory; Hans Eugster first lectured in geochemistry at Hopkins while he was still on the Laboratory staff. Later Hopkins students and faculty worked at the Laboratory for shorter or longer periods. George Fisher was at the Laboratory before he returned to Hopkins.

In many cases students, especially those whose theses were Survey sponsored, went from Hopkins to employment by the Survey and to a lifetime career. In other cases Survey personnel could retain their Survey positions and commute to Baltimore to work toward the Ph.D. Examples of the latter include M. I. Goldman, R. F. Black, and R. William Bromery. Conversely, some of the Hopkins faculty have had part-time Survey appointments and worked both for Hopkins and the Survey, as for example, Waters and myself. The school's proximity to Washington has made a difference.

In looking back at the Hopkins story one is struck by several things. First, the Hopkins Department of Geology has always been very small, consisting of only two persons in the earliest days and never more than six until about 1957, when the total was seven. Despite its size it had an enviable reputation. Three of its earlier faculty were members of the National Academy of Sciences—Berry, Clark, Reid—and three in the sixties were academicians—Eugster, Cloos, Pettijohn. Two others, Water and Raup, were elected after they had left Hopkins.

Also noteworthy is the long tenure of the early faculty and the much shorter tenure of those in recent years. Singewald had the longest unbroken association with Hopkins—fifty-seven years, from his A.B. degree in 1906 to his death in 1963. Reid was a member of the faculty for thirty-five years. There has been much greater instability since World War II. Is it that there is less loyalty to institutions today? People seem to switch allegiance without a qualm.

Looking back, one is struck with the general stability of the curriculum. Its basic components were mineralogy and petrology, geophysics and structural geology, paleontology and historical geology, and economic geology (ore deposits). Instruction in field methods and actual field studies, both informal and formal, were part of the Hopkins program. The most significant changes were the recognition as separate subdisciplines of sedimentology in 1952 and geochemistry in 1957. With the introduction of the latter there was a significant change in facilities, courses, and prerequisites. There were also changes in the manner of teaching and content of the older program—in petrology and mineralogy in particular, and in more recent years in paleontology and structural geology. Economic geology or ore deposits was abandoned, as was paleobotany.

## SEDIMENTOLOGY AT HOPKINS

Before I arrived in 1952 there was no regular instruction in sedimentology, though once or twice Anderson had taught a course in sedimentary petrography. Nonetheless it was at Hopkins that Goldman received his training. Marcus Isaac Goldman received his degree in 1913; his thesis dealt with the sediments of the Upper Cretaceous of Maryland. This study was later published as "The Petrography and Genesis of the Sediments of the Upper Cretaceous of Maryland" in the *Cretaceous* volume of the Maryland Geological Survey in 1916. It was a landmark paper, a prime example of how sediments should be investigated, unparalleled elsewhere in America at that time and not often matched today. I first encountered it in 1927 as a student in G. D. Louderback's seminar on sedimentation at Berkeley. Louderback chose it for reading and discussion as a model to be emulated.

Goldman was a very unusual student. He had studied with A. W. Grabau at Columbia, where he became interested in sediments. He spent some time abroad and visited J. Thoulet at Nancy and Lucien Cayeux at Paris, two of Europe's leading authorities on sediments and sedimentary rocks. He also consulted Johannes Walthur at Halle, and he acknowledged their aid in teaching him how to study sediments. He traveled extensively and participated in the excursions of the International Geological Congress at Stockholm as well as in those made when the Congress met in Canada in 1913. Some years after I came to Hopkins I found some of the collections Goldman made on these excursions, and these have been incorporated into the Hopkins collection of sedimentary rocks. Clearly, when Goldman entered Hopkins in 1911 he was well prepared to make his study of the Cretaceous sediments. He unquestionably became America's leading sedimentary petrographer.

When I arrived in Baltimore I fell to work at once, going on every field trip that came along—collecting furiously—and teaching a group of interested students. I also began work on a revision of my Harper book, *Sedimentary Rocks*—a book that had proved very popular. Revision is perhaps the wrong word, for I was unable to patch here and there; I had to rewrite the whole book beginning with page 1. The second edition came out in 1957, five years after I moved to Hopkins; a third edition appeared in 1975.

It was not until I left Chicago that I got seriously interested in paleocurrents, a term applied to ancient currents of wind or water (or even ice), now vanished, that left a record of their direction of flow in the rocks. The impetus came from Paul Potter's work on the Caseyville sandstone of Pennsylvanian age of the Illinois basin. To be sure, there had been some earlier studies of cross-bedding, one of the first being that of Rubey and Bass, who mapped the cross-bedding in a channel sandstone of Cretaceous age in Kansas. Also notable were Shotten's work on the Lower Bunter sandstones of England and Parry Reiche's work on the Coconino Sandstone of Arizona, but curiously the potentialities of the subject did not sink in until Potter did his work on the Caseyville in 1953.

Paul Edwin Potter (left) and the author.

Paul Edwin Potter was both an undergraduate and a graduate student at Chicago in the early post–World War II period. He was originally from Cincinnati, and after a hitch in the military during the war he turned up at Chicago. Paul is tall and very outspoken. His bachelor status has given him more freedom to travel—to North Africa and Brazil in particular. At Chicago he became interested in sedimentology and did a commendable job on the Pleistocene Lafayette gravel of western Kentucky, in which he measured, among other things, the cross-bedding.

The impact of Paul's Caseyville study, however, was diluted by its being attached to an analysis of variance, an aspect worked out with Jerry Olson, another Chicago student. The emphasis on the latter tended to overshadow the cross-bedding study and put it in the role of preamble. Potter had become interested in statistical methods as applied to sedimentary data and took a year's leave of absence from his job with the Illinois State Geological Survey to pursue the subject at the University of Illinois in Urbana.

But even before I left Chicago I had had George Brett, a graduate student, study the cross-bedding of the Precambrian Baraboo quartzite of Wisconsin. Like Potter, he made many field measurements, the result of which was a paleocurrent map showing the current flow pattern during deposition of the quartzite. Unlike Potter, however, Brett had to take into account the rotation of the cross-bedding during the folding of the quartzite. The Caseyville is still in its original horizontal position.

The unique feature of these studies is the measurement of the cross-bedding and the construction of a paleocurrent map showing the direction of flow at each outcrop. Every field geologist had seen cross-bedding; almost nobody has measured its attitude; fewer still have mapped its orientation, though Henry Clifton Sorby did all this over one hundred years ago. But he published almost nothing about it.

Upon coming to Hopkins, where the whole Appalachians with many well-exposed and cross-bedded sandstones were at my back door, I set students to work. Bern Pelletier was the first. He tackled the Pocono formation, a thick, resistant sandstone of Mississippian age, one of the two ridge-makers in the region. He studied all aspects of the formation, but measurement of cross-bedding was the most important element in his study, producing a paleocurrent map and paleogeographic reconstruction. Lloyd Yeakel did a similar job on the Silurian Tuscarora quartzite, the other ridge-making formation in the central Appalachians. This study was followed by others, including Larry Meckel's work on the Pennsylvanian Pottsville formation and Bob Adams's study of the Loyalhanna. We also made studies of the turbidite sandstones and their sole markings, another paleocurrent indicator; Earle McBride worked on the Ordovician Martinsburg formation and Norman McIver on the Devonian "Portgage" beds.

The many student theses on the Paleozoic sandstones of the central Appalachians ultimately led to the problem of provenance and source area—in short, to the question of Appalachia. It had long been observed that the Paleozoic sediments were thickest in the Appalachians—that they thin out to the west into the interior of the continent and that the coarser clastics wedge out and pass into shales or limestones westward. These observations led to the conclusion that the sediment source lay to the east. To this hypothetical source Schuchert had given the name Appalachia.

As our work progressed, beginning with Bern Pelletier's study of the Pocono, it became clear that the cross-bedding and other primary current structures did indeed indicate east-to-west flow of the depositing currents during the Paleozoic—just the reverse of that of the present-day streams. But John Whitaker, one of Ernst Cloos's students, noted that the cross-bedding of the Weverton, an early Cambrian quartzite, recorded a west-to-east transport. And one of my students, John Glaser, showed from cross-bedding analysis a similar west-to-east transport of the sands of the Lower Cretaceous Potomac formation. Clearly the early Paleozoic and Cretaceous sands were derived from the interior of the continent; the mid- and late-Paleozoic sands came from an eastern source. There had been two dramatic reversals of flow.

But the concept of an eastern landmass, Appalachia, was being challenged. It was argued that the so-called Gulf Coast geosyncline was filled by sediment derived from the bordering continent; on the other side was open ocean—no need for an offshore landmass. Marshall Kay though conceding that some sediment was derived from the east, downgraded Appalachia to an island arc, a chain of volcanic islands. Our study of the sandstone, like those of Krynine, however, did not support a volcanic source. The volume of sediments was too great, and their composition was incompatible with an island arc source. The mineral composition of most of the Paleozoic sands indicated derivation from older sedimentary and low-grade metamorphic rocks, not volcanic rocks. Robert Dietz, in an article in the *Journal of Geology* (1963), went so far as to eliminate Appalachia altogether and consider the whole Appalachian accumulation a great continental terrace derived wholly from the continent or craton. According to his model, some of the earlier deposits were deformed and uplifted to form a tectonic ridge. The debris from this was shed back westward to form the later Paleozoic clastics, a kind of Kilkenny cats mechanism. But during the earliest Paleozoic the continental interior was covered with carbonate deposits and thus armored or plated, so this area could hardly have been a source for the Paleozoic clastics.

Kuenen had also wrestled with a similar source land problem. At Menton, on the French Mediterranean coast, he noted that the flow direction in the Cretaceous and Oligocene of the Maritime Alps was from south to north—from the Mediterranean toward the land. The presumed source land must have been where there is now only deep water. He believed, therefore, that the landmass had foundered—had sunk beneath the waves. To geophysicists this was an impossibility—to have lighter material sink into denser crust was a violation of the principle of isostacy.

The enigma appears to be resolved by the theory of plate tectonics. According to this concept Africa was, in the middle and late Paleozoic, joined to the east coast of North America. It was the eastern source of the sediment that filled the Appalachian trough. In early Paleozoic time there was an ocean, the predecessor of the Atlantic, that closed as Africa approached and collided with North America. In Triassic time the movement was reversed; rifting occurred along the junction, and Africa and North America split apart and were separated by a new Atlantic, widening as the continents drifted apart to their present positions. The paleocurrents and sandstone mineralogy made sense; the earliest from the west before collision, and again from the west after separation.

In the meantime Potter and I discussed the possibility of a book on the whole subject, bringing together all the literature on directional properties—on cross-bedding, sole marks, grain fabric, and the like. The book was to do for directional structures what Bob Shrock's book had done for the criteria of stratigraphic order—the criteria for "way up" in tilted beds. Ernst Cloos had done something like this with his Geological Society Memoir on lineation. But we hoped to do more than just describe and explain these structures. We hoped to show how they might be applied to sand bodies and to the sedimentary basin as a whole—to basin analysis. What do they tell us about the filling of the basin—its paleogeography—about the source lands? And so *Paleocurrents and Basin Analysis* came into being.

To carry out the project, Paul applied for and was awarded a Guggenheim Fellowship. He resigned his position at the Illinois Survey and came to Hopkins, where we spent a fruitful year on the project. This work demanded a thorough search of the literature; it forced us to evaluate the whole subject, assessing its worth and its relation to many other aspects of geology. We came to see its many possibilities.

One of our concerns was to find a publisher who would produce a quality book that would do justice to the photographic plates. McGraw-Hill heard about the project and sent us a contract. We needed to be convinced they could do the job, so we took the train to New York to discuss the matter with them. We submitted several photographs and asked them to make specimen plates. But Professor Clifford Truesdell of the Mechanics Department at Hopkins, knowing of our work, suggested we get in touch with Springer-Verlag, a well-known German publishing house. We sent them the same photographs. Springer's work was superb, so we signed a contract with them. The book, published in 1963, was well received; the plates had a quality seldom, if ever, seen in an American book. Apparently the timing was right, and paleocurrent studies became commonplace. The work stimulated reexamination of current structures in general and led to study of the dynamics of their formation. The paleocurrent volume was successful enough that a second edition appeared fourteen years later.

In the course of our work on the book, Potter and I had assembled a large collection of photographs of sedimentary structures, only a few of which were used in the paleocurrent volume. We conceived the idea of publishing these as an atlas. Springer was receptive to the idea, and the atlas became a reality: *Atlas and Glossary of Primary Sedimentary Structures.* The plate captions were in four languages, and we added a glossary in English, German, French, and Spanish. Again Springer did a beautiful job. In the meantime Potter left Hopkins to accept an appointment at Indiana University at Bloomington.

Plate tectonics—the concept of large mobile segments of the earth's crust, a revived and modified version of continental drift—has truly revolutionized geologic thought, affecting all branches of geology. It is the most profoundly revolutionary concept of this century. Hopkins played a role in its evolution. One of the key elements in the concept is paleomagnetism. Many rocks acquire a weak, albeit measurable, magnetic polarity, a property induced by the earth's magentic field at the time these rocks were formed. The orientation of this polarity gives an accurate fix on the position of the magnetic pole of the earth at the time of their formation. One of the first to investigate paleomagnetism, was John Graham, a geology graduate student at Hopkins. It was during the forties that John collected his oriented samples in the Appalachian area and elsewhere; these he took to Washington, D.C., to the laboratories of the Department of Terrestrial Magnetism, where with the proper equipment he could measure the orientation of their weak residual magnetism. Graham wanted to find out if the initial magnetism of a newly deposited sediment was permanent. If so, it should be possible to determine how the direction of the earth's magnetic field has varied through geologic time. To solve the problem Graham measured the magnetic poles of samples taken from various parts of a folded bed; these were then rotated around the fold axis to their prefolded positions—he unfolded the bed. They were found to have a common orientation, showing that the magnetism was acquired before folding. The procedure is now commonly referred to as the "Graham test" (1949, *Geophys. Res.* 54; 131).

Graham's work laid the foundation for studies of paleomagnetism—studies showing that the earth's magnetic pole has been in vastly different places in the geologic past, at times even near or on the present equator. This observation led to the concept of polar wandering. But for theoretical reasons the magnetic pole should coincide with or be near the pole of rotation (geographic pole). The notion of a wandering pole was therefore dismissed as impossible, or certainly most unlikely. The pole could not move, physics said, so Graham must be wrong. Moreover the paleomagnetic results were internally inconsistent—the pole position determined for a given period was not the same with samples taken from different continents. Graham's work was received with a good deal of skepticism. According to Cloos, even Merle Tuve, director of the Department of Terrestrial Magnetism, advised Graham that he was "wasting his time." As it turned out, the continents wandered, not the pole. Graham's early work is now given the recognition and respect it deserves.

In 1964 I received a letter from the Alberta Geological Society at Calgary asking me to organize a conference—actually a week-long short course—on sandstones. The course would be offered in collaboration with the University of Alberta and conducted at the Banff School of Fine Arts during May—after the ski season and before the summer programs began. Kuenen had been asked to organize this venture but had declined and suggested my name. The course, to cover all aspects of the subject, was designed mainly for petroleum geologists who had been out of school for some time and were not conversant with recent advances in the subject. I was interested and consented to come if I could persuade both Paul Potter and Ray Siever to join me. I felt that Potter and Siever could handle some aspects much better than I. So it was agreed, and the short course was set up as scheduled. Registration exceeded all expectation, and we had to limit the class to sixty. I had never been to Banff, in the Canadian Rockes almost due west of Calgary. I took my wife along. We left Baltimore on one of the first hot, muggy days, went to Washington to catch a plane to Canada, transferred to Air Canada, and arrived in Calgary in the midst of a snowstorm. We were driven to Banff without so much as seeing a mountain—the snow concealed everything. But the next morning the sun was out and the mountain peaks, freshly covered with snow, made a beautiful sight against the ever-so-blue sky. Banff itself was a delightful place in the pine-clad valley. The course went off as planned.

Shortly after, Potter suggested we repeat the course the following year at the Conference Center at Indiana University at Bloomington. After some negotiations the course was given there under the auspices of the Department of Geology and the Indiana Geological Survey. The second time around we greatly expanded the syllabus we had prepared for the class, and after some discussion we agreed to "flesh out" the syllabus into a book. We did so, and Springer-Verlag published our *Sand and Sandstone*. The book had a good reception and was reprinted a couple of years later as a paperback. The course at the Conference Center was handled very well by the university's Extension Division, of which my father had been director many, many years before. I had a chance to see Bloomington and the university again, but there was very little that was familiar.

I had continued my work for the United States Geological Survey for only one year after I was established at Hopkins when I received an inquiry from Bob Nanz about a possible consulting position with Shell Oil Company. I expressed interest and promptly received a letter from Noyes E. Smith, Shell vice-president and director of the Exploration and Production Research Laboratory at Bellaire, Texas, offering me an appointment. I would be expected to visit the laboratory once or twice a year, give a lecture to the geological staff, and spend a few days talking to various people about their research. I would be a consultant, not an employee. I accepted the Shell offer, resigned my Survey position, and remained with Shell for the next ten years.

The Shell arrangements were immensely valuable to me, though perhaps not so much so for Shell! I had a chance to look in on a major industrial research operation, to meet a good many geologists and discuss their problems. But most valuable of all, I was able to visit some of the research operations in the field. My first such experience was at Houston itself. Shell then had a program on the Holocene of Texas. Chief investigators were Hugh Bernard and Rufus LeBlanc, both students of Hal Fiske when he was at Louisiana State University, and Bob Nanz. Also attached to the project was Barney Wilson, a former Hopkins student. The notion behind the project was that the present is indeed the key to the past. Because the coastal plain of Texas contained fabulous deposits of oil and gas, it seemed prudent to investigate the present seaward edge of that plain to see how it had developed. Knowledge of the stream, delta, and barrier beach deposits of today would be a guide to similar accumulations in the older Tertiary strata that underlie the coastal plain. But Shell did not follow the usual pattern of studying modern sediments, a pattern that often seemed pointless and led nowhere. Instead, three sites were selected for intensive study: the floodplain of the Brazos River at Richmond, the Brazos delta, and Galveston Island, a barrier beach. At Richmond Shell leased some bottomland along the river and brought in a backhoe to cut deep trenches in the point bar deposits. It also put down a line of borings across the entire floodplain. As a result one got a three-dimensional picture of a modern fluvial deposit and a good look at the kind of bedding and structures of the sediments in it. Out of this grew the concept of a fining-upward fluvial cycle, a concept discovered much later by J. R. L. Allen in his studies of the Old Red Sandstone of the Welsh borderlands. Shell had published nothing on this work, and very little has appeared since it was done, though the essential results are now embodied in a guidebook that Bernard and associates prepared for an SEPM field trip to the area in 1970. However, the Shell viewpoint and philosophy had already appeared in an article in the 1965 *Bulletin* of the American Association of Petroleum Geologists entitled "Use of Vertical Profile in Environmental Reconstruction," by Glenn Visher, now of the University of Tulsa and formerly attached to the Shell Oil Company. Here was a way to identify the environment of an ancient sedimentary deposit. Each geological process leaves its own signature in the particular sequence of strata and embodied structures. Similar studies were made of the Brazos delta—a prograding structure—and the barrier beach of Galveston Island.

This approach to the study of modern sediments was set by the late Harold Fiske when he was at Louisiana State University. Fiske had made a monumental study of the deposits of the lower Mississippi and its delta using data collected by the United States Army Corps of Engineers. Fiske's influence in setting the nature and direction of the Shell study cannot be overemphasized.

I got to know Fiske fairly well when we were on the Council of the

Society of Economic Paleontologists and Mineralogists together in 1954. He had then left the university and joined the Exxon research group in Houston. Fiske was a dynamic person, full of ideas. Although his teaching career was short, he had a profound influence on his students Bernard and LeBlanc. Fiske had once been at the University of Cincinnati, where today there is the H. L. Fiske Laboratory of Sedimentology.

The Shell group also had a program on carbonate rocks, for carbonates as well as sandstones are important reservoirs of oil and gas. The program was twofold: first a study of modern carbonate sediments in the Florida Keys, and second a study of ancient Cretaceous carbonates in the Fredericksburg area of Texas. In my role as consultant I visited both areas. Bob Ginsburg was in charge of the first, Frank Lozo of the second. Ginsburg had an office and laboratory in Coral Gables and worked both in Florida and in the Bahamas. Bob Ginsburg had taken his Ph.D. at Chicago in 1953. He had, pretty much on his own, decided he wanted to study modern carbonate sediments and managed to start at the Marine Laboratory of the University of Miami and work on the sediments of Florida Bay. When he went to work for Shell he continued and expanded his Florida program. Bob was a great organizer and succeeded in putting together a good research team. Probably more geologists were introduced to modern carbonate sediments by Bob Ginsburg than by anyone else. And I was no exception.

I had a chance to go to the Bahamas with Ginsburg. Shell chartered an amphibian plane, the *Goose*, which took off from the Nassau airport and landed on the water on the west side of Andros Island. We waded ashore to study the carbonate mud flats. We also visited other places, including oolite shoals, Children's Key, and the Tongue of the Ocean, and had a look at the whole region from the air. It was an exciting trip indeed. No less impressive was a close look at the reefs off Key Largo in Florida, snorkling and seeing for the first time the diversity of coral and other reef life. There is no substitute for seeing firsthand!

A few years later, 1965–70, Bob Ginsburg came to Hopkins. In the course of his work on the Recent carbonates of Florida and the Bahamas he had conducted courses and field excursions for the benefit of Shell geologists. He was a born teacher, and by quick action on our part we were able to get him. Because of his work on Recent carbonates it was natural that his interest would lead to the ancient carbonates as well. During Ginsburg's stay at Hopkins stromatolites became a topic of great interest. These enigmatic structures are well displayed in the thick limestone sequences of early Paleozoic age in western Maryland. Bob soon organized a conference on the subject, sparked in part by the abundance of superb examples in Maryland but also by Ginsburg's observations on algal mats and their role in sediment modification in the

Bahamas. The study of stromatolites at Hopkins even extended to the Precambrian of the East Arm of Great Slave Lake, which perhaps has the finest display of stromatolites anywhere in North America. These were studied in detail by Paul Hoffman, who was then a graduate student at Hopkins. Paul later visited the extraordinary modern stromatolites in Shark Bay of Australia—an occurrence that had been described by Brian Logan. Hopkins had become, as it were, the stromatolite capitol of the world.

Bob was the instigator and organizer of still another conference, on recent developments in sedimentology. I was unaware of the plans for the conference and its organizational activities, since it was to be held on the occasion of my retirement (the first of three retirements, as it turned out). Some eighty-five persons attended, a large number being former students of mine at both Chicago and Hopkins. The conference was a two-day affair, held in January 1971, with a program of speakers; the papers were afterward collected and in 1973 were published as *Evolving Concepts in Sedimentology* by the Johns Hopkins Press. Contributors included Roger Walker, Hans Eugster, Ken Hsü, Earle McBride, Adolf Seilacher, and Paul Hoffman. Bob Ginsburg was editor.

Unfortunately for us, Ginsburg returned to Florida, this time on the faculty of the University of Miami, at the Marine Laboratory, where he continued his studies of recent carbonates, especially reefs. Brian Logan of western Australia took Ginsburg's place, but only briefly, for he soon returned to Australia.

My Shell experience let me see what goes on in an industry-supported research center. The resources available are immensely greater than those available to university-based scientists. One has the support of an army of technicians—photographers, draftsmen, chemical analysts, and the like; one also has the means to charter planes and boats and can employ power equipment to drill or trench. Yet, as Hal Fiske himself noted, the volume of material published by those engaged in industrial research is not commensurate with the money spent. Fiske did not think the usual excuses—proprietary rights and the like—were acceptable. Company restraints are not insuperable (Fiske, presidential address, *J. Sed. Petrol.*, 1955). Proof that Fiske is right is surely demonstrated by King Hubbert, himself a research geologist at the Shell laboratory, who published his milestone papers while employed by Shell.

Shell, I believe, was particularly successful, in its earlier years at least, in tackling basic questions and not limiting its research to immediate problems of exploration or production. It was thus similar to the Bell Laboratories, and the kind and character of research undertaken might have been done in a university. This sort of program is most likely to attract the best research talent. A good many of my students worked for

Shell research, including Bob Ginsburg, Norm McIver, Larry Meckel, Bob Nanz, and Lloyd Yeakel. "Research" means quite different things to different companies. Some take a very narrow view, and research may be no more than troubleshooting—finding out, for example, why the paint peeled on the last shipment of wheelbarrows. Others think of research as creating new products or developing new oil fields. Few, like Bell, regard research as seeking understanding. Shell as I knew it was closer to the latter.

Paul Krynine, in the early forties, saw the need for this kind of research by the petroleum industry and suggested that the industry establish and underwrite a research institute somewhat like the Geophysical Laboratory of the Carnegie Institution in Washington. But, as I noted elsewhere, the industry was so competitive-minded that a cooperative venture proved impossible.

The Shell approach had a profound effect on my thinking; it very much changed my view of the study of present-day sediments, from the usual two-dimensional, skin-deep approach to a three-dimensional model. Heretofore the study of a modern sediment had seemed to me to yield very little. The usual study started with collecting various bottom samples—samples of the top few inches of the deposit. These were analyzed for every conceivable attribute: grain size, sorting, mineral composition, organic content, pH, and the like. The results were commonly plotted on a map, and the numerical values were contoured. One might ask, when standing in front of an outcrop, what this did for us. The answer was, very little. But the identification of the environment of ancient deposits was greatly enhanced by a study of the vertical sequence of sedimentary structures and rock types—a far more promising approach than the earlier efforts at grain-size analyses and the search for other criteria of origin—the "fingerprint" philosophy.

The matter was brought home very forcefully on a 1957 field trip to the north coast of Devon in England, organized by Harold Reading and Roger Walker. Walker, a former student of Reading's at Oxford, was at that time a research fellow at Hopkins. We were both in England to attend the International Sedimentological Congress at Reading. So just before the meetings we went to a little town with the picturesque name Westward Ho!, where the Carboniferous sequence was beautifully exposed on the sea cliffs nearby. DeRaaf, Reading, and Walker had made a detailed study of these strata, paying close attention to the rock facies—their sedimentary structures and sequences. Several well-defined "packages" of strata or cycles could be identified that represented prograding deltas, each capped by a prominent sandstone. A year later Walker pointed out a similar prograding delta sequence in the Devonian Mahatango formation exposed along the Juniata River north of Harrisburg,

Pennsylvania. It was illuminating to see what had been just sandstones and shales fall into an organized pattern—to see the fossils, the sedimentary structures and bedding, and the rock types fit into a well-defined sequence. Several years later I put Bill Kaiser to work on these strata; he did an excellent job, and for the first time the Mahatango strata "made sense." J. R. L. Allen of Reading did the same thing for the various Catskill red beds of Pennsylvania. Geologists had looked at these strata for years but had failed to see the fining-upward fluvial cycles. Allen, who had seen these cycles in the Old Red Sandstone in the Welsh borderlands, was visiting professor at Brown, and during the course of his stay in America he pointed out what generations of geologists had failed to see. Then for the first time we understood what we were looking at—the fining-upward fluvial or point bar cycle, many times repeated, the very same cycle recognized in the present-day deposits of the Brazos River by the Shell geologists. Similar point bar sequences occur in the Mississippian Mauch Chunk near Pottsville, Pennsylvania; Meckel described them in the anthracite region of Pennsylvania. Only recently have we learned to see other vertical sequences, "packages," in the Cambrian carbonates of the Conococheague formation in the Great Valley—prograding tidal flats—and in the turbidites of the Ordovician Martinsburg formation near Hamburg, Pennsylvania—in this case a prograding deepwater turbidite fan.

I had been teaching my second course—sedimentology—very much as I had at Chicago. The class went into the field and collected samples of sand and gravel, perhaps also samples of an associated silt or clay bed. These were then analyzed in detail—the sands and gravels sieved, the size distribution in the clay determined by the pipette settling method, the shape and roundness of the pebbles measured, and the heavy minerals of the sand separated and studied under the microscope. Other heavy mineral assemblages were also examined so that each student learned all the common "heavies" at sight. But one day I was visited by a "delegation," Paul Hoffman and John Henderson, both students of mine. Paul was tall, outspoken and often very critical, not only of things geological but also of national policies, events, and persons—including the United States involvement in the Vietnam War, a criticism not too well received in the sixties. Paul was one of the best field geologists I ever had as a student, one of only two persons I knew who could properly collect and trim rock specimens (Albert Johannsen was the other). Paul's work on the stratigraphy, structures, and geological history of the Coronation "geosyncline" was monumental. It was he who first applied the aulacogen concept anywhere in North America, first to the sequence in the East Arm of Great Slave Lake and later to the Arbuckle Mountains of Oklahoma. John Henderson, also a Canadian, was by contrast quiet-spoken, almost reticent. His self-effacing manner belied his real ability, for he was indeed an excellent field geologist, and his work on the Archean strata of the Yellowknife area was first rate.

Hence Paul was the spokesman; John was, I believe, a reluctant partner, for he said nothing. The gist of the visit was to inform me that my course was obsolete; it no longer was the kind of work being done. I was a bit taken back by the criticism, but on reflection, and on thinking about what I had observed at the Shell laboratories, I came to the same conclusion.

These observations had a great influence on my teaching at Hopkins and led to a complete restructuring of my course. I still devoted a good deal of time to thin-section study of sedimentary rocks, with emphasis on interpretation, but I expanded the scope and outlook. We were fortunate enough to have well-exposed Paleozoic sequences within an hour's drive of Baltimore. I could take my class into the field, have them measure a section, search out the sedimentary structures, identify the "packages," be they a prograding delta sequence or a fining-upward fluvial point bar cycle, collect samples of the several facies, then turn to analysis of thin sections from these collected rocks and finally to reading of the relevant literature. This introduced the student to the world of sedimentary deposits; it was a holistic approach. All other approaches seem to me to be partial and incomplete. One needs to begin in the field, for this is where the rocks are and where we get our problems.

Clearly our eyes have been opened as a result of the work of the Shell geologists in their studies of the Texas Holocene—studies made in the early fifties. This was a veritable revolution in sedimentological analysis and, like the "turbidite revolution" started by Kuenen in 1950, was done by looking at strata in the field, not by sophisticated laboratory analysis with expensive instruments. It is a lesson for those who think fieldwork is passé and the "kind of thing we are trying to get away from."

The work in sedimentology was picked up by L. A. Hardie on my retirement. Hardie's interest in the subject began in Durban, South Africa, where he did his undergraduate studies. At Hopkins he worked with Eugster and studied the deposits at Saline Valley, California, especially the anhydrite/gypsum relations. He later became involved, with Bob Ginsburg and Owen Bricker, with the recent carbonate sediments of Andros Island in the Bahamas and later, through his own students, in the early Paleozoic carbonates of the central Appalachians.

## The Demise of Geology and Birth of a New Department

Ernst Cloos did not get quite the faculty he had hoped for when he became chairman. Waters came to Hopkins, as did I; Jim Gilluly did

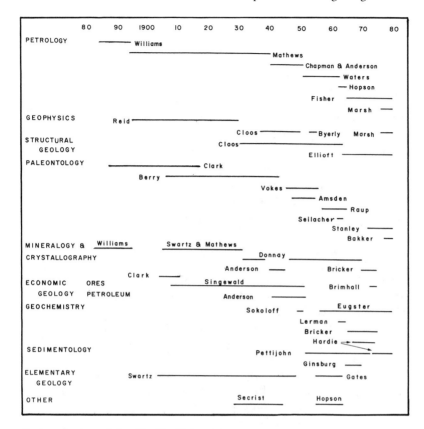

Geology faculty at Johns Hopkins University, 1883–1980.

not. But Donnay was still very much a part of the program, and when Raup and Eugster joined the group the department was again worthy of the Hopkins tradition.

The first threat to the integrity of the group came with the departure of Waters. Aaron had come from the West Coast. His research was still in the lava fields of Oregon and Washington; so when there was a chance to return, to join the department at Santa Barbara, it was too much. He left. Fortunately Cliff Hopson, one of Waters's students, was still at Hopkins and readily stepped into the job, so there was no interruption in our program. But to our dismay, one year later Hopson left to join Waters at Santa Barbara—as one wag put it, the longest umbilical cord in America had not yet been severed. Hopson's departure left us without a petrologist. We had to make do with an interim appointment of John Nolan, a postdoctoral student of Eugster's. But later George Fisher, also a student of Waters, then a research fellow at the Geophysical Laboratory, took over, first part time then full time.

When Cloos retired I became chairman. The chairmanship was not a job I wanted, but since I was senior member of the department it was offered to me. There seemed to be no choice; I took it as a duty to the department and the university. My most serious problem was due to our failure to keep 'Dolf Seilacher, who had been a visiting lecturer, or to replace him with another paleontologist. This led to the resignation of Dave Raup. I did succeed, however, in getting Bob Ginsburg, who was leaving Shell. Bob added a great deal to the department and program; unhappily, for very personal reasons Bob left after four years.

In 1968, while I was chairman, it was proposed that a new department be formed by the merger of the existing departments of geology and oceanography and the addition of several members of the Department of Mechanics who were interested in meteorology and geophysical fluid mechanics, including George Benton, a meteorologist. Benton was in the old Civil Engineering Department, a strange place for a meteorologist. When the engineering curriculum was revamped, Civil Engineering disappeared and became the Department of Mechanics, with strong emphasis on fluid mechanics. It was Benton who conceived the idea of the merger. Owen Phillips, also a professor in the Mechanics Department, initiated discussion of the proposal. Phillips himself was an applied mathematician who had become interested in geophysical fluid mechanics and other earth-related problems.

The Oceanography Department was receptive to the idea. Don Pritchard, chairman, was being pushed to secure more university support for the work in oceanography. Originally Pritchard and his colleagues were members of the Chesapeake Bay Institute, first situated near Annapolis, where the institute's vessels were moored. But Pritchard wanted to be on the Homewood campus, and very shortly the institute was relocated on the top floor of Maryland Hall, an Engineering building. The relocation made it possible for the institute staff to offer courses in oceanography, so very shortly a Department of Oceanography came into being. But the difficulty was that the university gave it virtually no support. All its funds came in the form of grants and contracts—mostly from the National Science Foundation—for specific research projects, not for teaching. The teaching program was in a sense a "bootleg" operation, not exactly legal. In time, oceanography got National Science Foundation funds for a building (and also for a larger research vessel, the catamaran *Warfield*). But the foundation insisted that the university increase its level of support. Hence Pritchard looked on the merger as a way to legitimize the teaching program in oceanography and gain the needed support.

There were some obvious advantages from a merger. Two small departments plus the additions from Mechanics would form one large department—give it greater visibility, put it on a par with the other science departments, give it greater "clout." The merger would presumably provide a broad-spectrum program in related fields, thought to be a more attractive package for students. And so the Department of Earth and Planetary Sciences came into being. The name was suggested by George Benton, who became its first chairman. Perhaps the name was chosen to capitalize on the current great interest in space science, perhaps with an eye to possible financial support. But the name was misleading. True we did have, for a short time, one member interested in the cratering of the moon, but with his departure nothing remained of space science. And, as Donnay pointed out, the name was redundant. After all, the earth is a planet. Ernst Cloos was unhappy with the name, for upon its adoption "geology" disappeared at Hopkins—where it had occupied an honored place for nearly one hundred years. Despite other unhappiness with the name it has remained, mainly because no agreement on another has been found.

The merger brought problems. Owen Phillips shortly succeeded Benton as chairman. Largely through his efforts some funds were obtained to make additional appointments in the field of oceanography. The department could not agree on the choice of candidates. One major problem was the *Warfield*, a costly operation. Funds to support it came from faculty-sponsored grants. The question always arose, Would a prospective faculty appointee use the ship and thereby help fund its operation? This was a good example of a tool—the ship—becoming a factor in decisions about faculty appointments. In effect it was an albatross.

The problem was eventually solved by removing the Chesapeake Bay Institute from departmental jurisdiction and casting it loose with its own director and budget. The Institute has since left the Homewood campus and returned to Annapolis, back where it began. We have come full circle.

But all this brings me too close to the present for comfort, so I will conclude the Hopkins story at this point and leave it to others to finish the tale.

# 9

## Reflections

### On Sedimentology

As the reader will have noted, I came to be a sedimentologist rather by accident. I accepted that appointment at Chicago, where, in addition to teaching elementary geology, I taught a course in sedimentation. It took some time to shift my interest from "hard rock" geology, especially the Precambrian, to sedimentation. In fact, I never abandoned the one for the other—I combined the two and became a Precambrian sedimentologist.

It is an interesting observation, perhaps, that as a sedimentologist almost all of my research was on Precambrian sediments: the Archean sediments first at Minnesota and then at Chicago, and the Proterozoic sediments both at Chicago and at Hopkins. Essentially all I know from firsthand study was learned by studying the Precambrian.

My experience with the United States Geological Survey did much to enlarge my understanding, especially of the younger Precambrian. My interest did not end with the termination of my Survey appointment or my move from Chicago to Johns Hopkins. Several Hopkins students worked on Precambrian sediments, and their work gave me the opportunity to see their areas of study and expand my knowledge of the subject.

But the course in sedimentation at Chicago forced me to turn in new directions. One of these was the laboratory analysis of sediments—primarily of present-day unconsolidated sediments, a line of work vigorously pursued in the thirties. The illusion that to quantify the subject was to make it a science spurred us on. The innumerable grain-size analyses by sieving and other methods have not, however, led to unambiguous identification of either the agent or the environment of

240

deposition, despite some lingering faith that they can. Even if such analyses ultimately prove successful with modern sands, application to thoroughly silicified sandstones or quartzites would be difficult indeed. The sampling problem itself is most formidable. The study of the surface textures of sand grains was given a new lease on life by the scanning electron microscope, but even such studies have not proved themselves, though we now have a photomicrograph of a sand grain some three meters square, made of eleven hundred individual pictures (1980, *Sedimentology* 27: 449).

A second new direction was the concentration on thin-section analysis of sedimentary rocks, bringing to the study of these rocks the same techniques that petrographers had utilized so successfully for years in their study of the "hard rocks." The compound microscope, one of the oldest laboratory tools, and the study of thin sections have continued to make large and important contributions, particularly to the study of sandstones and limestones. Though clearly used with great skill by Sorby a century ago, it was not until the forties that the study of thin sections of sedimentary rocks became widespread in America. With but few exceptions, few or no thin-section studies were prosecuted before World War II. The study came to be embedded in the teaching at Chicago and Penn State in the thirties, where a new generation of sedimentologists was trained in this old technique. As a result of such studies we now have enlightened systems of nomenclature and classifications of sandstones—classifications that reflect the prevailing concepts of genesis of these rocks. But more than that, we have a generation of sedimentologists capable of reading a great deal of the history of the rock from a close study of the fabric and mineralogy that can be seen only in thin section under the microscope. As a result we have a better understanding of the cementation and diagenetic changes that have taken place.

The study of the "heavy minerals," or the minor accessory fraction of sands, which was more commonplace in the twenties and early thirties, has waned. Primarily the earlier studies were made to enhance stratigraphic correlation from subsurface samples. The electric and other geophysical logging techniques rendered the study of heavy minerals obsolete, though they remain a valuable guide to provenance—and to a lesser extent paleocurrents. The new tools for geophysical logging have, however, revolutionized subsurface stratigraphy.

We have also made great progress in the study of limestones and lime carbonate sediments in general, based on field studies of modern carbonate sediments coupled with thin-section studies of the ancient carbonate rocks. We have come to recognize the role of sediment-binding algae and the stromatolitic structures they produce, the role of algae in precipitation of aragonite, the role of organisms in pelletization, and in general the role of waves and currents in redistributing carbonate debris—a role so widespread and pervasive that many limestones are in fact texturally sandstones and siltstones. We now have several schemes of limestone classification that recognize these realities and constitute a significant advance of the past twenty or thirty years. All this is a product of "conventional" methods or techniques—all observational or descriptive and largely, though not wholly, nonquantitative. This is not to say that mass spectrometers or microprobes have made no contributions, but by and large they have been supplemental, not basic to our advances.

A third new direction began at Chicago but reached its zenith at Hopkins. This was the study of sedimentary structures and paleocurrents, a study sparked by Kuenen's visit to Chicago and his milestone paper on turbidity currents and graded bedding and, a little later, by Potter's work on the cross-bedding in the Pennsylvanian Caseyville sandstone. This led to paleocurrent analyses of both Precambrian and Appalachian Paleozoic sandstones, incorporated in student theses.

The concept of turbidity currents and their deposits—the turbidites—is a revolutionary concept with major consequences. No longer are sands per se a criterion of shallow water. The turbidite revolution was brought about largely by field studies—the observations of Natland on displaced foraminifers in California and the field studies by Migliorini in Italy—coupled, however, with the observations of Kuenen in his flume at Groningen. Repetitive graded bedding was recognized as the hallmark of turbidite sedimentation and a major sedimentary facies.

The field mapping of directional current structures—cross-bedding, ripple markings, sole marks, and the like—led to the construction of paleocurrent maps. Though the concept was expressed by Sorby over one hundred years ago, it was not until the postwar era that the idea became widely accepted. Such paleocurent studies are now routine and have contributed significantly to paleogeographic reconstructions.

The fourth phase grew out of my association with the Shell research group. The Shell approach to the study of Holocene sediments led to recognition of sequences or "packages" produced by some geologic process such as meander migration or prograding deltas. These produce a characteristic upward sequence of sediment types and sedimentary structures. They are in a sense cycles, and the study of cycles is of course not new. What is new, perhaps, is the close correlation between the sequence or cycle and the actual process. This type of analysis received a great boost from the studies of the Shell research group at Houston in the early fifties. This was again primarily an observational study in the field.

One important aspect of the study of sediments in which I had no part, which had a major impact on sedimentology, was sedimentary geochemistry and crystal chemistry. Chicago had all the ingredients to pursue this field, but for the most part no one did so. It was developed elsewhere.

Where does this leave all the avant garde geology? The mass spectrometers and the study of radioactive and stable isotopes, the microprobe, and spectrographic analysis and trace elements? These are the new and most expensive tools, which require the services of a chambermaid and a megabudget to support—tools that produce mountains of data from a shoebox full of samples gathered on a weekend collecting trip, data that a computer must record and digest. These sophisticated tools are, in the last analysis, just expensive hand lenses to look at a rock and tell us what's there. They enable us to see things we cannot see with the naked eye, but tools for observation is still all they are. They are not an end in themselves or a solution to any problem. We tend to forget that.

Isotopic analyses have given us a clock and a thermometer—both often of questionable reliability. Of the first, the $C^{14}$ analyses are by all odds the most successful and widespread albeit limited to the past few tens of thousands of years of geologic history. Pleistocene stratigraphy has unquestionably been the beneficiary. Success is more limited in the older strata; only rarely have we reliable dates of deposition, and even the K/A dating of glauconite is limited in scope. The thermometer is even more restricted in scope and reliability. The use of isotopes to discriminate between fresh and marine deposition also has had only partial success. The same can be said for the use of trace elements, particularly the boron content of shales.

The understanding of chemical sedimentation, however, has been considerably enhanced by the experimental studies of Garrels and the application of the principles of physical chemistry to brines and salt deposits. But even here the results have been wide of the mark when basic sedimentology—field observations—has been ignored. A large part of the advances in our understanding of salt deposits has come from very conventional field studies.

Of all the modern tools, the X-ray has been most useful. It extends our powers of observation beyond that of the polarizing microscope in mineral identification. Clay mineralogy has been greatly advanced by its use. But, alas, it cannot do for us what the microscope does in understanding rock history by close study of the rock fabric and the relations of the minerals to one another. It does not distinguish between primary minerals and those that are "secondary"—due to infiltration, diagenetic alterations, or weathering.

In summary, the day has not yet arrived when one can chip off a sample and send it to the laboratory to learn the age, temperature of formation, or environment of deposition. We still have to depend on our field boots, hammer, and eyes. Nor, for that matter, have the new tools settled the dolomite problem or the chert problem, or the problem of the iron formation. The solution to these still has to come largely from "classical geology."

## ON MAPPING AND FIELD GEOLOGY

As I look back at my work on the Precambrian, it is clear that mapping was the major focus of my early studies (and a major part of even my later work also). Geological mapping has fallen out of favor in some quarters; it is regarded as a routine activity, not oriented to the solution of some problem or the answer to a significant question. It is just "coloring a piece of paper." Perhaps there is some truth to this view. But a geologic map is essential to many problem-oriented studies. "Map it and it will all come out right" is Lapworth's trenchant advice on how to solve a difficult geological problem (quoted by Knopf, 1941, in *Geol. Soc. Amer. Fiftieth Anniversary Volumes,* p. 347). It is difficult for some to realize that mapping needs to be redone from time to time. It is not that the rocks have changed; it is that our ideas about them have grown and require different and better maps.

A common fallacy among laymen, and also among some geologists who should know better, is the notion that the era of geologic mapping is largely over or at least that the end is in sight. According to this view, nothing remains except to subdivide the units already mapped and to remap on larger and larger scales. The future lies in the laboratory; fieldwork will be reduced to collecting trips. If the history of our science means anything, nothing could be further from the truth, for geologic maps become obsolete and hence the job of mapping is never done. Why do maps become obsolete? And what is the "life expectancy" of a geologic map?

By "geologic map" I mean any map that depicts geologic information produced by field survey. The usual maps show the distribution of formations, rock bodies, or types by appropriate patterns or colors. But special-purpose maps can also show metamorphic zones, geologic facies, structure, and the like.

My own experience with the Precambrian of the Lake Superior region and northwestern Ontario is most instructive. Many of the earlier maps were primarily lithologic maps—maps showing the distribution of rock types, not stratigraphic units. William McInnes's map of the Manitou Lake region, published in 1902 by the Geological Survey of Canada, was

Much of the material for this section is based on my contribution to *Advancing Frontiers in Geology and Geophysics* (Hyderabad, India: Osmania Press, 1964), pp. 51–57.

such a map. One cannot decipher the chronology or draw a structure section. As noted by Marland Billings (1950, *Geol. Soc. Amer. Bull.* 61:435), the key to understanding an area, even one of metamorphic rocks, is stratigraphy. Billings's principal contribution to the geology of New England is largely due to his emphasis on stratigraphy and the field determination of relative ages of the rocks. Hence the second stage in the evolution of the geologic map is depicting time-equivalent formations rather than lithology and recognizing that a formation may be a slate in one place but a mica schist in another. Clearly the failure to distinguish between metamorphic facies and stratigraphic entities renders a map obsolete. It is instructive to compare McInnes's map with that of the same area by J. E. Thomson, published in 1934 (*Ontario Dept. Mines Ann. Rp.*, Vol. 42), a little over thirty years later.

As Billings noted (p. 436), "many graduate students . . . have a warped attitude toward the study of metamorphic rocks. They think that petrography, physical chemistry, structural geology, and structural petrology will give answers to problems that can be solved only by stratigraphy." Or, as he expressed it, "One clear contact or key bed is more valuable than 100 petrofabric diagrams." As Billings might say today, it is "worth more than as many trace-element or isotopic analyses."

Many of the maps published before 1900 and even many published afterward show nothing of the attitude of the beds; they are devoid of strike and dip symbols. Moreover, the early investigators commonly mistook cleavage for bedding. The result has been controversy and misunderstanding. In the Harper's Ferry area, for example, only after Cloos (1951, *Washington County, Maryland Geol. Surv.*, pp.141–43) pointed out the difference beteen the two were the stratigraphy and structure properly worked out. It is obvious that a map in which cleavage is mistaken for bedding is in error, and that remapping will lead to a new interpretation, not merely a refinement.

Likewise the early workers, before 1920 at least, failed to utilize the internal structure of beds to determine their stratigraphic position. The stratigraphic order in vertical-standing, nonfossiliferous beds is not self-evident. Of the internal structures, cross-bedding and graded bedding are the most useful in sediments. Lake Superior geologists were aware of the utility of these features, as inspection of Leith's writing (*Structural Geology* [New York: Henry Holt, 1913], p. 132) will show. And I learned about them from Frank Grout—crawled with him on hands and knees looking for grading in the Coutchiching schists on Rainy Lake in 1927. Yet not until I pointed out grading in the schists of Bear Island in the Potomac River, in 1952, was Ernst Cloos, one of the keenest observers, aware of the structure. In 1927 E. B. Bailey joined the Princeton summer field excursion in a trip across Canada, during which he was shown and convinced of the usefulness of grading. Upon his return to Scotland, he applied what he had learned to Highland geology and found his earlier interpretation to be in error. A simple discovery can render a whole generation of work obsolete.

Only in the 1930s did American geologists learn from their Canadian colleagues, H. C. Cooke (1931, *Geol. Surv. Canada Mem.* 166:48) in particular, that the Archean greenstone complex could be mapped and the stratigraphy and structure unraveled if the criteria for top and bottom—primarily the shapes of the pillows in the ellipsoidal lavas— were carefully recorded. A. C. Lawson had seen pillow structures in the Keewatin greenstones of the Lake of the Woods region and thought them concretionary (1885, *Geol. Surv. Canada, Ann. Rpt.* 1:51–53). Van Hise and his associates described and photographed them in their classic work on the Lake Superior region in the late 1890s and in the first decade of this century. They correctly understood their volcanic origin, yet not one saw their obvious use in stratigraphy even though the top direction is clearly evident in their published photographs (see Clements, 1903, *U.S. Geol. Surv. Mon.* 43, plate IV). Consequently much of the stratigraphy and structure is incorrect, and their maps, valuable as they were, are in error and must be redone.

It is thus obvious that an outcrop, even if seen many times before, can still yield new information. I am reminded of the response of Hans Cloos to a student who declined to join a field excursion to a particular place because he "had already been there once." As Cloos noted, we go out into the field time and time again—often to the same outcrop—where "we studied the same stratification, or the same interpenetration of rocks, and yet each time advanced one step further, because of what we had learned on the last visit, because the previous impression had had time to settle, or because this time our eyes were a little keener and now observed what hitherto had excaped them" (*Conversation with the earth* [New York: Knopf, 1953], p. 28). The same thought was expressed by Jim Thompson (1964, *Geol. Soc. Amer. Proc.*, p. 214) in his response upon receiving the Arthur L. Day Medal for distinguished application of physics or chemistry to geology. He said, "In the application of chemistry and physics to, say, petrology, we must not in our enthusiasm, lose sight of rocks. They are the source of our problems and the final court in which our hypotheses must be tried—at least if they are to be anything more than purely chemical or physical hypotheses. It has been claimed by some in recent years that observational or descriptive geology has little more to contribute. I cannot believe that this is so. It certainly is not so in my own experience. An outcrop that was drab and uninteresting when studied in a routine manner, through sense of duty, may prove a treasure house of discovery when revisited months or years later and seen again through enlightened eyes. It is simply that we rarely find more than what we are looking for or expect."

Mapping techniques have also changed. The use of two-tone colors to discriminate between actual outcrops and inferred distribution of formations is to be commended, especially in glaciated terranes. How many times have I gone to see a formation only to find a cultivated field or a meadow? The distinction between what is seen and what is inferred enables the map user to better evaluate a map and the interpretations shown on it. The use of two-tone maps became common in the Ontario Department of Mines about 1936. Only since the early sixties has the United States Geological Survey used this technique. I would regard large-scale maps of the Precambrian of the Canadian and Baltic shields that failed to make this distinction as obsolete and unsatisfactory even if constructed today. The Canadians also made a significant advance when they showed, by appropriate symbols, the top position of sediments and lavas where observed. Such is not yet generally done. The practice of showing the criterion (graded or cross-bedding, etc.) and the place where seen by specific map symbols seems again to have been initiated by the geologists of the Ontario Department of Mines. The common practice of using just a symbol for overturned beds is most unsatisfactory, since the evidence of the overturning is nowhere shown on the map.

One can say that maps without strike and dip symbols, those that do not distinguish between cleavage and bedding, and those without symbols to designate top and bottom are obsolete. How many maps of Precambrian terranes pass these tests?

Although I have emphasized geologic mapping—the most basic of all geological activity—the reader should not lose sight of another equally important aspect of field study. Reexamination often opens new insights on important geologic problems. The First World War disrupted the fieldwork of the German geologists, who had carried their studies to the far parts of the earth. Confinement to the older, better-mapped areas proved a fortunate thing for Hans Cloos. He was obliged to examine again the granite plutons of Germany, and so was born a new school of "granite tectonics," based on the mapping of the primary features of these seemingly homogeneous and uninteresting rocks. This approach is best known to English-speaking geologists through the publication by Robert Balk (1937, *Geol. Soc. Amer. Mem.* 5) of his memoir "Structural Behaviour of Igneous Rocks" and the memoir of Ernst Cloos (1946, *Geol. Soc. Amer. Mem.* 18), "Lineation." These students of Hans Cloos have shown how it is possible to map igneous and metamorphic rocks, to delineate various planar and linear features that record a frozen movement plan. It is no longer sufficient to depict a granite pluton by a single uniform color. Many symbols denoting linear and planar elements dot the map, from which a new interpretation of emplacement follows.

A parallel development has taken place in the study of sedimentary rocks—especially sandstones. Although cross-bedding has been known for over a hundred years, it has generally been used to tell top from bottom only in the past fifty years and has been systematically mapped to show paleocurrent flow only in the past thirty. Although Rubey and Bass mapped cross-bedding in a Cretaceous channel sand in Kansas in 1925 (*Kansas Geol. Surv. Bull.*, Vol. 10), and Bausch van Bertsbergh, a student of Hans Cloos, mapped other directional features in the Devonian sediments in the Rhine Valley in 1940 (*Geol. Rundschau* 31:326), only since 1944 has mapping of primary structures become commonplace. The movement plans thus shown, or paleocurrent systems as they are now referred to, have given us new insight into paleogeographic problems. Such studies are field studies whose result is a map, albeit a specialized type of map.

Is this the end? Can we suppose that this long evolution—with its revolutions—of fieldwork and geologic mapping has suddenly terminated? It would be naive to suppose so. I believe, therefore, that it behooves any university department to maintain an active program of fieldwork—of mapping, not just casual excursions—and to build up a staff some of whom are field-oriented, not just laboratory-minded. Most important of all is development of some competence in field mapping for *all* students of geology, whether they go into the field or remain in the laboratory. For only by a firsthand acquaintance with the primary phenomena of geology, obtainable only by field study, can significant research be distinguished from the trivial.

Sometimes maps yield unexpected results. Collins's work on the North Shore of Lake Huron proved to be a classic example of mapping done with a purely scientific goal that later proved to have immense practical value (1925, *Geol. Surv. Canada Mem.* 143). About twenty-five years after publication of Collins's memoir the quartz conglomerates of the Mississagi formation were found to be uranium-bearing. And because nuclear fission had been discovered and put to practical use, uranium was in great demand. The discovery precipitated an exploration and mining boom. Since the uranium deposits were strata-bound, the early work of Collins proved the key to the exploration of uranium ores. It is of interest that John McDowell, one of my doctoral students at Hopkins, later demonstrated again the value of pure science—science not originally directed to immediate practical ends. In 1956 he mapped the cross-bedding in the Mississagi quartzites in the North Shore area. The ore-bearing channel conglomerates were oriented parallel to the general current pattern shown by the cross-bedding. This fact made it possible to predict the extension of the ore bodies beyond their known limits. The initial paleocureent studies had no economic motivation; they were done to satisfy scientific curiosity.

## ON ACADEMIA

Some schools are strong; others once were. The latter have the potential to regain stature by virtue of their tradition. Tradition is an elusive thing—it is the aura or spirit that permeates a place. Usually it is associated with one or two prominent personalities—leaders who were, in their time, intellectual giants and gave the place its orientation and direction. We can, for example, speak of the Chamberlin and Salisbury tradition at Chicago, of Pirsson and Schuchert at Yale, Daly at Harvard, Lawson at Berkeley, and Van Hise at Wisconsin. Schools that are not identified in this manner are not in the forefront; they are not the pace setters. In some schools the early tradition is lost to be regained later, as at Hopkins. G. H. Williams played this role in the early days at Hopkins; Berry, perhaps, played it in the middle years; and certainly Cloos did so in later times. Schools without tradition have a very difficult time establishing a graduate program in geology.

A number of schools have tried to make it into the "big league." They have put money into new buildings, greatly enlarged their faculty, and added the most modern equipment without really achieving a breakthrough. Money alone is not enough. The only way to succeed is to secure, at the same time, two or three distinguished scholars who provide the direction and leadership. This is exactly what Hopkins and Chicago did when they were founded, and in so doing they were catapulted into the top rank of departments.

What is it that makes one department a creative, stimulating place—an exciting place where the lights burn late into the night, where students and faculty often appear on Sundays and holidays—while another place has a nine-to-five mentality and work is a job to be done, not an exciting game? I have reflected on this question—thought about it many times. Twice in my career have I been associated with departments at those moments of intense creativity and excitement. Once was at Chicago just after World War II, when N. L. Bowen was there and Barth, Rankama, and Ramberg joined the geology faculty, and when Harold Urey, Willard Libby, Harrison Brown, and Cyril Smith were there in the institutes. They attracted such students as Sam Epstein, Jerry Wasserburg, Harmon Craig, and Heinz Lowenstam. Chicago was at its zenith. The group was truly exceptional: nine or more were elected to the National Academy of Sciences.

I was also at Hopkins in the mid-fifties when it attained a similar state of creativity with Ernst Cloos, J. D. H. Donnay, Dave Raup, Hans Eugster, and A. C. Waters—a much smaller group then at Chicago and all in the Geology Department. But, like Chicago, Hopkins attracted an exceptional group of students, including Cliff Hopson, Jim Moore, and Gary Ernst. Six of the group at Hopkins achieved Academy status. At that time one could walk around the campus at night to see where the action was. The two places that were lit up until midnight or beyond were Latrobe Hall, housing Geology, and Mergenthaler, the Biology building—the two strongest science departments on the campus.

But these groups are fragile affairs and may have a short life. Chicago is a case in point. Under T. C. Chamberlin's leadership the original department was a distinguished one. T. C. and later his son R. T. Chamberlin, J. P. Iddings, and C. R. Van Hise were of Academy stature. After Chamberlin turned the chairmanship over to Salisbury, the department became ingrown—most of its faculty were Chicago products. It was a good department but not a distinguished one. With the coming of Bowen and the revitalization after World War II, the department again reached a high point. But then, as noted elsewhere, it fell upon troubled times.

To some extent this is also the story of other departments—those that have attempted to "modernize," to incorporate the new tools and fields. All too often the attempt at modernization is made by bringing chemists or physicists to teach geochemistry and geophysics. It is very difficult to make a geologist out of a physicist or chemist—one can more readily make a geochemist out of a geologist. Persons who do not understand the nature and methods of geology do not see the significance of their work in the larger context. They are unable to understand the nonmathematical aspects of earth science and tend to "look down" on those who pursue them. This tends to split the department into factions, polarizing it, and to break it up into closed groups competing for funds and policy decisions. The curriculum tends to be drastically revised, producing narrow-visioned specialists. The support of "classical" geology is eroded; field studies and instruction become casualties. Only by having a chairman with both top-notch credentials as a scientist and a broad vision—one who also has tact and understanding and the confidence of his faculty—can the department be held together. The chairman, moreover, needs to be one who can deal with the deans, especially those from the "exact" sciences, and show them that geology is not just applied physics and chemistry. He must have such stature that his judgment is respected. Lacking these qualifications, it takes only a couple of resignations plus a retirement or two to make a top-flight department rapidly disintegrate.

# REFERENCES

## Memorials
## and Other Historical Materials

Anderson, A. L. 1955. Memorial to Edson Sunderland Bastin. *Geol. Soc. Amer., Proc.* (1954), 87–92.

Bascom, Florence. 1927. Fifty years of progress in petrography and petrology. In *Fifty years of progress in geology*, 33–82. Johns Hopkins Studies in Geology. Baltimore: Johns Hopkins Press.

Berry, E. W. 1945. Memorial to Harry Fielding Reid. *Geol. Soc. Amer., Proc.* (1944), 293–98.

Byerly, P., and Taliaferro, N. L. 1960. Memorial to George David Louderback. *Geol. Soc. Amer., Proc.* (1960), 137–42.

Clarke, J. M. 1919. Memorial to W. B. Clark. *Nat. Acad. Sci. Biogr. Mem.* 9:18.

Cloos, Ernst. 1956. Memorial to Robert Balk. *Geol. Soc. Amer., Proc.* (1956), 93–100.

———. 1964. Memorial to Joseph T. Singewald, Jr., *State Geol. J.* 16:314.

———. 1974. Edward Wilbur Berry. *Nat. Acad. Sci. Biograph. Mem.* 45:57–95.

Cloos, Hans. 1953. *Conversation with the earth.* Trans. E. B. Gerside. New York: A. A. Knopf.

Croneis, Carey. 1940. Memorial to Adolph Carl Noé. *Geol. Soc. Amer., Proc.* (1939), 219–27.

Dunbar, C. O. 1960. Memorial to William Henry Twenhofel. *Geol. Soc. Amer., Proc.* (1960), 151–56.

Eugster, H. P. 1980. Norman Levi Bowen, 1887–1956. *Nat. Acad. Sci., Biograph. Mem.* 52:35–79.

Fisher, D. J. 1963. *The seventy years of the Department of Geology, Univeristy of Chicago*. Chicago: University of Chicago.

Folk, R. L., and Ferm, J. C. 1966. A portrait of Paul D. Krynine. *J. Sed. Petrol.* 36:851–63.

French, J. C. 1946. *A history of the Hopkins founded by Johns Hopkins*. Baltimore: Johns Hopkins University.

Hawkins, H. 1960. *Pioneer: A history of the Johns Hopkins University, 1874–1889*. Ithaca, N.Y.: Cornell University Press.

Holmes, C. D. 1959. Memorial to George David Hubbard. *Geol. Soc. Amer., Proc.* (1958), 143–46.

Howland, A. L. 1975. W. C. Krumbein: The making of a methodologist. *Geol. Soc. Amer., Mem.* 142:xi–xiii.

Krumbein, W. C. 1975. Memorial to Hakon Wadell. *Geol. Soc. Amer., Proc.* (1975), 53.

Levorson, A. I. 1950. Memorial to William Harvey Emmons. *Geol. Soc. Amer., Proc.* (1949), 151–58.

Mason, J. F. 1974, Memorial to John Hazzard. *Bull. Amer. Assoc. Petrol. Geol.* 58:754–56.

Pabst, A. 1958. Memorial to George David Louderback. *Amer. Mineral.* 48:454–59.

Pettijohn, F. J. 1963. Memorial of Albert Johannsen. *Amer. Mineral.* 48:454–59.

———. 1964. The geological map: An historical essay. In *Advancing frontiers in geology and geophysics*, 51–57. Hyderabad, India: Osmania Press.

———. 1970. R. T. Chamberlin. *Nat. Acad. Sci., Biograph. Mem.* 41:89–110.

———. 1977a. Memorial to Gordon Rittenhouse, 1910–1974. *Geol. Soc. Amer., Memor.*, vol. 6.

———. 1977b. Memorial to Ernst Cloos, 1879–1974. *Geol.' Soc. Amer., Mem.*, vol. 6.

———. 1977c. Andrew Cowper Lawson. In *Dictionary of American biography*, suppl. 5, *1951–55*, 415–17. New York: Chas. Scribner's Sons.

———. 1981. Geology at Oberlin in the 1920's. *Oberlin Alumni Mag.* 77, no. 2:37–40, 59.

Schwartz, G. M., ed. [1972]. *A Century of geology, 1872–1972, at the University of Minnesota*. n.p.

Shrock, R. R. William Henry Twenhofel, 1875–1957. *Amer. Assoc. Petrol. Geol., Bull.* 41:978–80.

Swartz, C. K. 1945. Memorial to Edward Bennett Mathews. *Geol. Soc. Amer., Proc.* (1944), 259–64.

Thiel, G. A. 1958. Memorial to Frank Fitch Grout. *Geol. Soc. Amer., Proc.* (1958), 129–30.

Vaughan, F. E. 1971. *Andrew C. Lawson: Scientist, teacher, philosopher.* Glendale, Calif.: Arthur H. Clark.

Waters, A. C. and S. M. Stanley. 1980. Ernst Cloos, 1898–1974. *Nat. Acad. Sci., Biograph. Mem.* 52:95–119.

Williams, E. G. 1965. Memorial to Paul D. Krynine. *Geol. Soc. Amer., Proc.* (1965), 63–67.

Williams, Talcott et al. 1896. *George Huntington Williams.* Privately printed.

Wilson, J. L. 1972. Memorial to Carey Croneis. *Bull. Amer. Assoc. Petrol. Geol.* 56:2088–89.

Woodring, W. P. 1977. Memorial to M. I. Goldman. *Geol. Soc. Amer., Bull.* 77:53.

# INDEX

## Cast of Characters